THE WORLD MUST KNOW

The History of the Holocaust as Told in the

THE WORLD

Little, Brown and Company

Boston · New York · Toronto · London

United States Holocaust Memorial Museum

MUST KNOW

A Publication of the United States Holocaust Memorial Museum

Written by Michael Berenbaum
Arnold Kramer, Editor of Photographs

First Edition

All photographs of artifacts are by Arnold Kramer and from the Collection of the United States Holocaust Memorial Museum.

The author is grateful for permission to quote from the following:

From *The Muses Flee Hitler: Cultural Transfer and Adaptation, 1930–1945*, Jarrell C. Jackman and Carla M. Borden, editors. (Washington, D.C.: Smithsonian Institution Press, 1983), p. 18, by permission of the publisher. Copyright 1983 by Smithsonian Institution.

From *The Good Old Days: The Holocaust as Seen by Its Perpetrators and Bystanders*, Ernst Klee, Willi Dressen, and Volker Riess, editors, translated by Deborah Burnstone. Copyright © 1988 by S. Fischer Verlag GmBH. Translation, Copyright © 1991 by Deborah Burnstone. Reprinted with the permission of The Free Press, a Division of Macmillan, Inc.

Library of Congress Cataloging-in-Publication Data

Berenbaum, Michael, 1945–
    The world must know: the history of the Holocaust as told in the United States Holocaust Memorial Museum / Michael Berenbaum.
        p.   cm.
    Includes bibliographical references.
    0-316-09135-9 (hc)
    0-316-09134-0 (pb)
    0-316-09131-6 (museum hc)
    0-316-09293-2 (museum pb)
    1. Holocaust, Jewish (1939–1945) 2.
Holocaust, Jewish (1939–1945) — Exhibitions. 3.
U.S. Holocaust Memorial Museum — Exhibitions.
I. U.S. Holocaust Memorial Museum.   II. Title.
D804.3.B464   1993
940.53′18′074753 — dc20   92-32813

10 9 8 7 6 5 4

RRD-OH

Design by Susan Marsh

Published simultaneously in Canada
by Little, Brown & Company (Canada) Limited

Printed in the United States of America

THE YAFFA ELIACH SHTETL COLLECTION

The photographs at the beginning of the book and on pages 151–153 were made between the years 1900 and 1941, at a small town near the old border between Poland and Lithuania, called Eishishok in Yiddish. Eishishok was a typical Eastern European Jewish community, or *shtetl*.

In the museum, hundreds of these photographs form a tower representing the Jewish lives that were and are no longer.

Most of the pictures on display in the musem were taken by Yitzhak Uri Katz, his wife, Alte Katz, and their assistants, B. Szrejder and R. Lejbowicz, all professional photographers in Eishishok. In the studio, the streets, and the meeting places of the town, at parties and ceremonies, at homes and public buildings, their work portrays the life of the community.

The photographs, gathered from sixty-five families, have been collected by Dr. Yaffa Eliach, a native of Eishishok and granddaughter of Yitzhak Uri and Alte Katz. Dr. Eliach is a professor of Jewish Studies at Brooklyn College, New York.

PAGE II: Two students of Dr. Kaleko-Barkali, November 1, 1922, in Virbolin, near Kovna. Photo by Modern Kowno.

PAGE III: Sara Zlotnik died in 1915 during a typhus epidemic.

PAGE IV: This family photo was taken in 1927 on the occasion of Dora Zlotnik's (center row, third from right) departure for Palestine. Except for Dora and two young male cousins pictured here who also moved to Palestine, all were murdered in Ejszyszki in September 1941. Photo by Yitzhak Uri Katz.

PAGE V: Dora Zlotnik, standing second from left, with friends and cousins from Ejszyszok, Vasilishok, and Olkenik. The photo was made in Vilna in 1924 where they were students at the Hebrew gymnasium and teachers' seminary.

PAGE VI: Bluma Juris and niece Leah'le Dugaczinski strolling on Vilna Street, Ejszyszok, 1930s. Leah'le and her parents were murdered in Ejszyszki. Bluma survived the war in Russia. Photo by Rephael Lejvowicz.

PAGE VII: Moshe Sonenson and his daughter Yaffa Eliach on the road leading to their summer cottage (*dacza*) in Titiance, 1941. After liberation he was arrested by the NKVD (KGB) and exiled to Siberia. Photo by Zipporah Sonenson.

PAGE XII: Eliyahu Berkowitz in the late 1930s. Youngest of six Berkowitz brothers, he was murdered in Ejszyszki with his parents and grandfather, Reb Itche Berkowitz, who was over one hundred years old. Photo by Ben Zion Szrejder.

In memory of those who were consumed in the Holocaust

May their memory serve as a blessing—and a warning

And in honor of the men and women who created the United States Holocaust Memorial Museum

and thus made remembrance of the past a legacy for the American future

CONTENTS

FROM THE DIRECTOR

The United States Holocaust Memorial Museum is the American national memorial to the victims of the Holocaust. It is dedicated to the memory of the six million Jews and millions of non-Jews who were murdered by the Nazis and their numerous helpers. However, contrary to most memorials dedicated to historical events, and notwithstanding its extraordinarily impressive building, the museum fulfills its commemorative function primarily through a multifaceted effort at mass education rather than merely through sculptural aesthetics. All its major institutional components — the permanent exhibition, the special exhibitions, the Learning Center, the educational programs for students and adults, as well as the Holocaust Research Institute with its library and documentary archives — are tools of education. The museum has been built to tell America and the world the factual story of this most terrible event in modern history, and to illuminate the crucial moral lessons it entails.

In its emphasis on relating the Holocaust story, the United States Holocaust Memorial Museum differs from most traditional history museums, which usually do not teach history. As a rule, they collect, preserve, and selectively display objects relating to history, but do not attempt to tell comprehensively the story of the historical events to which their collections and displays relate. This observation is not meant to diminish the importance of traditional history museums. By collecting and preserving history-related objects and works of art, they, on the whole, preserve immensely important historical evidence, and thus fulfill an important role in human culture.

The main task of the United States Holocaust Memorial Museum is to present the facts of the Holocaust, to tell the American public as clearly and comprehensively as possible what happened in that darkest chapter of human history. To educate, the museum has first to convey knowledge. The museum has reconstructed the history of the Holocaust through multiple visual means — the meaningful arrangement of Holocaust-related objects as well as the presentation of documentary photographic and cinematographic materials. This museum holds the world's largest and most diversified collection of Holocaust-related objects; but in its display it is a "conceptual museum" rather than a traditional, object-oriented one: its primary purpose is to communicate concepts, complex information, and knowledge, rather than merely to display objects of the Holocaust, unrelated to the historical context of each individual exhibit.

The museum does not undertake to explain why the Holocaust has happened. This question has yet to be answered by the historians, and it is doubtful whether such answer will ever go beyond the limits of unprovable hypothesis and speculation. However, to quote the eminent German Holocaust historian Hans Mommsen, "the actual course of events has now been largely established . . . at most, there is marginal controversy about the exact number of victims." The museum restricts itself meticulously to answering the question of *how* it happened, i.e., to presenting the well-established actual course of events.

Scarcity of space inevitably led, however, to a somewhat selective approach. So, too, did insurmountable difficulties in obtaining displayable documentary material about some aspects of the Holocaust. Perforce, it proved impossible to include or to present everything that happened during this historical period. It is the task of the museum's special exhibitions as well as the Learning Center to supplement the inevitably incomplete overall picture presented by the permanent exhibition.

Unquestionably, there is a great measure of truth in the caveat that only a survivor of the Holocaust can fully know and understand what happened in those terrible years, but the world has to know the story of the Holocaust, the story has to be remembered, and in order to be remembered it has to be seen — and told.

The museum consciously avoided including in its permanent exhibition or its Learning Center genocidal events other than those that occurred in the framework of the Holocaust of 1933-1945. This does not mean that the planners of the museum were unaware of the strong intellectual and moral relevance of many such events to the Holocaust. However, it was their mandate to build a Holocaust museum rather than a museum dealing generally with genocide in human history. However, by no means does this thematic distinction preclude the inclusion of materials pertaining to other genocidal events, such as the Middle Passage of African slaves, the Armenian massacres in Turkey in 1915, or the Cambodian events after the Vietnam war, in the museum's library and archives or in its educational activities.

To preclude definitively revisionist declarations by antisemitic pseudo-scholars who try to "prove" that the Holocaust never happened, the museum considered it necessary to restrict itself in the choice of its exhibits solely to genuine artifacts and documentary photographic material with proven provenance (though the permanent exhibition includes eight full-scale replicas,

cast in fiberglass, of large objects that could not be transferred from Europe to the United States, but that can always be inspected on the actual site). Moreover, all visual details of the exhibition, as well as all its textual explanations, were thoroughly scrutinized by leading Holocaust historians to ensure their factual accuracy.

To educate its visitors, the museum does not have to indoctrinate moral conclusions. They are inherent in the historical story which the museum relates. The emotional impact of Holocaust history forces the museum's open-minded visitors to ponder how they would have acted had they found themselves in the position of a Jew in the Warsaw ghetto or in the Auschwitz concentration camp or, conversely, in the position of a German soldier ordered to kill innocent women and children, or how they would have behaved in the position of a witnessing bystander. The understanding of the passive bystander's inadvertent guilt is probably the most important and most relevant moral lesson the museum can teach its visitors. Its importance lies in its broad applicability to contemporary historical and social phenomena as well as to occurrences in everybody's daily life.

A visit to the museum, or reading this book, will be an interesting and challenging learning experience but, at the same time, it also will be a thought-provoking, disturbing, and personally upsetting one. And so it should be.

Jeshajahu Weinberg, Director
United States Holocaust Memorial Museum

INTRODUCTION

This book is related to an event, an institution, and a mission. The event is the Holocaust — the systematic state-sponsored murder of six million Jews by the Nazis and their collaborators during World War II; as night descended, millions of others were killed in its wake. The institution is the United States Holocaust Memorial Museum, charged to be a living memorial to the victims of the Holocaust by telling the story of their deaths — and their lives — to the American people. The mission of the institution is to memorialize the past by educating a new generation partly in the hope of transforming the future by sensitizing those who will shape it.

Ordinarily, the opening of a museum would be celebrated by a catalogue in which the institution displays its holdings, the treasures it possesses. Such a book would deal mainly with the museum and its collections. But the Holocaust Memorial Museum is no ordinary museum. Its opening cannot be a celebration, nor its catalogue self-regarding. Thus this work is not a catalogue, but a study of history. It focuses not on the museum, but on the story of the Holocaust that is told in the museum.

Here we seek to introduce you to the museum through the study of the Holocaust. You will learn of the event through the resources of the museum: text, artifacts, photographs, oral histories, maps, documents, film, and music.

This work does not seek to replicate the experience of the museum. Nothing can do that.

Instead, the book is meant to stand on its own as an exploration of the Holocaust for those who seek to learn the history of the event independent of a visit to the museum. For visitors to the museum who seek additional information and a more in-depth survey of history, this book will intensify their experience. It comments on what you have seen, and says in words what you have experienced in diverse media, three-dimensional objects, environments, and exhibitions. The images we use are presented in the museum; the artifacts are the museum's artifacts. The book fits the contours of the permanent exhibition. It follows the narrative of the story around which the museum exhibitions are built.

We have used one word again and again in this book, as we have in the museum. It is the accepted word by which historians and scholars, poets and writers, presidents and ordinary men and women refer to the cataclysmic events of 1933–1945. But despite its widespread usage, the word is inappropriate. That word is, of course, *Holocaust*. The word is Greek in origin. The Septuagint, the Greek translation of the Hebrew Bible, translates the Hebrew word *olah* as *holokauston*. The Hebrew literally means that which is offered up; it signifies a burnt offering offered whole unto the Lord. The word itself softens and falsifies the event by giving it a religious significance.

The Nazis called the murder of the Jews "The Final Solution to the Jewish Problem." It was their way of speaking euphemistically. Defining Jews as a problem or a question demands a resolution. The word *final* was only too accurate. Their intention was total — to end Jewish history, to eliminate all Jewish blood.

A family portrait at a Jewish wedding in occupied Belgium. *Yad Vashem, Jerusalem, Israel.*

The murder of the Jews was filled with apocalyptic meaning. It was, in the eyes of the Nazi perpetrators, essential to the salvation of the German people.

Yiddish-speaking Jews used the word *churban*, destruction, to signify the Holocaust. It is also the word that ancient Jews used to speak of the destruction of the first and second Temples and their exile from Jerusalem. In the years following World War II, Israelis spoke of *Shoah ve'gevurah* — Holocaust and heroism — as if the two were synonymous, which they are not. More recently, *Shoah* has been used alone, to signify a whirlwind of destruction. Raul Hilberg, the preeminent Holocaust scholar of this generation, called his major book *The Destruction of the European Jews*, an apt description. The Jews were murdered systematically. In Eastern Europe only a remnant remains — an aging group of men and women, heirs of a long past with no future. Cities that once were vibrant with Jewish life are without Jews. Historian Lucy Dawidowicz called the Holocaust *The War Against the Jews*, and perhaps she is right. In these pages, you will read of the second battlefront of World War II. The planned destruction of an entire people was a war the Nazis came close to winning. Had Allied policymakers recognized the double nature of the war that occurred during 1939–1945, they might have been more responsive to the victims of the Holocaust and not restricted attention to battlefields, weapons, and armies.

Still, the word *Holocaust* has come to signify the event, and despite its limitations it will be used. We will, however, resist at all points treating the victims as an offering to the Lord of History. This would be unworthy of God — and of us.

When the museum was first proposed in 1979, a problem arose that threatened to derail the project before it could begin: Who were the victims of the Holocaust? Are the word and the event it signifies restricted to Jews alone or do they encompass all the Nazi victims? The debate had political meaning and religious implications to many of the participants. Many hours of deliberation took place, debates were divisive, and even today, more than a decade after the project first began, the question is unresolved.

Within the Holocaust Memorial Museum, a simple practice is honored. All of the Nazis' victims are included and respected. At the center of the tragedy of the Holocaust is the murder of European Jews — men, women, and children — killed not for the identity they affirmed or the religion they practiced, but because of the blood of their grandparents. Near that center is the murder of the Gypsies. Historians are still uncertain if there was a single decision for their complete annihilation, an enunciated policy of transcendent meaning to the perpetrators. Nevertheless, historians have recognized — both in the museum and elsewhere — the victimization of the Gypsies who were killed in very substantial numbers, and also homosexuals, political prisoners, Soviet POWs, and slave laborers. We cannot understand the evolution of either the concept of genocide or the technology that made it possible without addressing the victimization of people other than Jews.

So while a museum is not a proper place to resolve ideological and historiographical issues, this work and the institution include the totality of victims without dejudaizing the Holocaust (and thus falsifying history), or overlooking any group victimized by the Third Reich.

The museum, as you will read elsewhere, is an American institution, chartered by the Congress and built on federal land. This book is an American work, designed to move us a continent away and take us back a generation in time. We see the events of the Holocaust through a variety of perspectives: those of victims, perpetrators, bystanders, and rescuers. Time and again we refer to the United States both as an actor in the drama and as a point of reference along our journey.

The history described here cuts against the grain of the American ethos. We learn of evil unredeemed, of death, of destruction. The Holocaust offers no happy ending, no transcendent meaning, no easy moralism. And even if we pause occasionally to learn of courage and valor, of heroism and decency, the overriding theme of the Holocaust is evil perpetrated by individuals, organizations, and governments. While we impart no singular meaning to the events of the Holocaust, we see in their perpetration a violation of every essential American value. Yet, perhaps in the deepest sense, the work is American for it calls upon the best of American values, seeking to reinforce the ideas of inalienable rights of all people, equal rights under law, restraint on the power of government, and respect for that which our Creator has given and which the human community should not take away.

A word on methodology. This work attempts to be both an overview and an in-depth view of historical events. The synthesis is informed by the great historians of this generation, but is the product of this writer's scholarship and perspective. It is methodologically eclectic. We touch on diverse fields of learning: literature and psychology, history and political science, theology and sociology as well as philosophy. Personal narrative is woven into the text so history is made incarnate through the experience of men, women, and children who went through the event and who told of what they had seen. There is a bibliographical essay at the end, but the text is uninterrupted by footnotes.

In the darkest hours of the Holocaust, Jews struggled with despair. On the walls of a Hasidic synagogue in the Warsaw ghetto, words were scribbled: "Jews do not despair, do not give up." In a synagogue in Cologne, it was written: "I believe in the sun even when it is not shining. I believe in love even when I don't feel it. I believe in God even when He is silent." There are two accounts of the death in 1941 of the great Jewish historian Simon Dubnow in the ghetto of Riga. According to one story, he was murdered by a Gestapo officer, his former student. According to another version, Dubnow's last words were *screibt und farscreibt*, write and record. To the end, he believed in the power of history, in the triumph of memory.

Survivors speak of one commandment that transcended everything that came from the lips of those who perished and seared the souls of those who remained: Remember: Do not let the world forget.

This book and the institution it represents seek to fulfill that commandment. *The World Must Know.* That was the commitment that underscored Jan Karski's mission to the West, Gerhard Riegner's desperate cables, Rudolph Vrba's escape from Auschwitz, the last stand of the Warsaw ghetto fighters, and, a generation later, President Jimmy Carter's call to create a national memorial. Now, in the heart of this nation's capital, within feet of the Washington Monument — and in the work you hold in your hand — the world can know.

What will be done with that knowledge, we cannot say.

But we can hope that the recollection of the past can prevent its recurrence, as it did in 1979 when then Vice-President Walter Mondale began the International Conference on the Boat People by invoking the failure of the Evian Conference:

"The boat people." "The land people." The phrases are new, but unfortunately their precedent in the annals of shame is not. Forty-one years ago this very week, another international conference on Lake Geneva concluded its deliberations. Thirty-two "nations of asylum" convened at Evian to save the doomed Jews of Nazi Germany and Austria. On the eve of the conference, Hitler flung the challenge in the world's face. He said: "I can only hope that the other world, which has such deep sympathy for these criminals, will be generous enough to convert this sympathy into practical aid." We have each heard similar arguments about the plight of the refugees in Indochina.

At Evian, they began with high hopes. But they failed the test of civilization.

Mondale continued: "Let us not reenact their error. Let us not be the heirs to their shame. To alleviate the tragedy in Southeast Asia, we all have a part to play. The United States is committed to doing its share, just as we have done for generations." The United States took the lead and the boat people were brought to these shores and others throughout the world, where they rebuilt their lives. An elemental lesson of the Holocaust had been learned — at least for a time.

Permit a story from the inferno. A veteran prisoner in Sachsenhausen would inform new arrivals of the rules of camp life, of the difficulties they would have to endure, of the darkness that awaited them. He told them what was to be — honestly, directly, and without adornment. He concluded his remarks with the words:

*I have told you this story not to weaken you.
But to strengthen you.
Now it is up to you!*

Michael Berenbaum
Washington, D.C.

THE NAZI ASSAULT

AMERICANS ENCOUNTER THE CAMPS

In the final days of the hard-fought Allied march toward Berlin early in the spring of 1945, American soldiers entered Nazi concentration camps. Ohrdruf, Nordhausen, Buchenwald, Dachau, Mauthausen: as far as the soldiers knew, these were merely the names of towns on campaign maps. The camps were unanticipated, almost accidental discoveries.

Ten months earlier, Soviet troops advancing on Germany through Poland had come upon the infamous death camp of Majdanek, with its crematoria and gas chambers. They had publicized what they discovered. Western correspondents had entered the death camp and written stories about it. H. W. Lawrence, a correspondent for the *New York Times*, wrote: "I have just seen the most terrible place on earth." These revelations were not given much credence. The very existence of something as awful as a death camp seemed impossible. Even graphic films of the camp shown in Britain and the United States were dismissed as propaganda.

Ohrdruf, a Nazi slave-labor camp near the underground V Rocket factories, thirty-seven miles southwest of Buchenwald, was the first to be discovered by the Americans. Army soldiers entered the town on April 6. Next came Nordhausen, then, on April 11, Buchenwald. Buchenwald is near Weimar, the home of Goethe, the embodiment of the German Enlightenment of the eighteenth century. Weimar was also the birthplace of the constitutional democracy that had been crushed by Hitler in 1933.

Toughened by months of combat, the soldiers thought they knew everything war had to show — ferocious infantry fighting, the destruction of bombing raids, the ugliness of death. But entering the camps was to stumble into a world beyond anything they had seen or could have imagined.

Bodies were strewn indiscriminately, rotting in the April sun. Those prisoners who survived were living skeletons. The stench of death was everywhere. Soldiers were stunned and sickened. "Buchenwald is beyond all comprehension," one American said. "You just can't understand it even when you've seen it." Another soldier who entered Buchenwald described what he saw:

I had been in the service and I had seen men die before. I've seen dead bodies before, but not stacked up like cordwood . . . a stack of bodies about 20 feet long and as high as a man could reach, which look like cordwood stacked up.

Only a few days before the Americans arrived, twenty-five thousand prisoners were taken out of the camp. Few of them survived. With American tanks visible on the horizon at 2:30 on the afternoon of April 11, starved and emaciated prisoners stormed the watch towers. By 3:15 a white flag hung from the main gate. The SS had gone. Two days later, the U.S. Army took control of the camp.

As American troops approached Dachau on April 29, 1945, they found thirty coal cars filled with bodies, all in an advanced state of decomposition. These victims had been brought to Dachau for cremation when time ran out.

Curtis Whiteway was one of the American soldiers who entered a concentration camp. He does not even remember which camp. It may have been Hadamar, near Giessen in Germany. He remembered storming the gates and then encountering hell:

As we burst into the camp and spread out, I saw in front of me a row of wooden one story barracks. . . . One of my men came for me. And he asked me . . . "You'd better come with me." His tone of voice was very serious.

I followed him across the yard to a building — to the best of my memory, a masonry building. The windows were all sealed up. Outside . . . eight automobiles, all up on blocks. The wheels had been taken off. The exhausts were piped in through the wall of that building. We went inside the door.

In the room . . . there was human excretion, vomit, urine, blood all over the room. I did not understand.

And there were shower heads and faucets, all over the wall. One of my men called out to me. He said: "What the hell's going on here?" He said: "There's no water."

We entered the back room filled with benches and

tables. And on one of the tables there were thousands of gold wedding rings . . . piles of human teeth with gold fillings. . . . It was obvious that someone was in there counting them.

We went outside into the yard. In front of me I could see human hair. There were piles of boots, shoes, suitcases, eyeglasses. To my left was four-wheel hay wagons and two-wheel push carts. Only these wagons contained nude bodies . . . men, women and children, even babies. All nude, all dead, all piled as high as they basically could pile them.

The journalist Fred Friendly described Mauthausen, the last of the camps liberated by the Americans, to his mother. He tried to make it real for her: "This was no movie, no printed page," he wrote. "Your son saw this with his own eyes and in doing this aged ten years."

I saw the shower room where 150 prisoners at a time were disrobed and ordered in for a shower which never gushed forth from the sprinklers because the chemical was gas. When they ran out of gas, they merely sucked all of the air out of the room.

I talked to the Jews who worked in the crematory, one room adjacent, where six and seven bodies at a time were burned. They gave these jobs to Jews because they all died anyhow.

I saw their emaciated bodies in piles like cords of wood. I saw the living skeletons, some of whom, regardless of our medical corps work, will die. I saw

A starved concentration-camp prisoner receiving a post-liberation meal. Buchenwald, Germany, 1945. *National Archives, Washington, D.C.*

where they lived, I saw where the sick died, three and four in a bed, no toilets, no nothing. I saw the look in their eyes.

Friendly was the son of Jewish immigrants from Europe. "There but for the grace of God," he wrote. "For if there had been no America, we, all of us, might well have carried granite at Mauthausen."

To be so surrounded by death was numbing. "Before I left the camp that evening," a soldier recalled, "I saw it reduced to such ordinariness that it left me with nothing, not even sickness in my stomach." Even the survivors were frightening. Emaciated by starvation, weakened by disease and harsh labor, their bones were protruding, their bodies distended. They were bald and unshaven. Their soiled clothes and their unwashed bodies smelled. They seemed hardly human. "You try to avoid seeing them too much. It is too hard to handle," a veteran soldier said.

A medic with the 45th Infantry Division wrote: "What I saw and experienced at Dachau — the atrocities, the cruelty — was something which if I had not seen with my own eyes, I would not believe had happened in civilized nations."

The American army, which had been trained for combat, now had the task of healing the survivors and bringing them back to life. Many of the survivors were too weak to live, and thousands died after the liberation of the camps.

Later, the accidental liberators assumed another responsibility — to tell the story of what they had seen. Liberators and survivors asked the same question: How could this have happened?

On April 12, 1945, the day that President Franklin Delano Roosevelt died in Warm Springs, Georgia, Generals Dwight Eisenhower, Omar Bradley, and George Patton visited Ohrdruf concentration camp. Though conditions were horrible by any conventional standards, Ohrdruf was far from the worst of the Nazi camps. Eisenhower turned white at the scene inside the gates, but insisted on seeing the entire camp. "We are told that the American soldier does not know what he was fighting for," he said. "Now, at least he will know what he is fighting against."

After leaving Ohrdruf, Eisenhower immediately wrote to Chief of Staff General George Marshall, attempting to describe things that "beggar description." The evidence of starvation and bestiality was "so overpowering as to leave me a bit sick," Bradley later wrote about the day: "The smell of death overwhelmed us." Patton, whose reputation for toughness was legendary, was overcome. He refused to enter a room where the bodies of naked men who had starved to death were piled, saying "he would get sick if he did so," Eisenhower reported. The Supreme Commander of Allied forces in Europe, however, visited "every nook and cranny." It was his duty, he felt, "to be in a position from then on to testify at first hand about these things in case there ever grew up at home the belief . . . 'that the stories of Nazi brutality were just propaganda.'"

Eisenhower issued an order that American units in the area were to visit the camp. He also issued a call to the press back home. A group of prominent journalists, led by the dean of American publishers, Joseph Pulitzer, came to see the concentration camps. Pulitzer

initially had "a suspicious frame of mind," he wrote. He expected to find that many of "the terrible reports" printed in the United States were "exaggerations and largely propaganda." But they were understatements, he reported.

Within days, congressional delegations came to visit the concentration camps, accompanied by journalists and photographers. General Patton was so angry at what he found at Buchenwald that he ordered the military police to go to Weimar, four miles away, and bring back one thousand civilians to see what their leaders had done, to witness what some human beings could do to others. The MPs were so outraged they brought back two thousand. Some turned away. Some fainted. Even veteran, battle-scarred correspondents were struck dumb. In a legendary broadcast on April 15, Edward R. Murrow gave the American radio audience a stunning matter-of-fact description of Buchenwald, of the piles of dead bodies so emaciated that those shot through the head had barely bled, and of those children who still lived, tattooed with numbers, whose ribs showed through their thin shirts. "I pray you to believe what I have said about Buchenwald," Murrow asked listeners. "I have reported what I saw and heard, but only part of it; for most of it I have no words." He added, "If I have offended you by this rather mild account of Buchenwald, I am not in the least sorry."

Life magazine photographer Margaret Bourke-White recalled that people often asked her how she could photograph such atrocities. "I have to work with a veil over my mind," she said. "In photographing the murder camps the protective veil was so tightly drawn that I hardly knew what I had taken until I saw prints of my own photographs."

What so shocked the American observers in April 1945 was in fact only a small part of the vast system of camps established by the Nazis in Europe. Not until much later was the magnitude of the Holocaust understood: six million Jews had been murdered and two millennia of Jewish civilization in Europe had been brought to an end.

How could this have happened?

BEFORE THE HOLOCAUST

Jews had lived in Europe for more than two thousand years, ever since the time of the Roman Empire. Jews were found in every European country, from Portugal to the Soviet Union, from Greece and Italy to Scotland and Ireland. Descendants of the Hebrews of the Bible, Jews trace their origins to the patriarch Abraham, who lived in Mesopotamia in the seventeenth century B.C.E. Their religion is rooted in the formative experience of the miraculous Exodus from Egyptian slavery and the revelation to Moses at Sinai. The God of Israel was an exclusive God. His people were commanded: "Thou shalt have no other gods beside me." God and Israel were linked by a covenant. The covenant was expressed in the commandments, which encompassed both ritual laws and ethical rules. The sign of the covenant among males was indelible circumcision.

After the revelation at Sinai, twelve Israelite tribes traveled to the promised land of Canaan, where in time they established a nation with David as their king. Its capital was Jerusalem. From the beginning, the history of the Jewish people has been a story of exile, survival, and return. The first exile followed the destruction of Jerusalem by the Babylonian king Nebuchadnezzar in the sixth century B.C.E. After a generation of exile in Babylonia, the Israelites returned to their land. The second exile, which began in 70 C.E. when the Romans sacked Jerusalem and destroyed the Temple, defined Jewish existence for the next 1878 years.

There were two kinds of Jewish response to the defeat of 70 C.E. In the first, the Zealots fought a full-scale military battle against Rome. Three years later, at Masada, the last Zealot garrison chose suicide over surrender. The second course — which was to dominate Jewish life for two millennia — was one of political accommodation in order to preserve the spiritual integrity of Judaism. It is illustrated by the legend of Rabban Yochanan Ben Zakkai, the first-century rabbi who escaped from the besieged city of Jerusalem and went to see the victorious Roman general, Vespasian. In the story, historical fact has been embellished by the rabbinic imagination.

Yochanan is said to have addressed Vespasian as "Caesar," a title far above his actual rank. Soon word of Vespasian's elevation to Caesar arrived from Rome, and, seeking to reward the rabbi for his prophecy, Vespasian asked what he wanted. "Give me Yavneh and its wise men," answered the rabbi. (Yavneh is a small town some thirty-five miles southwest of Jerusalem, where Yochanan founded an academy.) He was willing to surrender the political independence of his people in return for their religious autonomy. Yochanan transformed Judaism from a land-centered political entity with a Jerusalem-based Temple practicing sacrificial worship to a religion in which the Torah and the study of the Torah were preeminent. The synagogue and the religious academy were the portable institutions of an exiled people. Yochanan's surrender marked the foundation of rabbinic Judaism, which has dominated Jewish life through the twentieth century. It is still too early to tell if the emergence of the state of Israel will bring this era to an end.

The loss of political independence, which was sealed by the defeat of the Bar Kokhba rebellion against Rome in 135 C.E., was only part of the challenge to Jewish life that emerged in the first century of the common era. The other came from the other great religion, Christianity, born in the wake of Jerusalem's destruction. Neither the situation of Jews in twentieth-century Europe nor the death camps and the Holocaust itself can be understood apart from the vexed and painful relationships between Jews and Christians since the birth of Christianity, and the hostility of Christianity toward Judaism.

Jesus of Nazareth was a practicing Jew. His followers were Jews, and the Last Supper was a Passover seder. Christianity is rooted in the Jewish teaching of monotheism. It affirms that God had revealed Himself to the Israelites at Sinai, formed a binding covenant with them, and bade them be His servants. Jesus was crucified for being a messianic pretender by Pontius Pilate, who executed him according to contemporary Roman practice.

Historians agree that the break between Judaism and Christianity followed the Roman

Jewish carpentry
workshop in Vilna.
Vilna, Poland, 1922.
Zionist Archive, New York.

Class in a Jewish
community school,
1920-1930. *Central
Archives of the History of
Jewish People, Jerusalem, Israel.*

A Zionist group at an
agricultural training
farm, Romania, 1933.
*Beth Hatefusoth Museum of the
Diaspora, Tel Aviv, Israel.*

Goldenberg grocery, rue
de Rosiers. Paris, France,
interwar period. *Memoire
Juive de Paris (France, c. 1930.)*

destruction of Jerusalem in the year 70 C.E. In the aftermath of this devastating defeat, which was interpreted by Jew and Christian alike as a sign of divine punishment, the Gospels were recast to diminish Roman responsibility and emphasize Jewish culpability in the death of Jesus. Jews were depicted as killers of the son of God.

Christianity was bent on replacing Judaism by making its particular message universal. The New Testament was seen as fulfilling the "Old" Testament; Christians were the new Israel, both in flesh and spirit. The God of justice had been replaced by the God of love. Thus, the early church fathers taught that God had finished with the Jews, whose only purpose in history was to prepare for the arrival of His son. According to this view, the Jews should have left the scene. Their continued survival seemed to be an act of stubborn defiance. Exile was taken as a sign of divine disfavor for the Jews' denial that Jesus was the Messiah and for their role in his crucifixion.

Enmity toward the Jews was expressed most acutely in the church's teaching of contempt. From Augustine in the fifth century to Luther in the sixteenth, some of the most eloquent and persuasive Christian theologians excoriated the Jews as rebels against God and murderers of the Lord. They were described as companions of the devil, a race of vipers. During the Middle Ages, Jews were accused of the blood libel: Jews supposedly murdered Christian children as an act of ritual worship or to prepare unleavened bread for the Passover seder. Church liturgy, particularly the scriptural readings on the crucifixion for Good Friday, stirred up this hatred. It was no coincidence that acts of violence against Jews often took place in the spring, the season of Easter and Passover.

As Christianity became the dominant religion of Europe, Jews were forced to the margins of society. They accepted their minority status because of their own religious belief that they were chosen by God for a special purpose and destiny. The covenant could not be repudiated. Religious attitudes were reflected in the economic, social, and political life of medieval Europe. In the late eleventh century, the first crusade unleashed a

Yiddish school in Kharkov. The slogan on the board reads: "One who does not work does not eat." Soviet Union, 1922. *YIVO Institute for Jewish Research, New York.*

wave of antisemitic violence across the continent. Jews were expelled at various times from England and France, as well as from Spain in 1492, and were the objects of massacres and pogroms from the fifth to the twentieth centuries. Still, Jewish survival was important to Christianity, for in the end of days when Jesus would again return, at least a remnant of Jews would be required to affirm him as the Messiah.

At the heart of Christian hatred was rage inspired by the one unforgivable crime: the Jews had killed Christ. That alone justified whatever was done to them. The great twelfth-century mystic, Bernard of Clairvaux, who preached a vision in which every Christian could experience God's love, also ranted about the Jews' bestiality, "the more than bestial, which caused them . . . to rush headlong into that crime, so enormous and so horrible, of laying impious hands upon the Lord of Glory."

But where they were needed, Jews were tolerated. Living as they did at the margins of society, Jews performed economic functions that were vital to trade and commerce. Because premodern Christianity did not permit usury, and Jews could not own land, Jews played a vital role as moneylenders and traders. Where they were permitted to participate in the larger society, Jews thrived. During the golden age in Spain, Jewish philosophers, physicians, poets, and writers

HOPITAL DE HIRSCH ✡ שפיטאל די הירש

The staff of the Jewish hospital in Salonika. Salonika, Greece, c. 1930. *Beth Hatefusoth Museum of the Diaspora, Tel Aviv, Israel.*

were among the leaders of a rich cultural and intellectual life shared with Muslims and Christians. In collaboration with Arab scholars and thinkers in this tolerant society, they were instrumental in transmitting the intellectual heritage of the classical world to medieval Christendom. But by 1492, both Muslims and Jews were driven out by militant Christian rulers.

Christian teachings that the Jews were evil persisted in the Protestant Reformation. Martin Luther's reliance on the Bible as the sole source of Christian authority only fed his fury toward Jews for their rejection of Jesus. "We are at fault for not slaying them," he wrote. "Rather we allow them to live freely in our midst despite their murder, cursing, blaspheming, lying and defaming."

Luther's diatribes in the sixteenth century are an eerie foreshadowing of Nazi practices four centuries later. He advised:

First, to set fire to their synagogues and schools, and to bury and cover with dirt whatever will not burn so that no man will ever again see a stone or a cinder to them.

In Deuteronomy 13 Moses writes that any city that is given to idolatry shall be totally destroyed by fire and nothing of it shall be preserved. If he were

alive today, he would be the first to set fire to the synagogues and houses of the Jews.

Such views were finally renounced by the Roman Catholic Church decades after the Holocaust, with the Vatican II proclamation of *Nostra Atatae* in 1965, which revamped Roman Catholic teaching with regard to Jews and Judaism. The Vatican accepted the legitimacy of Judaism as a continuing religion and exonerated Jews for the murder of Jesus. As a result, Good Friday liturgy was changed to make it less inflammatory with regard to Jews. Similar transformations have also occurred in Protestant teaching.

Though the Enlightenment movement of the eighteenth century changed the nature of Jewish life in Europe, at least in the West, it did not necessarily reduce antisemitism. While the major Enlightenment figures championed the light of reason in debunking what they regarded as the superstitions of Christian belief, their thinking did not lead to any greater acceptance of Jews. Instead of holding Jews responsible for the crucifixion of Christ, Enlightenment leaders blamed them for Christianity and for all the crimes and perversities committed in the name of monotheistic religion. Some of the most prominent, including Diderot and Voltaire, pilloried the Jews as a group alienated from society, who practiced a primitive and superstitious religion.

Until the French Revolution of 1789, the status of Jews on the continent remained tenuous. Treated as outsiders, they had few civil rights. They were taxed as a community, not as individuals. Exclusion from the larger society reinforced their religious identity and strengthened their communal institutions, which served judicial and quasi-governmental functions. In the French Revolution, with its promise of liberty, equality, and fraternity, the rights of citizenship were extended to Jews. Still, emancipation was conditioned on the willingness of Jews to abandon their age-old customs and their communal identity. This was the meaning of the slogan "To the Jews as individuals, everything, to the Jews as a people, nothing."

France was in the vanguard of the movement that gave civic and legal equality to the Jews. Napoleon's conquest of the German states led to emancipation there, but after his defeat, legal equality ended. It was not restored until the unification of Germany in 1871 under Bismarck. Even in France itself, emancipation did not diminish antisemitism, but merely transformed it. Now antisemitism took on the racial overtones that characterized anti-Jewish thought during the nineteenth century and beyond. Jews became the target of the conservative right and the radical left in France. Pierre-Joseph Proudhon, the leading French socialist theoretician, wrote:

The Jew is the enemy of the human race. One must send this race back to Asia or exterminate it . . . by fire or fusion or by expulsion. The Jew must disappear. . . . Tolerate the aged, who are no longer able to give birth to offspring.

Richard Wagner, the renowned German composer, sought to eliminate the Jews from the creative sphere. "I hold the Jewish race to be the born enemy of pure humanity and everything noble in it. I am perhaps the last German who knows how to hold himself upright in the face of Judaism which already rules everything."

In this new climate, antisemitism became a powerful political tool, as the politicians were quick to discover. In the 1890s Karl Lueger won the mayoralty of Vienna — a city of diverse cultures including many Jews — with his antisemitic campaigns.

French society was polarized by the case of Captain Alfred Dreyfus, the only Jewish officer attached to the army's general staff. Dreyfus was tried and convicted on the basis of a trumped-up accusation of treason. During his trial, a mob chanted "Death to the Jews" in the streets outside the courtroom. The Dreyfus affair continued to fragment the country for years, as evidence was brought forward to show that Dreyfus had been framed. He was finally pardoned, but the lesson was clear: Jews were not secure even in the most advanced nation in Europe.

Mass meeting of Jewish colonists. The Yiddish streamer on the wall reads "Dictatorship of the proletariat is the only form of national liberation." Soviet Union, 1920–1928. *YIVO Institute for Jewish Research, New York.*

At the beginning of the twentieth century, Jewish life was caught up in radical change. In 1881 Czar Alexander II was assassinated by revolutionaries. Jews were blamed and an era of promise came to an end in Russia. Pogroms and persecutions erupted that set off a massive migration to the West as millions of Jews migrated to the New World. The Jewish population of the United States — which had from the beginning given full equality under law to all males who were not slaves and where there had never been any religious test for holding office — increased from fifty thousand in 1881 to four million in 1919 as waves of immigrants came to escape antisemitism, poverty, and despair. The shores of the United States were open to receive those needing a haven, those yearning to be free. (When the persecution under nazism began in 1933, the gates of the New World were closed.) A smaller group, impelled by Zionist ideology, sought to rebuild the ancient Jewish homeland in the Middle East. Only those Jews who emigrated from Europe escaped the ravages of the Holocaust.

It is tempting but inaccurate to read back into past Jewish history the extreme powerlessness of the Holocaust era. David Biale summarized the Jewish predicament:

From biblical times to the present day, Jews have wandered the uncertain terrain between power and powerlessness, never quite achieving the power necessary to guarantee long-term security, but equally avoiding, with a number of disastrous exceptions, the abyss of absolute impotence. They developed the consummate skill of living with uncertainty and insecurity.

As the nineteenth century ended, Jewish life was in ferment throughout the East. In Eastern Europe, many Jews lived in shtetls, villages that were predominantly Jewish. They spoke Yiddish, read Yiddish books, both sacred and secular, and attended Yiddish theaters and movies. Many wore traditional black caftans and continued to observe the practices of their grandparents. Jewish religious life in all its forms was fervent. The religious community was piously observant; the secularists ardently secular, seeking to overturn the power of religious authority and to embrace the ideological movements of communism and socialism. Many a young Jew left the yeshiva to enter a German university, casting aside traditional garb and practice and passionately adopting the teachings of the West. Despite antisemitism and cultural constraints, Germany was the place where Jews were best able to participate in intellectual and cultural life. They assimilated rapidly. Intermarriage was widespread; so was conversion.

A vibrant Sephardic culture flourished in North Africa in Algeria, Tunisia, Libya, and Morocco, where the dominant cultures were Arabic and French, and the most significant religious influence that of Islam.

At the beginning of the new century, civil equality was guaranteed by law, but social barriers were slow to fall. Sigmund Freud's revolutionary teachings on sexuality were delivered to the B'nai B'rith chapter in Vienna. His psychoanalytic teachings were dismissed as "a Jewish science," and he desperately courted a non-Jew, Carl Jung, to promulgate his new theories. Still, Jewish artists, writers, scholars, and scientists thrived in a new climate of openness. Einstein launched a new era in physics, as Freud had in psychology. Chagall and Modigliani were in the forefront of modern art. Einstein was only the first

among peers: between 1905 and 1931, the Nobel Prize in a variety of scientific fields was awarded to ten German Jews.

Most Jews, of course, were neither prominent nor affluent. Contrary to the image that all Jews lived like Rothschilds, most Jews lived in very ordinary circumstances. Many were poor. They were stevedores in Salonika, Greece; factory workers in Lódź, Poland; small shopkeepers in Amsterdam; yeshiva students in Kovno, Lithuania; and professors in Berlin. They worked to create a home and sustain their families.

When the Nazis came to power in 1933, more than nine million Jews lived in the twenty-one European nations later occupied by the Germans in World War II. The six hundred thousand Jews who lived in Germany itself were less than one percent of the population. Within a dozen years, two out of three of the nine million were dead.

THE TAKEOVER OF POWER, 1933

Adolf Hitler's appointment as chancellor of Germany on January 30, 1933, sealed the destruction of constitutional government in Germany. A month later, in Washington, D.C., Franklin Delano Roosevelt took the oath of office as president, swearing to uphold the Constitution of the United States. Both men led their countries for the next twelve years. Both died in the same month, April 1945, Hitler by his own hand in an underground bunker amid the rubble of a broken and defeated nation.

In 1933, both Germany and the United States were in the grip of a severe worldwide economic depression accompanied by massive unemployment, social unrest, and the loss of national confidence. In Germany, the harsh provisions and high reparations imposed by the Treaty of Versailles that followed Germany's defeat in World War I were an additional cause of national bitterness.

Citizens in both countries who were frightened and uncertain of the future looked for a strong leader to guide them out of despair. In his inaugural address, Roosevelt

Hitler waving to crowd from Chancellery on the day he assumed office. Berlin, Germany, January 30, 1933.
Bettman / Hulton, New York.

told the American people they had "nothing to fear but fear itself." Hitler and his National Socialist (thus Nazi) party used fear as the vehicle to seize and maintain power.

For a decade the Nazis had based their political campaigns on terror, first street-brawling and thuggery, then a calculated policy of intimidation, hatred, and violence. Five years before the Nazi takeover, their master propagandist, Dr. Joseph Goebbels, said: "We come like wolves descending upon a herd of sheep."

Hitler's first hundred days in power were marked by the mass arrest of trade-unionists; the suppression of free speech and all political opposition; the opening of the first concentration camps, where those arrested were held without trial; the purging of opponents of the regime from the civil service — which included teachers; the gutting of the judicial system and the establishment of a People's Court answerable only to Hitler; and the first steps of an orchestrated policy of persecution of German Jews.

How did Hitler — a failed Austrian artist who headed a small, discredited band on the lunatic fringe of political life in the Weimar Republic — attain such power? His National Socialists became a significant minority party only in 1930, when they won 107 seats in the Reichstag, the German legislative body. As economic conditions worsened, Hitler attracted a wider following. He was a spellbinding orator and a skilled organizer. Thousands of jobless young men put on the brown-shirted uniform of the Nazi storm troopers (for *Sturmabteilung*, or SA). Their job was to mount frightening demonstrations and terrorize political opponents.

At the end of January 1933, Hitler was named by President Paul von Hindenburg as Chancellor of a coalition government with the right-wing Nationalist party. New Reichstag elections were called for March. The eighty-six-year-old von Hindenburg and his advisers hoped that Hitler could end the political chaos and still be controlled within a coalition. The responsibilities of office, von Hindenburg thought, would force the political outsider toward the center. Centrist parties, rendered impotent by inept political leadership, had collapsed under the pressure of economic crisis. Other politicians on both the right and left were equally naïve. Goebbels had clearly outlined the Nazis' tactics: "We will become members of the Reichstag in order to disable the Weimar order with its own acquiescence. . . . We come as enemies." But no one took Hitler or his program seriously until it was too late.

A fatal flaw in the Weimar Constitution was the source of its own destruction. Two emergency provisions — articles 25 and 48 — allowed the president to usurp the powers of the state governments, suspend the constitutional guarantees of civil liberties, and dissolve the Reichstag. The Reichstag could also grant temporary legislative power to the chancellor by a two-thirds majority of those present and voting. Hitler would use this opening to gather all power into his hands.

THE TERROR BEGINS

On the night of February 27, the Reichstag building was set ablaze. Hitler blamed the Communists. The morning after the fire, von Hindenburg was persuaded to invoke Article 48. The German government thus suspended individual and civil liberties, including freedom of the press, speech, and assembly. Homes could be searched without warrants and property confiscated without due process of law. Decrees issued at the same time also abrogated the power of the federal states and imposed the death sentence for a variety of crimes, including the vaguely defined "serious disturbances of the peace." These emergency decrees, which were never rescinded, became the legal basis for the concentration camps.

Four thousand Communist officials were arrested, as well as many Social Democrats and liberal leaders, including members of the Reichstag. A "shoot to kill" order encouraged police to fire on Communist demonstrators. The last days of the election campaign were

Hitler with the Nazi leadership. From left to right: Wilhelm Kube, Fritz Saukel, Wilhelm Frik (seated), Joseph Goebbels, Ernst Roehm, Hermann Göring, Walter Darre, Heinrich Himmler, and Rudolf Hess. Berlin, Germany, January 31, 1933. *National Archives, Washington, D.C.*

The Reichstag [German parliament] building on fire. Berlin, Germany, February 27, 1933. *Ullstein Bilderdienst, Berlin, Germany.*

Police search on a street. Berlin, Germany, 1933. *Spaarnestad Fotoarchief, Haarlem, Netherlands.*

19

Arrest of Communists by the members of the Nazi Sturmabteilung (SA). Berlin, Germany, March 6, 1933. *Bundesarchiv Koblenz, Germany.*

Political violence became official when the Nazi private army was enlisted into the regular police. Here, a member of the SS patrols the streets with a regular policeman. Berlin, Germany, March 5, 1933. *Bundesarchiv Koblenz, Germany.*

marked by uncontrolled violence by Nazi storm troopers. Still, the Nazis won only 44 percent of the vote.

When the Reichstag reconvened late in March, an Enabling Act was passed that gave dictatorial powers to Hitler. The vote of 441 to 94 (all of these cast by Social Democrats) was deceptively overwhelming: all of the 81 Communist and 26 of the Social Democrats were prevented from attending the meeting. Hitler was able to claim that he had come to power legally. For the next twelve years, Germany was ruled by the Führer.

Racism was the central and pervasive theme of Nazi ideology. It shaped social policy in Germany between 1933 and 1939, was a major factor in Nazi conduct of World War II, motivated German policy in occupied countries, and, when carried to its ultimate conclusion, resulted in the Holocaust.

Hitler's obsession with racial purity, his hatred of both Marxism and democracy, his beliefs in German racial supremacy, and the notion of an Aryan master race that would take over the world should have come as no surprise when they became state policy after March 1933. He had stated them clearly not only in his speeches, but in his book, *Mein Kampf* (*My Struggle*), which was first published in 1925. It was the "sacred mission of the German people . . . to assemble and preserve the most valuable racial elements . . . and raise them to a dominant position."

The Nazis regarded the Germans as racially superior, and considered Slavs, Gypsies, and blacks to be inferior. At the bottom of this scale were the Jews, the most dangerous of races, in part because they parasitically lived off the other races and weakened them.

"All who are not of a good race are chaff," Hitler wrote. As a young man, he had been repelled by the cosmopolitan diversity of Vienna: a mixture of "Czechs, Poles, Hungarians, Ruthenians, Serbs and Croats, and . . . the eternal mushroom of humanity — Jews." The Aryan race was destined to be superior, therefore the German people "are the highest species of humanity on earth." In the racial struggle of history, the "master race" would dominate if it preserved its purity. Otherwise, it would be polluted, corrupted, and destroyed by inferior races.

It was necessary for Germans to "occupy themselves not merely with the breeding of dogs, horses and cats but also with care for the purity of their own blood." These notions were not original. Hitler simplified racial doctrines propounded in the nineteenth century, particularly in the writings of the French aristocrat Joseph Arthur de Gobineau and the English-born disciple of Wagner, Houston Stewart Chamberlain.

Whatever the theoretical underpinnings of Hitler's racial beliefs, Nazi racism under his direction was far from theoretical. Blood mixture was abhorrent. Procreation by inferior races was to be discouraged, at first through forced sterilization, later by systematic murder.

BOYCOTT

Official persecution of Jews began on April 1, 1933. At ten o'clock on that Saturday morning, the Nazis initiated a boycott of Jewish businesses and shops in cities and towns throughout Germany. Until then, violence against Jews had been individual and sporadic. The boycott was the first salvo in a nationwide campaign against the entire German Jewish community.

Storm troopers were stationed menacingly in front of Jewish-owned shops. The Star of David was painted in yellow and black across thousands of doors and windows. Signs were posted saying: "Germans! Defend Yourselves! Don't Buy from Jews," "The Jews Are Our Misfortune," or simply "*Jude.*"

The boycott was Hitler's response to foreign criticism of his regime. Reports of Nazi violence against Jews and Jewish businesses in Germany had prompted talk of an American boycott of German goods. On March 26, Hitler summoned Joseph Goebbels, now the minister of Public Enlightenment and Propaganda. Goebbels described Hitler's instructions: "We must . . . proceed to a large-scale boycott of Jewish businesses in Germany. Perhaps the foreign Jews will think better of the matter when their racial comrades in Germany begin to get it in the neck."

The boycott was a Nazi party operation. Julius Streicher, the master Jew-baiter, was given the title of leader of the Central Committee for Counteracting Jewish Atrocity Tales and Boycotts. When the boycott began, the police were instructed not to hinder it in any way, but rather to "view the boycott with magnanimity."

The reaction of non-Jews was mixed. In some cities, the boycott inspired greater eruptions of violence against Jews, but some Germans made it a point of honor to enter Jewish shops or telephone their Jewish friends. Some German Jews were quick to see the boycott as a sign of things to come. A few fled; others took their lives in despair. But many Jews were more optimistic and appealed to the German public's sense of justice through leaflets and advertisements, urging them not to respect the boycott.

SA storm troopers blocking the entrance to a Jewish-owned shop with signs demanding that Germans buy only at German shops. Berlin, April 1, 1933. *National Archives, Washington, D.C.*

The end of German Jewry has arrived.

RABBI LEO BAECK

Still others were openly defiant. Robert Weltsch, the editor of a German-language Jewish newspaper, refused to accept the Nazis' use of the Star of David as a sign of shame. German Jews, he said, should wear the yellow badge with pride.

The boycott, which was scheduled to last for five days, was called off after twenty-four hours. The boycott committee remained in existence and the boycott was made compulsory for Reich agencies and party members. A week later, the government announced the first of a series of laws singling out Jews. The Civil Service Law of April 7, 1933, dismissed all non-Aryans from the civil service, including notaries and teachers in state schools. (Communists were removed four days later.) It was the first of four hundred separate pieces of legislation enacted between 1933 and 1939 that defined, isolated, excluded, segregated, and impoverished German Jews.

Soon after Hitler came to power, Leo Baeck, the most prominent rabbi in Germany, wrote: "The end of German Jewry has arrived." Baeck's words were prophetic, although many German Jews found this impossible to imagine in the spring of 1933.

Before the advent of Nazi rule, Jews felt comfortable as Germans. They were active and successful in theater and the arts, science and literature, industry and the professions. Ever since the late eighteenth century, Germany had represented culture and freedom to the European Jewish community. Germany had epitomized the best of Western civilization.

Although they encountered social discrimination and were often restricted in their professional careers, Jews were confident of their future as Germans. Many Jews converted to Christianity, and even more had shed their ancestral religious practices. Intermarriage with non-Jews was common. Their language was German, and they identified with the German nation. It was their home.

German Jews had demonstrated their loyalty to the fatherland during World War I. More than one hundred thousand — one of every six Jews in the population — served in the army, 80 percent in combat roles. Thirty-five thousand were decorated for bravery, and twelve thousand lost their lives. Under the Weimar Republic, Jews served in high office, held important places in the civil service and the judiciary, and studied and taught in Germany's great universities. Their influence in German intellectual life was enormous considering their relatively small proportion of the population. Of the thirty-eight Nobel Prizes won by Germans between 1905 and 1936, fourteen were received by Jews.

Joseph Goebbels, the Nazi master propagandist, during a rally supporting the boycott. Berlin, Germany, April 1, 1933.
National Archives, Washington, D.C.

SA storm troopers distributing boycott pamphlets. Berlin, Germany, April 1933.
National Archives, Washington, D.C.

Bookburning at
Opernplatz. Berlin,
Germany, May 10, 1933.
Bettmann Archive, New York.

THE BURNING OF BOOKS

Hitler moved swiftly to gather all state power in Nazi hands, eliminate potential opposition to his rule, and carry out the nazification of German culture. On April 7, the governments of the federal German states were dissolved and new Nazi governors appointed. May 1 was declared a workers' holiday, with labor leaders invited to participate in parades and celebrations. The next day, the Nazis arrested trade-union leaders and occupied their headquarters. Within the month, all labor unions were destroyed.

On the night of May 10, 1933, thousands of Nazi students, along with many professors, stormed universities, libraries, and bookstores in thirty cities throughout Germany. They removed hundreds of thousands of books and cast them onto bonfires. In Berlin alone, more than twenty thousand books were burned. The book burnings were part of a calculated effort to "purify" German culture. Since April 12,

the Nazi German Student Association had been purging libraries, working from lists of books deemed "un-German." The authors of some of the books were Jews, but most were not.

Like many Nazi propaganda efforts, the book burnings were designed as a spectacle featuring torchlight parades, frenzied dancing, ritualistic chants, and massive bonfires. In Frankfurt, books were brought to the pyre in manure carts drawn by oxen to the accompaniment of Chopin's "Funeral March." At the Opera House opposite the main entrance to the University of Berlin, Goebbels triumphantly told the crowd that "The age of hairsplitting Jewish intellectualism is dead. . . . The past lies in the flames."

Jewish authors whose books were burned included Albert Einstein, Sigmund Freud, and Stefan Zweig. The works of Nobel Prize winner Thomas Mann, Germany's best-known writer (and a Protestant), were cast into the flames. Mann would soon leave Germany, one of more than two thousand writers and artists who could no longer regard Nazi Germany as home. Other eminent German-language writers whose books were burned were Bertolt Brecht, Franz Werfel, Erich Maria Remarque, and Max Brod.

Also cast into the flames were books by non-Jewish American novelists Jack London, Ernest Hemingway, Upton Sinclair, John Dos Passos, Theodore Dreiser, and Sinclair Lewis, the only American writer to have then won a Nobel Prize. In the city of Kiel, the books of the American anthropologist Franz Boas were burned, less than a year after he had received an honorary doctorate from the university there.

Works by the Communist theorists Karl Marx, V. I. Lenin, Leon Trotsky, and Rosa Luxemburg were torched. Dr. Magnus Hirschfeld's sympathetic studies of homosexuality were reduced to ashes, along with the writings of the American women's rights activist Margaret Sanger. The books of Helen Keller were also burned. Born deaf and blind, Keller had overcome these disabilities and was known throughout the world as a heroic figure and respected writer. When told of the book burnings, she said: "Tyranny cannot defeat the power of ideas."

Where one burns books, one will, in the end, burn people.

HEINRICH HEINE

In the United States, public opinion was outraged by the book burnings. *Time* called it a "bibliocaust." *Newsweek* described the event as a "holocaust," a name that would forever be linked with the Nazis and their flames. American writers protested en masse. Public rallies in New York, Philadelphia, Chicago, and St. Louis attracted hundreds of thousands of participants. The political commentator Walter Lippmann wrote: "There is a government in Germany which means to teach its people that their salvation lies in violence," a description that Hitler and Goebbels would not have disputed.

The last word on the book burnings had in fact been written a century before by Heinrich Heine, a German poet of Jewish origin: "Where one burns books, one will, in the end, burn people." The distance between burning books and burning people would be eight years.

Nazi Party officials confiscate books in preparation for a pyre in Hamburg on May 15. Hamburg-Eimsbüttel, Germany, May 15(?), 1933. *Bildarchiv Preussischer Kulturbesitz, Berlin, Germany.*

As Hitler had promised, Nazi rule brought about a revolution in every aspect of German political and cultural life. Under the Weimar Republic, Germany had been a federal nation. Now the autonomy of the various states was ended as Hitler's national government assumed total control of state governments, appointing Nazis as local governors.

The judiciary was also brought under tight Nazi control. By early May of 1933, a new People's Court was established to try treason cases. Proceedings were secret, and there was no avenue of appeal except to Hitler. Sentences of death were handed down routinely. Concentration camps were set up to hold political opponents without trial. Between May and July, all opposition political parties were dissolved, and on July 14, the National Socialist party was declared the sole party in Germany. By then, 26,789 people were in "protective custody" in the concentration camps.

Also on July 14, the Law for the Prevention of Hereditary and Defective Offspring was proclaimed. It authorized the surgical sterilization of people who were mentally retarded, schizophrenic, alcoholic, or who had genetic diseases.

NAZI PROPAGANDA

In a period of a few months Hitler had established a one-party state. The next step was to win the allegiance of the German people and unite them behind his rule. Hitler had more than an intuitive understanding of the power of propaganda. Two chapters of *Mein Kampf* deal with the subject. To be successful, propaganda had to present a simple message to a mass audience. The German people had to believe they were involved in an urgent struggle with an evil enemy, a struggle of apocalyptic drama.

Dr. Joseph Goebbels (he had a Ph.D. in literature and philosophy from the University of Heidelberg) became the Nazis' master propagandist. As head of the Ministry of Public Enlightenment and Propaganda, he

Free distribution of radios in honor of Joseph Goebbels's birthday. Berlin, Germany, October 29, 1938.
Süddeutscher Verlag Bilderdienst, Munich, Germany.

controlled the flow of public information through the press, radio, and film.

All newspapers in the Reich were licensed. Those that refused to endorse the Nazi line were shut down. Editors had to be racially acceptable — of Aryan descent and not married to a Jew. Some of the most venerable newspapers in Germany were closed because they were owned by Jews, or were forced to get rid of their Jewish publishers and editors.

Twice a day, Goebbels's ministry held a press briefing where reporters were told which events were to be covered. Editors were informed how a story was to be treated. Ministry officials read and censored all papers. Everyone understood the ground rules: failure to please the ministry by printing anything "to weaken the strength of the German Reich . . . or offend the honor and dignity of Germany" could result in heavy fines, even imprisonment in a concentration camp.

Goebbels also turned the state-owned broadcasting system into a propaganda vehicle. The Nazi government was the first to exploit the new technology of radio. (President Roosevelt also used the radio to successfully further his own political goals. Fireside chats brought him into the living rooms of the ordinary citizens and were effective in establishing an intimate rapport between the president and the American people.) The Nazis marketed a cheap wireless

Crowd responding to pageantry at Nazi Party Congress. Nuremberg, Germany, November 1938. *Hugo Jaeger, Life Magazine, Time Warner Inc., New York.*

set — the *Volksempfänger*. Local radio wardens encouraged neighbors to buy radios. Later, they reported on those who listened to foreign broadcasts, who were then subject to arrest. Radio reached a mass audience and became the most pervasive source of Nazi propaganda. German radio devoted most of its airtime to playing martial music, telling human-interest stories about good deeds done by the noble young Aryan men of the Hitler Youth organization, and carrying Hitler's speeches.

Hitler was a powerful and spellbinding orator. In photographs, he does not appear to be a prepossessing person. But in the flesh he was able to exert a magnetism that persuaded even sophisticated Germans that he was not to be underestimated. Albert Speer, who later served as minister of armaments, recalled his first encounter with Hitler:

Three hours later I left that beer garden a changed person. I saw the same posters on the dirty advertising columns, but looked at them with different eyes. A blown-up picture of Adolf Hitler in a martial pose that I had regarded with a touch of

amusement on my way there had suddenly lost all its ridiculousness.

The Nazis systematically created the cult of the Führer, the great charismatic leader. To veterans, Hitler was portrayed as the heroic corporal who had fought valiantly for the fatherland; to artisans, as an artist who had torn himself from his studio to answer the call to serve his nation. At public rallies, Hitler worked himself up to a pitch of near hysteria, and carried his audience with him. His experience as a street-corner speaker paid off: Hitler knew how to touch his audience, how to gain their sympathy and play on their fears.

Demonstrations were held at night in a sports stadium. Thousands of men carried banners. Torchlights illuminated the stadium, making it seem like a cathedral of light, or a tribal ceremony. The audience was held in breathless tension. Hitler's speech was punctuated again and again by shouts of "*Sieg Heil*" from the frenzied crowd. William L. Shirer, the American journalist who reported from Berlin for CBS News, wrote that Hitler's

German propaganda poster explaining the development of the United States. Uncle Sam kicking out the Indians and then a Jew kicking out Uncle Sam. The poster indicates that in "1885 a Jewish historian predicted that a strong Jewry will arise in the 20th century. It has happened exactly that way. The Jews have reached their goal. They pushed the American people into the war." *USHMM.*

Ei.. weitblickender E..glä..der

sah im Jahre 1909, also vor 33 Jahren, die Entwicklung der Vereinigten Staaten voraus, als er diese Zeichnung veröffentlichte.

Viel früher schon, nämlich im Jahre 1885, entschlüpfte dem bekannten jüdischen Historiker Heinrich Graetz in einem Vortrag in London folgendes bemerkenswerte Geständnis:

„**Das jüdische Volk wird einst in Amerika, in dem Lande der Freiheit und Gleichheit, aufblühen. Ein großes, mächtiges Judentum wird entstehen im 20. Jahrhundert.**"

HISTORY OF THE UNITED STATES

Genau so ist es gekommen! In den Vereinigten Staaten haben die Juden ihr Ziel erreicht. Juden und Judengenossen sind die wahren Herren in USA. Sie haben das amerikanische Volk in den Krieg getrieben, um ihre Macht jetzt auch über Europa und die übrige Welt auszudehnen. **Dagegen setzen wir uns zur Wehr!**

Wir werden die Waffen nicht eher niederlegen, bis das Judentum und seine Helfershelfer zu Boden geschlagen und sein Einfluß endgültig vernichtet ist.

Mit der Herrschaft des Judentums wird Schluß gemacht!

A German propaganda poster, which proclaims that the Jews want war and that Franklin Delano Roosevelt is considered by Jews as the modern Moses.

Roosevelt has assumed the mantle of an "apostle of peace for all people." How stupid, the poster asks, does Mr. Roosevelt really think we non-Jews are? *USHMM.*

audiences were caught up in emotion that took on the quality of a religious experience:

> They reminded me of the crazed expressions I saw once in the back country of Louisiana on the faces of some Holy Rollers who were about to hit the trail. They looked upon him as if he were a Messiah, their faces transformed into something positively inhuman.

Nazi propaganda was designed to shape a folk community bonded to its leader. Allegiance to Hitler was direct, personal, and absolute; it superseded all other loyalties.

Hitler's frequent companion Leni Riefenstahl, the beautiful film star and pioneering director, glorified the Führer in *The Triumph of the Will*, a film that is still studied and shown as a prime example of brilliantly effective propaganda and suasion. Even the opening narrative frames the film as an epic:

> September 5, 1934. Twenty years after the outbreak of the World War, 16 years after Germany's crucifixion, 19 months after the commencement of the German renaissance, Adolf Hitler flew to Nuremberg again to review a column of his faithful adherents.

Leni Riefenstahl, Nazi film director and producer, at work on a documentary on the Nazi Party. Germany, 1934. *Spaarnestad Fotoarchief, Haarlem, Netherlands.*

The hour-and-a-half-long film is devoted to the 1934 Nazi party rally at Nuremberg. No effort was spared to accommodate Riefenstahl. Pits were dug in front of the speakers' platform so she could get the camera angles she wanted. Tracks were laid so that her cameraman could take traveling shots of the crowd. Aerial views of Hitler's arrival were shot from planes, and a blimp high above the stadium captured the massive crowd. More than 170 people were on the production staff. When the rough cuts were not quite right, major party leaders and high-ranking public officials were forced to reenact their speeches in a studio. All this was in order to set the scene perfectly before Hitler began his oration, which was the centerpiece of the film.

While Riefenstahl's work was a masterpiece of elegant technique, propaganda in the popular press was intended to be crude. Julius Streicher's tabloid, *Der Sturmer,* featured antisemitic cartoons and fanciful stories in which Jews were shown constantly engaged in international conspiracy, as ruthless businessmen whose god was money cheating honest Germans, and as sex-crazed monsters violating German women and children. Riefenstahl's epic works might appeal to cultured sophisticates, but coarse movies such as *The Eternal Jew* were featured in theaters and schools.

Perhaps the most impressive achievement of Nazi propaganda was the international public relations effort that surrounded the 1936 Berlin Olympics. Germany hosted athletes from fifty-two countries at an event staged on a colossal scale. It was an occasion to showcase the new Germany that had risen from the ashes of the Weimar Republic and the humiliating defeat of World War I. The Olympics gave the Nazis the opportunity to convince the international community that the new regime had been unfairly treated by the press and that stories of antisemitism and the suspension of political freedom had been overstated by journalists and diplomats alike.

In the United States and other countries, participation in the 1936 Berlin Olympics was

German children view *Der Sturmer* and war propaganda posters. Germany, about 1937. *International Film Foundation, New York.*

RIGHT:
Avery Brundage with a Nazi official. Berlin, Germany, July 1936. *Ullstein Bilderdienst, Berlin, Germany.*

a matter of controversy. Those who believed that American participation would be taken as tacit approval of the Nazi regime urged a boycott. Others made the case for the purity of a sports competition, arguing that sports and politics should not mix. They warned that a boycott could trigger antisemitism throughout the United States and would threaten the future of amateur sports. Despite the setting, the Olympics were an international, not a German event, they insisted.

The American Olympic Committee received assurances that all German athletes had a chance to participate on the German teams. In fact, Protestant and Catholic sports clubs had been closed down. Only Nazi sports clubs continued to operate. Jews were expelled from gymnastics clubs and dropped from the Davis Cup team. Jewish athletes were totally excluded from participation. Avery Brundage, the president of the American Olympic Committee, publicly stated that he had witnessed no antisemitism in Germany, and that his impression of tolerance was confirmed in private meetings he had held with the Jewish community in Germany. He neglected to say that these meetings had been held in the presence of Nazi officials.

In anticipation of the Olympics, Berlin was cleaned up. Antisemitic billboards and posters were taken down, the pace of persecution slowed, and even the rhetoric of Nazi leaders toned down. Hitler was a constant presence throughout the games. His arrivals and departures were dramatically staged, and he made a point of personally congratulating the German medal winners.

American schoolchildren learn that Jesse Owens, the superb African-American sprinter who won an unprecedented four gold medals in 1936, spoiled Hitler's plans for an Aryan triumph. Exhausted after his track feats as both a sprinter and broad jumper, and more than content with his victories, Owens had not planned to run in the 400-meter relay. Two Jewish runners, Marty Glickman and Sam Stoller, had competed and qualified for the event, and Owens felt that they had earned the right to compete. Mack Robinson, whose brother Jackie was to break the color line in major league baseball a decade later, was the third member of the relay team. Afraid that a victory by Jewish athletes would further offend the German hosts, a solicitous Avery Brundage excluded the two Jewish runners and ordered Owens to take the baton. In those

days, athletes did as they were told. Glickman described the emotion that came back to him as he revisited Berlin some fifty years later:

I stopped and looked across at the stands, and saw where Hitler, Göring, Goebbels, Streicher and Himmler had sat. And suddenly a wave of anger swept over me so that I thought I was going to pass out. . . . How could these dirty bastards do this to any eighteen-year-old kid, keep him from competing in the Olympic Games?

President Roosevelt, who had remained silent throughout the Olympic debate, reassured his friend Rabbi Stephen Wise, president of the American Jewish Congress. Tourists returned from Berlin had reported to Roosevelt that "The synagogues were crowded and apparently there is nothing very wrong."

THE SCIENCE OF RACISM

In *Mein Kampf*, Hitler proclaimed that the "state must set race in the center of all life. It must take care to keep it pure." The state "must see to it that only the healthy beget children."

Forced sterilization, which had been made legal in 1933, began in January, 1934. In the next decade, more than 200,000 people were sterilized in a widely publicized program administered by physicians and supervised by the courts. Early targets were the "Rhineland Bastards," children fathered by black French colonial soldiers who had served in the French occupation forces after Germany's defeat in World War I.

Nazi Germany was not the first country to sterilize those considered abnormal. In the United States, several states permitted forced sterilization. But under nazism, eugenics became national policy. So-called racial sciences were taught in the universities. The teaching of medicine, biology, history, anthropology, and sociology was perverted to support the pseudo-science of racial theory. The Nazi regime eventually established thirty-three university and research institutions, eighteen university professorships, and four research divisions within the Reich Health Offices dedicated to "racial hygiene." The Nazi appointed rector of the University of Berlin (a veterinarian and member of the storm troopers) introduced twenty-five courses in "racial science" into the curriculum.

The sole serious and sustained opposition to the sterilization program came from the Roman Catholic Church. The German Protestant churches were generally silent on the issue.

Sterilization was only the prelude. In 1939, under the guise of a so-called euthanasia program, the Nazis began the systematic murder of Germans who were insane, handicapped, or mentally retarded.

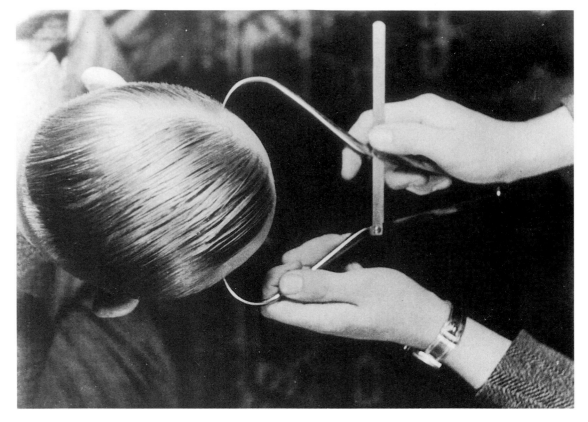

A "scientific" examination of skull width. Germany, 1937. *Bildarchiv Preussischer Kulturbesitz, Berlin, Germany.*

A "scientific" examination of nose width. Germany, 1938. *Hulton-Deutsch, London.*

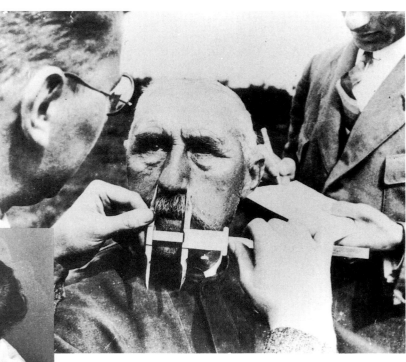

Eye-color examination with comparative chart. Germany, 1936. *Abraham Pisarek Collection, Berlin, Germany.*

THE NUREMBERG RACE LAWS, 1935

The end of German Jewry came gradually. In the spring of 1933, Jews were removed from the civil service; in the fall, non-Aryan editors were dismissed from German newspapers; and by year's end, Jewish artists, musicians, filmmakers, and writers were expelled from the guilds set up under the Reich Chamber of Culture by Goebbels in order to make sure artists were politically acceptable to the Reich.

Martin Heidegger, the renowned existential philosopher who served as rector of the University of Freiburg, set an example of obedience to nazism, first by publicly swearing to support Hitler, then by hastening to dismiss Jews from the faculty.

In 1935, German Jews were stripped of their citizenship. Two laws promulgated at the annual Nazi party rally in Nuremberg on September 15 — the Law for the Protection of German Blood and the Reich Citizenship Law — became the centerpiece of Hitler's anti-Jewish legislation. Those laws, which were soon known throughout the world as the Nuremberg Laws, restricted citizenship in the Reich to those of "German or kindred blood." Only citizens, racial Germans, were entitled to civil and political rights. Jews were merely subjects of the state.

In order to "protect German blood and honor," the marriage of Jews and "citizens of German or kindred blood" was forbidden. So were sexual relations between Jews and Aryans. Women under the age of forty-five could not work in Jewish households. Jews could not fly the German flag. Categorization had consequences. Definition was the first step toward destruction.

For the first time in history, Jews were persecuted not for their religious beliefs and practices, but because of their so-called racial identity, irrevocably transmitted through the blood of their grandparents. (Once resolved, the question of definition was closed, and a precedent had been set.) The Nuremberg Laws were later imposed on lands occupied by the Nazis and served as a model for the treatment and eventual extermination of the Gypsies.

But who was a Jew? Although the Nuremberg Laws divided the German nation into Germans and Jews, neither the term *Jew* nor the phrase *German or kindred blood* was defined. Since the laws contained criminal provisions for noncompliance, the bureaucrats had the urgent task of spelling out what the words meant. The civil service and the Nazi party were at loggerheads in their efforts to define a Jew. The civil service wanted to protect the "German" part of the half-Jew, while the party viewed part-Jews as even more abhorrent than full Jews.

It was the notion of the mixing of blood that had driven Hitler into the frenzy expressed in *Mein Kampf* and, as Führer, in nationally broadcast speeches telling Germans they would triumph only if their blood was pure. The mongrelization of the Germanic race "has robbed us of world domination," he said. From now on, the German nation must be protected from racial contamination.

Two basic Jewish categories were established. A full Jew was anyone with three Jewish grandparents. That definition was fairly simple. Defining part-Jews — *Mischlinge* (mongrels) — was more difficult, but they were eventually divided into two classes. First-class *Mischlinge* were people who had two Jewish grandparents, but did not practice Judaism and did not have a Jewish spouse. Second-class *Mischlinge* were those who had only one Jewish grandparent.

In the end, the bureaucratic contortions were immaterial: anyone who had even one Jewish grandparent was technically Jewish and for all practical purposes no longer had full rights as a German citizen. According to the Nuremberg Laws, even Roman Catholic priests and nuns and Protestant clergy who were converts to Christianity, or whose parents had converted, were considered Jews. Jewish emancipation in Germany had ended.

Seven documents were required to prove German descent: a birth or baptismal certificate, certificates for both parents, and certificates of all four grandparents. Church offices, which had registered all births until 1875, were besieged with requests for documents proving German ancestry. A new cottage industry sprang up as hordes of "licensed family researchers" offered their services to an anxious clientele of Germans afraid of a skeleton in the family closet.

In the United States, the public thought the legislation was unfair, but few believed there was anything their government could do to challenge it. American Jewish organizations could not agree on how to respond. While working behind the scenes to help individual Jewish refugees enter the country, some of the major groups were opposed to either launching a public protest or lobbying for liberalizing the restrictive U.S. immigration laws. They were afraid of stirring up anti-semitism, both in Germany and at home.

Commentary in the international press condemned the Nuremberg Laws, but most reporters did not understand that the laws marked a new and ominous departure in Nazi treatment of the Jews. An editorial in the *Los Angeles Times* claimed that the laws did not signify much of a new problem for Jews because "generally speaking, nobody has any civil rights in Germany." Church leaders also criticized the Nuremberg Laws, but had little success in arousing the Christian conscience.

Neither President Roosevelt nor the State Department made any public comment on the Nuremberg Laws. Before the Nazi party meeting, the American ambassador to Germany, William Dodd, had alerted FDR that new laws would be issued ensuring "complete sub-ordination for the Jews." Dodd wanted the American, French, and British ambassadors to boycott the rally. The State Department rejected his proposal. Nevertheless, Dodd did not attend. He warned Washington that soon even more severe measures would be aimed at the "complete separation of the Jews from the German community."

FROM CITIZENS TO OUTCASTS

Those who predicted that the new laws heralded even worse persecution were right. After Nuremberg, the pace of ostracism was stepped up. Signs saying *Juden unerwünscht* (Jews unwelcome) were posted on public facilities — shops, theaters, restaurants, hotels, even pharmacies. Jews were forbidden to sit on park benches restricted to Aryans; they could sit only on benches set aside for them.

Jewish woman on a park bench labeled "For Jews only." Austria, shortly after the Anschluss, 1938. *Institute of Contemporary History and Wiener Library, London, England.*

The regime then set out to deprive Jews of any means of livelihood. All Jewish property was registered in 1937. In 1938, all Jewish businesses still in existence were Aryanized: Jewish workers and managers were dismissed, and Jewish stockholders disfranchised. The German business and banking community, which benefited richly, cooperated fully with the dismantling of Jewish firms.

Within a year, Germans had taken over the ownership of four out of five Jewish businesses, acquiring them at bargain prices prescribed by the Nazi Ministry of Economics. German banks made enormous profits from these forced transactions, first in commissions on the transfers, then through loans to the buyers and subsequent business contracts with the new firms. Many Jewish businesses were liquidated.

In July 1938, Jewish physicians were forbidden to treat non-Jews; in September, Jewish lawyers were forbidden to practice; and in October, at the request of the Swiss, who were fearful of being overrun by Jews fleeing Germany, Jewish passports were marked with the letter J, for *Jude*. On August 17, 1938, Jews had to take new middle

names: all Jewish men were to be called Israel; all Jewish women, Sara. In November came the pogroms known as *Kristallnacht*.

An article in the November 24 edition of *Das Schwarze Korps*, house organ of the SS, bluntly answered the question "Jews: What Next?"

Because it is necessary, because we no longer hear the world's screaming, and finally because no power in the world can stop us, we shall therefore take the Jewish question toward its total solution. It is: total elimination, complete separation.

JEWISH RESPONSES

As the foundation of Jewish life in Germany was undermined and then destroyed between 1933 and 1939, the response of the Jewish community included despair, dismay, disbelief, even, at first, accommodation. In 1933, speaking on behalf of German Jews, Rabbi Leo Baeck tried but failed to meet with Adolf Hitler. German

Jews would adjust "to every order of the state, willingly, if one leaves them their decency, work and freedom," he said.

We expect German Jewish questions to be solved on a legal basis and with the weapons of nobility, so that there will be created an honest understanding of our place and our way. The well-being of Germany, as well as the well-being of German Jews, insists on that.

The triumph of Nazism took Jews by surprise. It seemed inconceivable that there was no place for them in a nazified society. The new legislation cut against the grain of a hundred years of increasing assimilation. As German citizens, they pinned their hopes on law, even as the law was increasingly used to create and codify their status as pariahs.

The deterioration of the situation of German Jews is reflected in the evolution of the names of the central organization representing Jews. Between 1933 and 1939, the body, originally called the Reich Representation of Jewish Land Federation, assumed six different names. Even after the Nuremberg Laws, the Reich Representation of Jews in Germany (the body's title in 1935) was sanguine. The clarification of the legal status of Jews, it said, "must create a basis for a tolerable relationship between the German

and Jewish people." By 1939, it had gone from representing "German Jews" to becoming an "association" of Jews in Germany. Among the "Jews" in Germany included in the association were men and women who had abandoned Judaism and converted decades earlier, more than a generation ago.

The mainstream Jewish community still saw its future within Germany. Its members had traditionally been anti-Zionist, expressing nationalism as Germans, not as Jews. Even the Zionists, who pushed for Jewish emigration to Palestine, did not perceive Jews as an alien presence in Germany. They were affected by the pull of German culture and lulled by the apparent German-Jewish symbiosis of the Weimar period, when Jews saw themselves as full partners in German political, economic, and cultural life.

The diverse Jewish community spoke with many voices, particularly in the early days of the Reich. For Zionists, persecution made the case for migration to Palestine even stronger. He-halutz, the Zionist pioneer organization in Germany, established training farms where young people prepared themselves for life on a kibbutz. Youth Aliyah transferred children and young people from Germany to Palestine. Yet, for large numbers of Jews who believed themselves to be in the mainstream of

German society, the struggle to preserve Jewish rights in Germany seemed the right course. Their instinct was to reaffirm vigorously their ties to German culture, the state, the German language, and even the land itself.

For some, Nazi rule was unbearable. There was a rapid rise in the suicide rate among Jews. Many left. Between 1933 and 1939 one of every two German Jews emigrated, about 300,000 out of a population of 600,000.

Many of those who remained embraced their Jewish roots. Synagogue attendance rose dramatically as Jews who had been casually observant rediscovered the religious traditions of Judaism. Prayers took on a new meaning. The names of Pharaoh and Haman, the tyrants of the Hebrew Bible, were invoked as code words for life under Hitler. Jewish learning and education flourished as it never had before in post-emancipation Germany. The Jewish community came together and took on a new vibrancy even as life became more desperate. Joachim Prinz, who was then a young rabbi in Berlin, offered a course in Jewish history. The largest hall available seated thirty-five hundred people. Twice that number applied so the course was divided into two sections. Prinz spoke of those times: "To be a Jew was now a new discovery, and to emphasize one's Jewishness in the face of danger and disgrace became the thing to do."

A variety of Jewish organizations sponsored vocational training and agricultural settlements to prepare for emigration. The Kultur Society of German Jews made jobs for artisans and musicians. Jewish theological seminaries introduced a full university curriculum for students who were excluded from German universities. Jewish schools were opened to serve students who were no longer safe in German classrooms. The Jewish press became more important.

Martin Buber, Germany's most prominent Jewish philosopher, initiated a nationwide adult-education program to prepare the Jewish community spiritually for an unknown fate. He used commentary on the Bible to address the most contemporary of problems. Buber created what Ernst Simon, his disciple who returned from Palestine to work with Buber, called a new Midrash, a commentary

To be a Jew was now a new discovery, and to emphasize one's Jewishness in the face of danger and disgrace became the thing to do.

RABBI JOACHIM PRINZ

that could be grasped immediately by one's coreligionists but not by the enemy. Thus, in an October 1934 lecture to the Frankfurt Lehrhaus — the adult-education school began in the 1920s by Franz Rosenzweig as part of the renaissance of German Jews — later repeated at a public gathering in the Berlin Philharmonic, Buber said: "Blood and soil are hallowed in the promise made to Abraham, because they are bound up with the command to be a 'blessing' [Genesis 12:2]. 'Seed' and 'earth' are promised but only in that order so that . . . a new people may 'keep the way of the Lord and do righteousness and justice' in his land, and so begin building humanely." Buber's audience clearly understood the attack on the Nazi myths of blood and soil. So too did the Nazis, and Buber was soon forbidden to speak publicly. According to Ernst Simon, Buber taught "the meaning of spiritual resistance against identification with the aggressor. . . . He was and remained our teacher."

In the fall of 1938, on Yom Kippur, the Day of Atonement, the most sacred day of the Jewish year, a prayer composed by Rabbi Leo Baeck was read in synagogues throughout Germany:

Our history is the history of the grandeur of the human soul and the dignity of human life. In this day of sorrow and pain, surrounded by infamy and shame, we will turn our eyes to days of old. From generation to generation, God redeemed our fathers and He will redeem us and our children in the days to come. . . .
We stand before our God . . . we bow to Him, and we stand erect before man.

Rabbi Baeck stood erect before man, but there was no redemption for Jews in Germany.

Closing of the Reichstag session with the Nazi salute and anthem. Berlin, Germany, May 21, 1935. *Ullstein Bilderdienst, Berlin, Germany.*

Judges of the Berlin criminal court give the Nazi salute on the day they were required to wear the Nazi emblem on their court robes. Berlin, Germany, October 1, 1936. *Ullstein Bilderdienst, Berlin, Germany.*

NAZI SOCIETY, POLICE STATE

After five years in power, the Nazis had achieved total domination of German life. The state was supreme: government, society, and culture were under party control. At the center was the cult of the Führer, the leader, who had absolute power. Adolf Hitler was the incarnation of the German people's historic mission, and his will was law. The army, all civil servants, and the entire judiciary swore allegiance personally to Hitler, not to the constitution. His name was invoked in daily greetings. "Heil Hitler" prefaced formal meetings and intimate conversations; schoolchildren recited the phrase at the beginning of each class.

The Führer's exercise of power was unrestrained. "The law and the will of the Führer are one," Hermann Göring said in 1934. There were no checks and balances. Hitler was above the law, exercising legislative and judicial powers as well as the executive functions of government. Hitler's orders could overturn all legal norms and precedent; by his will, any deed could be sanctioned.

The Führer's instrument of terror was the Gestapo. Established in 1933 by Göring as a new political police unit, its official name was *Geheime Staatspolizei*, or Secret State Police. Known by the abbreviation Gestapo, it soon became synonymous with brutality. The Gestapo was also above the law. Its actions were not subject to review by any court.

At first, the Gestapo was used by Göring to do away with political opponents. The "temporary" state of emergency proclaimed in February 1933 after the Reichstag fire was never rescinded. Even after all political opposition to the Nazis had been crushed, the Gestapo enforced conformity at every level of German society.

It seemed to be present everywhere. Block wardens monitored their neighbors, waiters informed on their patrons, workers were alert to disparaging comments about the regime by their employers. Children were taught to watch their teachers, their pastors, even their parents. The Gestapo's reputation for cruelty only made it more feared, respected, and effective.

Heinrich Himmler and Rudolf Hess discuss Dachau concentration camp model. Dachau, Germany, May 8, 1936. *Bundesarchiv Koblenz, Germany.*

The Gestapo was authorized to hold people in protective custody, a euphemism for arbitrary arrest and imprisonment in concentration camps. In the first days of the Nazi regime, thousands of political prisoners were "taken into preventive protective custody" — arrested and placed in temporary camps. The main one was Dachau, which was established in 1933 and continued in existence throughout the twelve years of the Reich. Dachau served as the model for the SS controlled concentration camps and a training ground for personnel. After the initial wave of political arrests, the temporary camps were gradually put to other uses. But beginning in 1936, the Nazis established larger, more permanent concentration camps to replace them. Sachsenhausen was set up in 1936; Buchenwald a year later. Mauthausen and Flossenbürg began in 1938, and Ravensbrück, a special camp for women, was opened in 1939.

In June 1936, Reich SS leader Heinrich Himmler assumed the newly created position of chief of the German Police and set about to expand his empire. Himmler understood that the concentration camps had economic as well as political utility. Germany was moving toward a war economy. Production was expanding rapidly and labor was in short supply. Concentration camp prisoners were used to work on military and civilian

construction projects, and new camps were built near quarries and brickyards where prisoners could readily be used as laborers.

Terror went hand in hand with the enforcement of ideological conformity. From cradle to grave, the Nazi state laid claim to every stage of a German's life. The Hitler Youth and the League of German Girls trained boys and girls in their obligations to serve the party and the race. Young men were initiated into the state in the Labor Service. Army duty was obligatory. The calendar was filled with Nazi pageants and ritual observances honoring such events as Hitler's birthday and the anniversary of his assumption of office in 1933.

As German society became increasingly nazified at every level, the Christian churches also fell in line. The Roman Catholic Church believed it was protected by the 1933 concordat between Hitler and the Vatican granting freedom of practice to the Catholic Church in Germany, with the understanding that the church would not meddle in politics. Hitler did not live up to his part of the

bargain. The concordat, negotiated by Papal Secretary of State Eugenio Pacelli, the former papal nuncio in Berlin and the future Pope Pius XII, was widely regarded as a diplomatic victory for Hitler. It diminished the influence of the Catholic center party and Catholic labor unions in Germany. Notwithstanding its protests against Nazi euthanasia policy, the Roman Catholic Church became subservient to the regime.

With the exception of a few pastors who resisted Nazi domination, the Protestant churches were also caught up in the zealous nationalism sweeping Germany. The Nazi-inspired German Christians Faith Movement took over mainstream church offices, proclaiming: "In the person of the Führer we behold the One sent from God who places Germany in the presence of the Lord of history."

An opposition group, known as the Confessional Church, spoke out against the regime's Nazi racial and anti-Christian teachings. It was led by the Reverend Martin Niemöller, the most prominent of hundreds

Bishop Ludwig Müller gives Nazi salute. Müller was appointed by Hitler to the position of "Reich Bishop" with the mandate to unite all Protestant churches under a single Nazi-controlled organization. Nuremberg, Germany, 1934. *Presseillustrationen Heinrich H. Hoffman, Zeitgeschichtliches Bildarchiv, Munich, Germany.*

of pastors and laymen arrested beginning in 1936. In the last sermon preached by Niemöller before his arrest and consignment to Dachau, he said. "No more are we ready to keep silent at man's behest when God commands us to speak. . . . We must obey God rather than man."

The Reich Chamber of Culture controlled all forms of artistic expression: music, film, theater, literature, and art. Works by Jews or politically unacceptable writers and artists were banned. "Degenerate" modern art was seen as inimical to the Nazi state. Paintings by modern artists including German modernists Grosz and Kokoschka as well as Van Gogh, Picasso, and Gauguin were suppressed.

Intellectual life was also ruled by the state. German universities, which had been known for their scholarship and autonomy, expelled Jewish students and dismissed Jewish professors.

Reverend Martin Niemöller. Germany, 1937. Martin Niemöller (1892–1984) was a German anti-Nazi pastor whose oft-quoted condemnation of the bystanders has become a call to early action. He is reported to have said:

"First they came for the socialists, and I did not speak out — because I was not a socialist. Then they came for the trade-unionists, and I did not speak out — because I was not a trade unionist. Then they came for the Jews, and I did not speak out — because I was not a Jew. Then they came for me — and there was no one left to speak for me."

Bildarchiv Preussischer Kulturbesitz, Berlin, Germany.

TECHNOLOGY AND PERSECUTION

All governments gather information about their citizens. Census data, tax records, driver's licenses, birth certificates, and property transfers are significant raw material that the bureaucracy collects, organizes, uses, and disseminates in the course of its operation. Nazi Germany was no exception. But the Nazis used the neutral statistics in a lethal way: to hunt down those who did not fit into their vision of a perfect Aryan society.

The regime had a special interest in identifying, locating, and ultimately deporting Jews and other victims. It pursued its racial goals in a systematic and highly disciplined manner that incorporated sophisticated techniques of statistical analysis.

As early as 1934, government departments developed a series of card catalogues on people considered to be social deviants. By 1935, information was gathered on Jews, Gypsies, other "ethnic foreigners," and people who suffered from genetic diseases. Freemasons were also listed. They were seen as part of a secret conspiracy, and thus subversive. By 1936, the criminal police began a pilot project to register all Gypsies.

In 1939, the German government conducted a census. For the first time, explicit racial categories were part of the census form. Jews were not identified by their religious affiliation, but according to the racial criteria outlined in the Nuremberg Laws. The census was the basis for a national card catalogue of German Jews. All Jewish cards were marked with the letter J. The catalogue was the source used for compiling deportation lists. The Reich catalogue of Jews and *Mischlinge* was completed on December 10, 1942. Most of the men, women, and children it listed did not survive World War II.

The work of identifying and locating Jews was done efficiently with the help of the German-made American-engineered Hollerith machine, one of the earliest card sorters. The Hollerith was developed by Herman Hollerith, a German-American and an employee of the United States Census Office, who invented the first punch-card counting device. Its first major use was in the 1890 census. In 1896 Hollerith founded his own company, which he sold in 1911 to the Computing-Tabulating Recording Company (CTR), better known by its post-1924 name of International Business Machines (IBM). The Hollerith machines used by the Germans were developed by the Deutsche Hollerith Maschinen Gesellschaft (Dehomag), a company of which IBM controlled a 90 percent share. The Hollerith made it possible to process vast quantities of data in a relatively short time. During the war, the Hollerith was used to identify and allocate conscript labor. Whether the machine was used to compile deportation lists of Jews in Germany cannot be determined. But in many concentration camps, the political section of the Gestapo used the Hollerith to process the records of those who entered. The IBM technology was neutral; its use by the Nazi regime was malevolent. Clearly, its potential use was understood by the German manufacturer.

At the 1934 dedication of the new Dehomag offices in Berlin, Willy Heidinger, its founder, said:

We are recording the individual characteristics of every single member of the nation onto a little card. . . . We are proud to be able to contribute to such a task, a task that makes available to the physician of our German body-social the material for his examination, so that our physician can determine whether, from the standpoint of the health of the nation, the results calculated in this manner stand in a harmonious, healthy relation to one another, or whether unhealthy conditions must be cured by corrective interventions. . . . We have firm trust in our physician and will follow his orders blindly, because we know that he will lead our nation towards a great future. Heil to our German people and their leader!

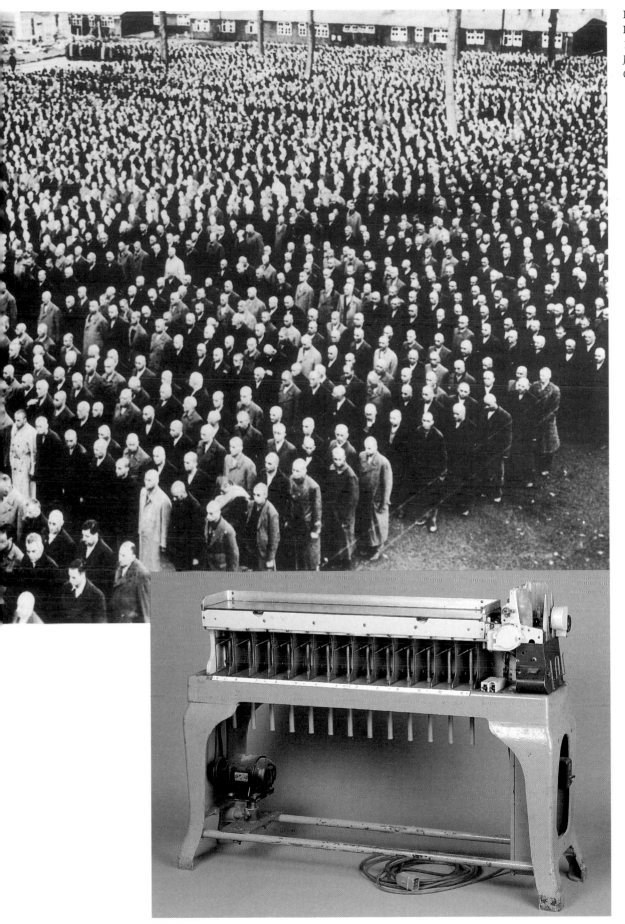

Roll call of prisoners. Buchenwald, Germany, 1938 or 1939. *American Jewish Joint Distribution Committee, New York.*

INSET:
Sophisticated technology helped the regime locate its victims quickly and efficiently. In the 1930s and 1940s, Holleriths were the best data-processing devices available. The machine sorted punch-cards according to specific criteria, such as residence, religion, or marital status. The tabulator counted the already-sorted cards. Hollerith machines tabulated national census data in 1933 and 1939; during the war, the SS used them to manage the huge numbers of prisoners shipped in and out of concentration camps. The machines were manufactured by a firm called Dehomag, for *Deutsche Hollerith-Maschinen Gesellschaft* (German Hollerith Machine Company). DEHOMAG had been a subsidiary of IBM since 1922. *Donated by the Museum für Verkehr und Technik, Berlin, Germany. Photo USHMM.*

Jewish boy being forced
to paint the word *Jude*
on his father's store.
Vienna, Austria, within
days of the Anschluss.
*Österreichische Gesellschaft für
Zeitgeschichte, Vienna, Austria.*

EXPANSION WITHOUT WAR

Hitler was determined to increase the territory of Germany — even if war was required. Until 1939, however, he was able to expand the Reich's borders without a fight.

Territorial expansion began with the Saarland area bordering on northeastern France, which had been temporarily severed from Germany following World War I pending a plebiscite. In January 1935, a 90 percent majority of Saarland voters favored reunification with Germany. In 1936 Hitler remilitarized the Rhineland in direct violation of the Treaty of Versailles.

On March 12, 1938, German troops occupied Austria, receiving a warm welcome from the native population. The following day, Austria was incorporated into the Reich, fulfilling what Hitler, who had been born in Austria, believed was the destiny of his native land. Nazi influence in Austria was pervasive well before the invasion, and a significant group favored unification with Germany. Soon after Hitler came to power, the Austrian chancellor, Engelbert Dollfuss, a Christian Socialist, dissolved parliament and banned all political parties except for his own Fatherland Front. Nevertheless, the Nazis remained active, and by 1938 the Austrian cabinet included Nazi party leaders. One of them, Artur von Seyss-Inquart, took his instructions directly from Berlin and proclaimed the union with Germany.

For Austrian Jews, annexation meant doom. Within a year, the Nazis accomplished what they had not been able to do in five years at home — total exclusion of the Jews. The speed and efficiency of Nazi persecution of Austrian Jews also served as a model used later in the territories conquered during World War II.

In Austria, nazism found a congenial climate of opinion. A long tradition of political antisemitism paved the way for Austrian Nazis and their supporters. Many parties tried to show that they liked Jews no more than did the Nazis. They exploited anti-Jewish sentiment and called for limiting Jewish influence in business, science, and the arts. The Catholic Church in Austria, which

Vienna residents greet Hitler. Vienna, Austria, March 11, 1938. *AP/ Wide World Photos, New York.*

Jews forced to scrub the sidewalks shortly after the Anschluss. Vienna, Austria, March 1938. *Dokumentationsarchiv des Österreichischen Widerstandes, Vienna, Austria.*

Viennese Jews waiting
in front of the Polish
consulate. Vienna,
Austria, April 1938.
*Österreichische Gesellschaft für
Zeitgeschichte, Vienna, Austria.*

was always uncomfortable with Jewish
"materialism" and liberalism, was silent about
rabid antisemitism among Catholic political
organizations. But it was the practical
application of German Nazi notions of racial
antisemitism that led to the doom of the
Austrian Jewish community.

At the time of the Anschluss (the German
takeover of Austria), there were 185,000 Jews
in the country, 90 percent of them living in
Vienna. They played a significant role in
Viennese intellectual and cultural life.

As soon as Germany took over, Jews were
physically attacked on the streets of Vienna.
The beards of pious Jews were forcibly
shaved. Jewish women were forced to scrub
sidewalks and clean gutters as crowds jeered
them. Apartments were looted. In the first few
weeks of the occupation, thousands of Jewish
businesses were taken over.

By the summer of 1938, the Nazis imposed
a version of "law and order." Street violence
was curbed, but antisemitism took a more
efficient and ruthless form. The persecution of

Austrian Jews followed the German pattern:
Aryanization of property, segregation, then
emigration. By the summer of 1939,
twenty-one thousand Jewish businesses were
closed and five thousand transferred to non-
Jewish ownership. Segregation was also
accomplished swiftly. By the end of 1938, 60
percent of all Jewish homes and apartments in
Vienna were taken over to be used by Aryans.

Jews began to leave Austria as soon as the
Nazis entered. By December 1938, sixty-six
thousand had emigrated. By the time war
broke out in September 1939, 75 percent of
the Jews had left.

An Office for Jewish Emigration was set up
under the SS (the dreaded initials were the
abbreviation for *Schutzstaffel*, elite guard). The
SS had originally been a small group of
black-uniformed loyalists who served as
Hitler's personal guard. Under the leadership
of Heinrich Himmler, the Reichführer SS, the
SS had become a vast and powerful police
network whose responsibilities included the
concentration camps. Soon after annexation,

Himmler saw to it that a new concentration camp was established at the town of Mauthausen to avoid the inconvenience of sending Austrians held in "protective custody" all the way to Germany.

Adolf Eichmann, the German-born, Austrian-raised SS "Jewish specialist," who later became one of the master bureaucrats organizing mass deportations, administered the Office for Jewish Emigration from a mansion that had been confiscated from the Baron Louis de Rothschild.

MUNICH: THE DISMEMBERMENT OF CZECHOSLOVAKIA

In March 1939, Germany took over Czechoslovakia, again without firing a shot. The fate of the most prosperous and most democratic country in central Europe had been sealed almost six months earlier at the Munich Conference, when Prime Minister Neville Chamberlain of Great Britain abandoned his country's ally in an effort to appease Hitler.

From the beginning, Hitler had called for the union of all Germans. Three million ethnic Germans lived in the Czechoslovak region of the Sudetenland, where they constituted a minority. After the annexation of Austria, Germany demanded concessions from the Czechoslovak government, calling for the "autonomy" of the Sudeten German population. When these were rejected, Hitler threatened an invasion, thus precipitating an international crisis. Although Hitler pretended to be concerned about the fate of the German minority, his real aim was to take over Czechoslovakia's industrial capacity, its resources of gold and coal, the strategic fortifications on its frontier with Germany, and, above all, *Lebensraum* — living space for the militantly expanding Reich.

On September 28 and 29, 1938, the leaders of Great Britain, France, and Italy met with Hitler at Munich to resolve the political status of the Sudeten Germans. No Czechoslovakian leaders were allowed to participate.

The French and British, who had treaty obligations to support Czechoslovakia in the event of an attack, were terrified that calling Hitler's bluff would lead to a German invasion, which would draw them into war. They agreed to Hitler's annexation of the Sudetenland. Hitler later regretted settling for half a loaf.

Chamberlain returned to England triumphantly to declare that he had brought "peace in our time." He told his people:

> How horrible, fantastic, incredible it is that we should be digging trenches and trying on gas masks here because of a quarrel in a faraway country between people of whom we know nothing.

Concessions only whetted Hitler's appetite. Almost six months after the Munich Conference, in March 1939, Germany overran Czechoslovakia. In another six months, Britain was at war with Germany and Chamberlain had been driven out of office, to be replaced by Winston Churchill in 1940.

Prague residents responding to German occupiers. Prague, Czechoslovakia, 1939. *Czechoslovak News Agency, Prague, Czechoslovakia.*

The chief concierge at the Hotel Evian is reported to have commented:

"Very important people were here and all the delegates had a nice time. They took pleasure cruises on the lake. They gambled at night at the casino. They took mineral baths and massages at the Etablissement Thermal. Some of them took the excursion to Chamonix to go summer skiing. Some went riding; we have, you know, one of the finest stables in France. But, of course, it is difficult to sit indoors hearing speeches when all the pleasures that Evian offers are outside."

The Hotel Royal at Evian. Evian-les-Bains, France, July 1938.
National Archives, Washington, D.C.

NO HELP, NO HAVEN: THE EVIAN CONFERENCE OF JULY 1938

Between 1933 and 1941, the goal of Nazi anti-Jewish policy was to make the Reich *Judenrein* (cleansed of Jews) through forced emigration. Jews were eager to leave Germany, and for a while German policy and Jewish self-interest in survival coincided. By 1938, perhaps as many as 150,000 Jews — one in four — fled the country. But in 1938, as conditions became more desperate, there were few havens left for Jewish refugees. The annexation of Austria in 1938 brought an additional 183,000 Jews into the Nazi orbit, incorporating overnight more Jews into the Reich than had left Germany in the previous five years. Where were they to go?

In the summer of 1938, delegates from thirty-two countries met at Evian on Lake Geneva to deal with the international refugee crisis. The conference had been conceived by President Roosevelt as a grand gesture in response to mounting pressure in the United States to do something about the refugee problem. His call for the conference was greeted warmly by the American Jewish community. Henry Feingold reports that Herbert H. Lehman, governor of New York, simply sent a note with a single word: "Splendid." President Roosevelt replied: "I wish I could do more." Not everyone was pleased by the president's action. Representative Thomas Jenkins, one of those who wanted to restrict immigration, accused the president of going "on a visionary excursion into the warm fields of altruism. He forgets the cold winds of poverty and penury that are sweeping over the 'one third' of our people who are ill clothed, ill housed, ill fed." American Jews and their allies were pressing the admission of greater numbers of immigrants. Restrictionist forces kept reminding the president of the Depression, of the domestic agenda, and of the need to put America first. Roosevelt sought to balance both concerns.

Domestic considerations did not operate in a vacuum. Roosevelt was reticent about pressuring the international community to accept refugees. His invitation to the Evian Conference made it clear that no country would be expected to receive more immigrants than were permitted under existing laws. Nor would any government be expected to subsidize refugees: all new programs would have to be funded by private agencies. The American quota system for immigrants would not be touched. Britain was given assurances that the question of Palestine, which was under British mandate, would not be discussed. Any international pressure by Roosevelt would have forced him to do more on behalf of the refugees at home. It was enough for the president to assuage the pro-immigration forces at home without alarming potential political opponents.

Two days after Roosevelt's announcement of the Evian Conference, Hitler issued a characteristic statement:

I can only hope that the other world which has such deep sympathy for these criminals (Jews) will at least be generous enough to convert this sympathy into practical aid. We on our part are ready to put all these criminals at the disposal of these countries, for all I care, even on luxury ships.

American participation at Evian was less than enthusiastic. The United States delegation was not headed by Secretary of State Cordell Hull or Undersecretary Sumner Welles. The president did not want such a high-powered delegation. Instead, FDR nominated Myron C. Taylor, a businessman who was one of his close friends. Foreign leaders grasped the message. The French premier told his British counterpart that the American president was acting to soothe public opinion. Under these circumstances, little was expected or accomplished.

For nine days the delegates met at the Hotel Royal, along with representatives of thirty-nine private relief agencies, twenty-one of them Jewish. The world press gave the event extensive coverage.

Delegates from each country rose in turn to profess their sympathy with the plight of the refugees. They also offered plausible excuses for declining to open their countries' doors. Britain had no room on its small island and refused to open Palestine to Jewish refugees. The United States spoke abstractly about "political" refugees, using the euphemism to glide over the fact that most of the refugees were Jewish.

The Australian delegate was more candid. "We don't have a racial problem and we don't want to import one," he said. For Canada, still in the midst of the Depression, "none was too many." Canada would, however, accept farmers — small comfort for the urbanized Jews seeking to leave Germany. Colombia's delegate could not resign himself to believe "that two thousand years of Christian civilization must lead to this terrible catastrophe." In any case, his country could offer nothing. The Venezuelan delegate was reluctant to disturb the "demographic equilibrium" of his country. No Jewish merchants, peddlers, or intellectuals were wanted in Venezuela.

Holland and Denmark were ready to extend temporary asylum for a few refugees. Only the Dominican Republic made a generous offer to receive 100,000 Jews. In the end, however, few came. Even though an intergovernmental group was established at Evian to coordinate policy, the tidal wave of refugees soon overwhelmed the few offers of assistance.

In an official response to Evian, the German Foreign Office was able to gloat:

Since in many countries it was recently regarded as wholly incomprehensible why Germany did not wish to preserve in its population an element like the Jews . . . it appears astounding that countries seem in no way anxious to make use of these elements themselves now that the opportunity offers.

It was clear that the policy of forced emigration would not work: no one wanted the Jews.

The *New York Times* cartoon on the Evian Conference. *New York Times,* **July 3, 1938.** *New York Public Library, New York.*

THE NEW YORK TIMES, SUNDAY, JULY 3, 1938.

WILL THE EVIAN CONFERENCE GUIDE HIM TO FREEDOM?

A British cartoon reflecting the hopes that are placed in the Evian Conference—This meeting, to be at Evian, France, on Wednesday to arrange for the emigration of political refugees, was called at the instigation of the President and Secretary Hull, and only Italy, out of thirty-three nations asked to join, refused to participate. Myron C. Taylor, industrialist, will represent the United States.

Although Jews were the primary targets of Nazi persecution, they were not the only ones. Other groups were victimized — some for what they did, others for what they refused to do, still others for who they were. According to Nazi ideology, the world was divided into Aryans destined as the master race, followed by the lesser races identified by color, ethnicity, culture, and nationality. After Jews, Gypsies inspired the most animosity. Gypsies were also treated as social outcasts.

In the first years of the Nazi regime, terror was directed at political opponents — Communists, Socialists, liberals, and trade-unionists — as well as members of the clergy who spoke out against the regime. Once these voices were silenced, terror actually increased as the Nazi state turned against whole categories of people, including Gypsies, Jehovah's Witnesses, Freemasons, homosexuals, and the mentally retarded, physically handicapped, or insane.

Gypsies: Gypsies (Roma and Sinti) had been subject to official discrimination in Germany long before 1933, but even the Nazi regime never promulgated a comprehensive law against them. Pure Gypsies were not targeted for extermination until 1942: the real threat to the "purity of the race" was from the potential "mixture" of Gypsy and German blood. In the case of the persecution of Gypsies, local initiatives came before policy decisions were made in Berlin. In 1935, the city of Frankfurt herded Gypsies into a fenced camp. A year later, the city banned new immigration and authorized "biological hereditary examinations."

In 1936, the Reich Interior Ministry issued guidelines "For Fighting the Gypsy Plague," requiring that all Gypsies be photographed and fingerprinted. This documentation of the Gypsy population was later used by the Nazis when persecution and incarceration no longer seemed sufficient and the Gypsies were targeted for systematic murder.

In 1937, Himmler ordered the Reich Center for Fighting the Gypsy Menace to draft

Roundup of Gypsies. Leipzig, Germany, c. 1938, *Bundesarchiv, Koblenz, Germany.*

racial definitions for Gypsies, a preliminary step to authorizing "preventive custody" — the euphemism for imprisonment in a concentration camp — for those who fit the new definitions of Gypsy.

According to Heinrich W. Kranz, who headed the Institute for the Preservation of Race, Heredity and Health at the University of Giessen, "In the long run, the German people will only be freed from this public nuisance when [the Gypsies'] fertility is completely eliminated." The logical way to accomplish this was through wholesale extermination.

Jehovah's Witnesses: The proselytizing sect of Jehovah's Witnesses was a small minority in Germany — only twenty thousand in a population of sixty-five million, but the

Else Woieziek, a Jehovah's Witness sentenced to death and executed in 1944. Dusseldorf, Germany, 1937–1938.

Nordrhein-Westfälisches Hauptstaatsarchiv, Dusseldorf, Germany.

Witnesses were a thorn in the side of the regime. They would not enlist in the army, participate in air-raid drills, or give up their meetings and proselytizing. The Witnesses viewed themselves as soldiers of Jehovah in the spiritual battle between good and evil. They taught that the forces of Jehovah would defeat Satan, personified in Germany by Nazi authority. Worst of all, the phrase "*Heil Hitler*" would never pass their lips. For the Witnesses, each instance of social conversation was an act of spiritual resistance.

Persecution of the Witnesses lasted from 1933 until 1945, and beginning in 1937, they were sent to concentration camps. Those who remained at large lost children, jobs, pensions, and all civil rights. Nevertheless, the Witnesses continued to meet, to preach, and to distribute literature. Posters and tracts were even delivered to Nazi party headquarters.

Five thousand Jehovah's Witnesses were sent to concentration camps. They were unique in that they were "voluntary prisoners." If they recanted, they could be freed. Some lost their lives in the camps, but few renounced their faith.

Homosexuals: As was the case throughout Europe, homosexual behavior had been against the law in Germany for hundreds of years. In the liberal climate of the Weimar Republic, however, homosexuality was tolerated and open. Works advocating homosexuality were published, and gay bars were found in all the major cities.

Within weeks of his assumption of office, Hitler banned homosexual groups. On May 6, 1933, only four days before the book burning, Professor Magnus Hirschfeld's Institute of Sexual Research, which defended homosexuality, was vandalized, its library and photo collection destroyed. During the summer of 1933, storm troopers began raiding gay bars. Homosexuals sent to concentration camps were forced to wear yellow bands inscribed with the letter *A* for *Arschficker*. Pink triangles would come later.

Nazi homophobia was based on several strains in Nazi ideology. Homosexuals were seen as a threat to Aryan breeding policy. Homosexuality was also identified with the lack of manliness that the Nazis associated with the humiliation of Versailles and with the permissive cultural ambiance of the Weimar years. Above all, the upholders of the macho-centered culture of nazism felt threatened by the very existence of homosexuality.

On July 1, 1934, the head of the SA, the storm troopers, Ernst Roehm, was shot to death on Hitler's orders as part of a power struggle between the army and the SA. Roehm, an open homosexual, had been a close associate of Hitler since the early days of street fighting. His murder, which was lauded and officially sanctioned, was a signal to intensify the antihomosexual campaign.

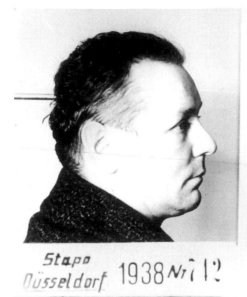

Stapo Düsseldorf 1938 Nr 7 12

Friedreich Althoff, arrested for alleged homosexuality. Dusseldorf, Germany, January 25, 1939. *Nordrhein-Westfälisches Hauptstaatsarchiv, Dusseldorf, Germany.*

Murder became the norm for dealing with political enemies of the regime. Soon, Himmler created a special criminal police office to fight homosexuality. By December 1934, homosexual "intent" was sufficient for criminal prosecution.

Freemasons: Freemasons were a secret fraternal order whose Masonic lodges were regarded by antisemites as a cover for a Jewish conspiracy to destroy Christianity. Started in 1717, from 1732 onward (almost sixty years before the French Revolution) Freemason lodges were open to Jews, and hence of added fascination to the antisemites.

Under nazism, Freemasons were regarded as an ideological foe of the Third Reich as well as part of the Jewish problem. The Nazis believed that Jews exploited the Freemasons' international connections to achieve world domination. The Nazi conception of "freemasonry" was quite elastic, and eventually grew to include potentially any secret brotherhood, including "old-Prussian" lodges, Scottish Rite Masons, the Rotary Club, the Order of the Grail, Rosicrucians, Theosophists, and Anthroposophists.

Nazi persecution of Freemasons was uneven and inconsistent. Initially, the pattern of persecution was virtually identical to that of the Jews, but it changed over time according to the needs of the state and the economy.

Throughout Germany in 1933 and 1934,

Masonic lodges dissolved themselves "voluntarily" or were closed by force. In 1935, all remaining Masonic lodges were abolished. Like Jews, Freemasons were purged from the civil service, forced into early retirement. During the "Night of Broken Glass," SA men were encouraged to paint anti-Masonic slogans on destroyed shops and synagogues.

But as the campaign against Jews intensified after 1938, the persecution of Freemasons slackened. The massive rearmament program of the late 1930s forced the Nazi regime to exploit every available resource, and many Freemasons were civil servants, merchants, or professionals whose skills were required. In April 1938, Hitler declared a partial "amnesty" for Freemasons, and in September some lower-ranking Freemasons were readmitted to the civil service. After this partial rehabilitation, persecution of Freemasons inside Germany was limited to "obdurate" practitioners and mainly took the form of ideological warfare against Freemasonry's humanitarian and supposedly Jewish influence. This cultural warfare took the form of a museum located in Nuremberg denigrating the Freemasons.

The amnesty did not, however, affect the treatment of Freemasons in the German-occupied territories of western Europe. In every German-occupied land, lodges dissolved themselves or were forced to close.

"NIGHT OF THE BROKEN GLASS," 1938

On the night of November 9, 1938, anti-Jewish violence erupted throughout the Reich, which now included Austria and the Sudetenland. What appeared to be a spontaneous outburst of national anger sparked by the assassination of a minor German embassy official in Paris at the hands of Herschel Grynszpan, a seventeen-year-old Jewish youth, was carefully orchestrated by the Nazi regime. Grynszpan's parents were Polish Jews living in Germany. They had been deported from Germany to Poland, but because Poland refused to accept its Jewish citizens, they were stranded in limbo. From the border town of Zbaszyn they wrote to their son in desperation. His immediate response was to seek revenge.

Just before midnight on November 9, Gestapo Chief Heinrich Müller sent a telegram to all police units letting them know that "in shortest order, actions against Jews and especially their synagogues will take place in all Germany. These are not to be interfered with." Rather, the police were to arrest the victims. Fire companies stood by synagogues in flames with explicit instructions to let the buildings burn. They were to intervene only if a fire threatened adjacent Aryan properties.

Within forty-eight hours, over one thousand synagogues were burned, along with their Torah scrolls, Bibles, and prayer books. Seven thousand Jewish businesses were trashed and looted, ninety-six Jews were killed, and Jewish cemeteries, hospitals, schools, and homes were destroyed. The attackers were often neighbors. Thirty thousand Jews were arrested. To accommodate so many new prisoners, the concentration camps of Dachau, Buchenwald, and Sachsenhausen were expanded.

When the fury subsided, the pogrom was given a fancy name: *Kristallnacht* — crystal night, or night of broken glass. It came to stand for the final shattering of Jewish existence in Germany. In the aftermath of *Kristallnacht*, the regime made sure that Jews could no longer survive in their country.

The cost of the broken window glass alone came to five million marks, the equivalent of well over two million dollars. Jews of German nationality, unlike Jewish-owned corporations from abroad, could not file for damages. Any compensation claims paid to Jews by insurance companies were confiscated by the Reich. The rubble of ruined synagogues had to be cleared by the Jewish community. A fine of one billion Reichmarks ($400 million) was imposed collectively on the Jewish community. After assessing the fine, Göring remarked: "The swine won't commit another murder. Incidentally . . . I would not like to be a Jew in Germany." On November 15, Jews were barred from schools. Two weeks later, local authorities were given the right to impose a curfew, and by December Jews were denied access to most public places. All remaining Jewish businesses were Aryanized.

The broken glass of the Jewish shops. Berlin, Germany, November 10, 1938. *Rijksinstituut voor Oorlogsdokumentatie, Amsterdam, Netherlands.*

Interior of Fasanenstrasse
Synagogue. Berlin,
Germany, about 1912.
Landeshildstelle, Berlin, Germany.

The Fasanenstrasse
Synagogue, destroyed
during *Kristallnacht*.
Berlin, Germany, April
16, 1941. *YIVO Institute for
Jewish Research, New York.*

Charred Hebrew prayer books damaged in a fire on *Kristallnacht* from a synagogue in Bobenhausen II, of the Vogelsberg district in Germany. *USHMM*.

The *Kristallnacht* pogrom was the last occasion of street violence against Jews in Germany. It appeared that Jews could leave and enter their homes in safety. But they no longer had any illusions. Life in the Reich was no longer possible. There was another wave of suicides. Most tried desperately to leave.

ifty years after *Kristallnacht*, a survivor, Sigmund Tobias, recalled what it meant to a Jewish child then:

Our family stayed at home and ventured outside only on the day after Kristallnacht. As we passed the entrance to the Ryke Strasse Synagogue, we saw a mound of simmering, smoking ashes in the center courtyard. To our horror, we realized that the smoldering mound consisted of the synagogue's prayer books. From the center of the mound the blackened, charred handles of sacred Torah scrolls protruded.

I had been taught great reverence for the Torah. If the Torah was dropped during services — even accidentally — the whole congregation would have to fast for 40 days. Yet the Nazis had brazenly destroyed the most holy, the most awesome objects of our faith.

I will never forget how terror struck this six-year-old at the realization that there was no safety for us anywhere.

OPPOSITE PAGE:
In response to the Anschluss, Jews desperately sought to emigrate. Jews waiting for the exit visas at a police station. Vienna, Austria, March 1938. *Österreichische Gesellschaft für Zeitgeschichte, Vienna, Austria.*

SEARCH FOR REFUGE

There was no place to go. Jewish emigration to Palestine was severely limited by the British. Neutral Switzerland was afraid of being overrun by Jews. The United States raised a formidable series of paper walls to keep refugees out.

A strict quota system limited the entry of immigrants to the United States according to their country of origin. To obtain a visa, a would-be immigrant had to fill out myriad forms and submit them to American consular officials in Europe, whose job was to issue visas sparingly. There were financial tests to weed out refugees who were likely to become a public charge. One of the requirements was a certificate of good conduct attesting to the exemplary character of the immigrant. This was supposed to be obtained from one's local police authority, in this case the Gestapo. Because American law at the time did not include any special provisions for admitting refugees fleeing persecution and since American law permits no distinctions on the basis of religion, after the outbreak of war in Europe in 1939, German Jews were barred as potential spies.

The United States, a nation of immigrants, was reluctant to become a haven for Jewish refugees. Reflexive nationalism went hand in hand with widespread antisemitism. The depression lingered on, and high unemployment made many Americans fearful of opening the doors to new immigrants, who represented competition in the job market. That these were victims of Nazi persecution fleeing for their lives did not seem a sufficient reason to let in more than a trickle of refugees. Only in 1938 and 1939 in the years between 1933 and 1945 was the quota for Germany and Austria filled, even though from 1932 to 1938 more people emigrated from the United States than came in as immigrants — the first time in all of American history that this had happened.

Public opinion polls taken at the time revealed widespread opposition to loosening the quotas, even among people who were critical of the Nazis. According to Roper polls taken in 1938 and 1939, while 95 percent of

Americans disapproved of the German regime, fewer than 9 percent supported changing the system to allow more refugees into the country. After *Kristallnacht*, even more Americans opposed any change.

American Jews, most of whom were themselves first- and second-generation immigrants, were hesitant about bringing pressure for a more generous refugee policy. As a community, they were splintered and powerless. They were afraid of stirring up antisemitism in the United States, and with good reason. Antisemitism in the United States reached a peak in the period between 1938 and 1945. Sixty percent of Americans polled by Roper in the late 1930s thought Jews had "objectionable qualities"; nearly half believed Jews had "too much power" in the United States; and as many as 20 percent said they would sympathize with an antisemitic campaign. In virtually every poll, Jews were cited as posing a major threat to the country.

Even efforts to rescue children were not successful. In February 1939, Senator Robert Wagner of New York and Congresswoman Edith Rogers of Massachusetts introduced a bill that would grant special permission for twenty thousand German children under the age of fourteen to come to the United States. The bill specified that the children would be supported privately, not by the government. At first, it seemed that the bill would pass easily. How could anyone be opposed to taking in children? But opposition came from the isolationists in Congress, who argued that American children should come first, and from groups who argued that it was "a Jewish bill" designed to help only Jewish children. President Roosevelt never said a word in support. The Wagner-Rogers Bill died in committee and never came to the floor of either the House of Representatives or the Senate.

The American journalist Dorothy Thompson wrote:

It is a fantastic commentary on the inhumanity of our times that for thousands and thousands of people a piece of paper with a stamp on it is the difference between life and death.

It is a fantastic commentary on the inhumanity of our times that for thousands and thousands of people a piece of paper with a stamp on it is the difference between life and death.

DOROTHY THOMPSON, AMERICAN JOURNALIST

THE VOYAGE OF THE ST. LOUIS

On May 13, 1939, the SS *St. Louis*, a luxury liner on the Hamburg-America Line, left Germany for Cuba carrying 936 passengers, all but six of them Jews. Each had a landing permit to Cuba. They seemed to be the lucky ones among the hundreds of thousand of Jews seeking to leave the Reich after *Kristallnacht*. In a few days they would reach freedom.

One day out of Havana, many of the passengers used the last of their "ship money" to send telegrams to relatives in Germany telling them, "Arrived safely." But when the *St. Louis* reached port on May 27, the Cuban government refused to honor the visas. The day before the ship had set sail, the president of Cuba had invalidated the landing certificates, a fact known to the shipping line, although not to the ship's captain. Bribes were solicited, with the asking price of five hundred dollars a person. As the ship sat in Havana harbor within yards of the shore, the ante was raised to one million dollars.

The American Joint Distribution Committee, the Jewish organization responsible for relief and rehabilitation work overseas, was in a dilemma. To pay such a huge ransom for nine hundred Jews would be an invitation for other governments to extort similar and even larger sums. At the same time, there was increasing pressure from the public — Jews and non-Jews alike — to meet the demand. The JDC continued to negotiate, while newspapers and radio gave daily reports on the fate of the passengers. Urgent appeals were made to the State Department, which decided not to intervene. The passengers sent a telegram to President Roosevelt. It went unanswered; the White House maintained its silence on refugee issues. A hand-wringing editorial in the *New York Times* said:

We can only hope that some hearts will soften and some refuge will be found. The cruise of the St. Louis cries to high heaven of man's inhumanity to man.

In New York, the JDC received discouraging replies from Colombia, Chile, Paraguay, and Argentina. On June 5, an agreement was reached that would allow the refugees to land in Cuba if $453,000 was deposited within twenty-four hours, a deadline the JDC could not meet.

When the *St. Louis* left Havana, the German captain, Gustav Schroeder, appealed in vain to the United States for a haven. As the ship sailed along the Florida coast, the passengers could see the lights of Miami. U.S. Coast Guard ships patrolled the waters to make sure that no one jumped to freedom. The *St. Louis* turned back to Europe.

Antisuicide patrols were organized. Children played a game in which two boys guarded a barrier constructed of chairs. Other children lined up and asked permission to pass through.

> *"Are you a Jew?"* asked one of the guards.
> *"Yes,"* answered the child at the barrier.
> *"Jews not admitted,"* snapped the guard.
> *"Oh, please let me in. I'm only a very little Jew."*

For a while, the sad voyage of the *St. Louis* seemed to have a happy ending. Belgium, the Netherlands, England, and France admitted the passengers. But within months, the Nazis overran Western Europe. Only the 288 passengers who disembarked in England were safe. Of the rest, only a few survived the Holocaust.

Denied entrance to Cuba, German refugees talk in Havana harbor to friends and relatives who are kept at bay. Havana, Cuba, May 27–June 2, 1939. *AP/Wide World Photos, New York.*

TO SAFETY

A few — too few — Jews found places of refuge. The United States received the largest number of refugees between 1933 and 1945, a total of 132,000. Until 1939, most refugees had gone to Palestine, but in 1939 a British White Paper limited the number of Jews who could settle there to fifteen thousand a year for five years. England did, however, take in ten thousand Jewish refugee children that year, something the United States was not willing to do.

Latin American countries received approximately eighty thousand refugees. Mexico, Argentina, Costa Rica, Brazil, Cuba, and Colombia were lands of refuge for those lucky Jews who escaped in time. Many German Communists who sought asylum in the Soviet Union were eventually sentenced to death under Stalin's terror campaigns.

Canada received only a handful of refugees. Canadian university faculties were not open to Jews. Of the thousands of European scholars who were forced to flee, only six found full-time jobs in Canadian universities. One of them, Gerhard Herzberg, a molecular physicist, became Canada's first Nobel laureate in science.

Until November 1, 1939, China required neither a visa nor a police certificate for entrance. Jews arrested after *Kristallnacht* could be freed from concentration camps on the condition that they left Germany within two weeks. Many went to Shanghai, a city of odd juxtapositions. Opium dens flourished in the vicinity of a distinguished university; thousands of Chinese died on the streets in a city that supported a symphony orchestra; caftan-clad Yiddish-speaking yeshiva students and German-speaking families who had been part of the Berlin cultural establishment lived alongside the Chinese.

The German Jewish refugees included ordinary people — shopkeepers, artisans, middle-class professionals — as well as distinguished writers, artists, scholars, and scientists who epitomized the flowering of high German and European

Arriving back in Europe with a Zionist delegation from the United States, Albert Einstein declared that he would never return to Germany. Antwerp, Belgium, 1933. *YIVO Institute for Jewish Research, New York.*

culture. Many had international reputations in their fields. Leaving their homeland to make a new life in a strange country was difficult. An Einstein was received royally, but other, less-renowned intellectuals were often treated shabbily, unable to find work suited to their abilities.

Not all the refugees were Jewish. Thomas Mann left Germany immediately after the Nazi takeover, and Paul Tillich, the brilliant young Protestant theologian, came to the United States in 1933.

Some of Europe's finest artists fled, including Jean Arp, André Breton, Marc Chagall, Marcel Duchamp, Max Ernst, Jacques Lipchitz, Andre Masson, and Henri Matisse. Eminent musicians included Georg Szell and Bruno Walter. Many established writers came to the United States, among them Franz Werfel, the novelist whose *Forty Days of Musa Dagh* conveyed the tragedy of the Armenians and was invoked by Jewish resistance fighters in Bialystok and Warsaw. Lion Feuchtwanger and Max Brod, the friend and biographer of Franz Kafka, were forced to flee.

In Vienna, Sigmund Freud dispatched his disciples around the globe. Psychoanalysis was no longer safe in the Reich. Analysts trained by Freud fled to New York and Los Angeles, Jerusalem and Johannesburg, Buenos Aires and Sydney. Freud himself left Vienna for London soon after the Nazis entered Austria. At a final gathering of his disciples in Vienna, Freud called on the memory of Yochanan Ben Zakkai, the first-century rabbi who had made Judaism portable and synagogue centered after the destruction of Jerusalem. Psychoanalysis would survive even if Freud was exiled from Vienna.

An Emergency Visitors Visa Program was established in the United States to rescue "persons of exceptional merit, those of superior intellectual attainment." Varian Fry, an emissary in France of the Emergency Rescue Committee, was dispatched, lists in hand, to save a cultural elite and relocate them in the United States. One hundred and fifty mathematicians came to the United States under the program. Hundreds of chemists came, eight of them Nobel Prize winners in the years before their arrival or in subsequent years.

In the humanities, the social sciences, and medicine and law — fields in which Jews had achieved prominence — many of the best and the brightest were forced to flee. Whole institutions of scholarship were relocated — for example, the Warburg Institute of Art, which moved from Berlin to London. Many of those who escaped found a haven, and often a home, in the United States. They taught at American universities, where their presence enriched American cultural life and left a permanent legacy. In fields as diverse as quantum physics and medieval history they reshaped American scholarship. Many of them could not easily find academic jobs, and a new institution, fittingly called the New School for Social Research, was established in New York City. Its faculty consisted almost entirely of refugees. The Manhattan Project, where atomic fusion first took place, would not have been possible without the contributions of the refugees.

Many of the German Jewish refugees who managed to enter the United States formed a community in New York City. More than twenty thousand of them lived in the Washington Heights area of upper Manhattan. Because they strenuously preserved *echt* (authentic) German culture and attitudes in the face of freewheeling American customs, the blocks between 160th and 180th streets

Sigmund Freud and daughter Anna Freud in Paris, en route to exile in England. Paris, France, June, 1938. *Popperfoto, Overstone, England.*

west of Broadway were facetiously called "The Fourth Reich." The émigrés published their own German-language newspapers, tried to live as they always had in Germany, and anguished for the brethren they had left behind. Among the children to grow up in this area was a young Jewish refugee, Henry Kissinger, who was later to become the first secretary of state of Jewish origin, a Nobel Peace Prize winner, and the architect of American foreign policy between 1969 and 1977.

Forced to begin anew in a strange world, the refugees had been wrenched from their language, their work, and their old lives. They could never forget those who did not survive. The playwright Bertolt Brecht described how it felt:

I know of course; it's simply luck
That I've survived so many friends. But last night
  in a dream
I heard those friends say of me:
  "Survival of the fittest"
And I hated myself.

THE WAR BEGINS

"War is life," Hitler wrote. "War is the origin of all things."

On September 1, 1939, the German armies invaded Poland. World War II had begun. The aim of German foreign policy, Hitler said, was to "secure for the German people the land and the spoils to which they are entitled on this earth." Austria and the Sudetenland had been taken into the Reich without a shot being fired, but the conquest of Poland required war. "Only thus shall we gain the *Lebensraum* [living space] which we need," Hitler told his troops.

Lebensraum was only one motive for going to war. Hitler's determination to carry out Nazi racial policy was of equal importance. In a speech on January 30, 1939, celebrating the beginning of his sixth year in power, Hitler issued an unequivocal warning:

If international-finance Jewry [Hitler's term for the supposed conspiracy of Jewish bankers] inside and outside of Europe should succeed once more in plunging nations into another world war, the consequence will not be the Bolshevization of the earth and thereby the victory of Jewry, but the annihilation of the Jewish race in Europe.

War made possible, Goebbels wrote, "the solution of a whole series of problems that could never have been solved in peacetime." War freed the regime from all restraints and at the same time united the German people against their enemies — both real and imagined. Hitler's war, which overnight reversed the humiliating defeat of 1918, restored the confidence of the nation that until recently had been still reeling from its defeat in World War I. Within a year of the attack on Poland, Germany achieved hegemony over an empire in the East.

The Polish army was destroyed within days of the Nazi invasion. Warsaw surrendered in less than a month. Great Britain and France declared war on Germany to fulfill their treaty obligations, but provided no military assistance to the beleaguered Polish government.

Germany and its new Soviet ally proceeded to carve up Poland. (In a stunning reversal of policy, Germany and the Soviet Union had signed a nonaggression pact less than two weeks before the attack on Poland.) Eastern territories were annexed to the Soviet Union; those in the west, including the city of Danzig, became part of the Reich or came under German rule. More than twenty-two million people were added to the Nazi empire.

On April 9, 1940, Germany invaded Denmark and Norway. Both were conquered swiftly. On May 10, German armies swept through Belgium and the Netherlands on their approach to France in an attack called the *Blitzkrieg*, or lightning war. The Netherlands fell in five days. Belgium capitulated in less than three weeks, forcing a British army of a quarter of a million to flee across the English Channel from the beaches at Dunkerque.

The French army, afraid of being totally destroyed, retreated. On June 13, Paris fell to the Germans. Under an armistice agreement, France was divided. The northern part of the country was occupied by Germany, while Hitler's ally, Italy, occupied part of the south. Part remained under nominal French control, ruled by the Vichy government, which was in fact a puppet of Germany.

During the summer of 1940, the Luftwaffe, the German air force, launched massive bombing raids on Britain as the prelude to a planned invasion, but met unexpectedly strong opposition from the Royal Air Force. Between July and October, the skies above England were ablaze with aerial combat; Germany lost 1,722 aircraft to the RAF's 915.

During the winter, the German army completed plans to invade the Soviet Union in May 1941. On April 6, 1941, Germany invaded the Balkan countries of Greece and Yugoslavia (Bulgaria and Romania had already come under German domination). The Greeks and Yugoslavs put up strong resistance, causing Germany to delay the invasion of the Soviet Union until late June, a postponement that was to have fateful consequences when the German armies were forced to campaign in the deadly Russian winter. Still, on the eve of the attack, the Soviet army was the only major land force on the European continent left standing against the Nazis. The triumphant German army looked invincible.

In the spring of 1940, the Nazi occupation government in Poland began a murder campaign against Polish priests, teachers, writers, artists, and suspected members of the resistance. These SS troops were photographed shortly before killing their blindfolded captives. Palmiry, Poland. *Main Commission for the Investigation of Nazi War Crimes in Poland, Warsaw, Poland.*

TERROR IN POLAND

The German High Command in occupied Poland received its orders directly from Hitler. In the Nazi racial hierarchy, Poles were considered *Untermenschen* (subhumans) standing in the way of German expansion. Prior to the attack, Hitler addressed his high command in Obersalzberg. Louis Lochner, a famous American correspondent in Berlin, received a copy of the notes of the meeting from Hermann Maass, a key contact of Admiral Wilhelm Canaris, director of the Abwehr, the counterintelligence department of the German High Command. (In 1944, Maass was a leader in the conspiracy against Hitler.) Hitler is reported to have said:

I have issued the command — and I'll have anybody who utters but one word of criticism executed by a firing squad — that our war aim does not consist in reaching certain lines, but in the physical destruction of the enemy. Accordingly, I have placed my deathhead formations in readiness — for present only in the East — with orders to send to death mercilessly and without compassion, men, women, and children of Polish derivation and language. Only thus shall we gain the living space [Lebensraum] which we need. Who, after all, speaks today of the annihilation of the Armenians?

German policy in Poland represented a departure from traditional warfare. Terror was intensified *after* a state was subdued and its people had surrendered. In the territories extending from East Prussia to Silesia, which were annexed outright by the Reich, the Nazis instituted a program of colonization. German settlers moved in and the native Polish population — including Jews — was forcibly resettled. Cities and towns were given German names. Whole regions were evacuated.

In what was known as the General-Government, the German-run but nonannexed territories of central Poland, members of the Polish intelligentsia and political leadership were systematically and brutally killed by the Nazis. The aim was to harness a leaderless, subservient population of laborers, who would be used to serve their German masters as migrant workers. Terror was central to this policy. The Nazi General-Governor Hans Frank said: "Poles will become slaves to the German Empire."

Executions took place daily in Warsaw's Pawiak prison and the Palmiry forest on the outskirts of the city. In Poznan, Fort VII became a place for the torture of university professors, politicians, and clergy.

The Roman Catholic Church had for centuries been inextricably linked with the Polish nationalist movement; therefore, it seemed logical to the Nazis that getting rid of Catholic priests was an effective way to weaken Polish nationalism. During the course of the war, 18 percent of all Polish diocesan priests were killed. In some regions, the death toll was even more devastating. Polish reports indicate that in Chelmno, 47.8 percent of the priests were murdered; in Lódź, 36.8 percent were killed; and in Poznan, 31.1 percent died. Within four months of the German invasion, 80 percent of the priests of the Wartaland region were expelled. Even if these figures are inflated, the reality of massive slaughter cannot be denied.

In prewar Poznan, thirty churches and forty-seven chapels had served a population of two hundred thousand. After the German occupation, only two churches remained open. In Lódź, a city of seven hundred thousand, only four churches remained.

Within a few weeks of the invasion, two hundred professors from Poland's ancient and venerated Jagiellonian University were murdered. Archives were plundered, art was stolen, and national treasures were taken to Germany. Even monuments to Poland's heroic figures — Chopin, Kosciuszko, and Pilsudski — were removed.

Those Polish children who were considered to be sufficiently Germanic were kidnapped and sent to Germany as part of a forced Aryanization program. "If a child is recognized to be of our blood," Himmler wrote, "the parents will be notified that the child will be sent to school and will remain permanently in Germany." As for ordinary Polish children, there was also a plan. In a top-secret memorandum, "The Treatment of Racial Aliens in the East," dated May 25, 1940, Himmler laid out the strategy:

For the non-German population of the East, there must be no higher school than the fourth grade of elementary school. The sole goal of this schooling is to

Execution of Piotr Sosnowski, a Polish priest. Piasnica, Poland, c. 1939. *Main Commission for the Investigation of Nazi War Crimes in Poland, Warsaw, Poland.*

teach them simple arithmetic, nothing above the number 500, writing one's name and the doctrine that it is divine law to obey the Germans. . . . I do not think that reading is desirable.

Himmler was equally blunt about his attitude toward Polish adults. "The conditions in which these people live . . . are a matter of complete indifference to us," he said. "They interest me only to the extent that we need them as slaves for our culture."

MURDER OF THE HANDICAPPED

Mass murder began with the death of a few individuals. In September 1939, Hitler signed an order empowering his personal physician and the chief of the Führer Chancellery to put to death those considered unsuited to live. He backdated it to September 1, 1939, the day World War II began, to give it the appearance of a wartime measure. In the directive:

Reich leader Philip Bouhler and Dr. Brandt are charged with responsibility for expanding the

The Hadamar euthanasia center. This picture was taken in the summer of 1941. In all likelihood the smoke is from the crematoria. Hadamar, Germany, 1941. *Hessisches Hauptstaatsarchiv, Wiesbaden, Germany.*

authority of physicians, to be designated by name, to the end that patients considered incurable according to the best available human judgment of their state of health, can be granted a mercy killing.

What followed was the so-called euthanasia program, in which men, women, and children who were physically disabled, mentally retarded, or emotionally disturbed were systematically killed.

Within a few months, the T-4 program (named for Berlin Chancellery Tiergarten 4, which directed it) involved virtually the entire German psychiatric community. A new bureaucracy, headed by physicians, was established with a mandate to "take executive measures against those defined as 'life unworthy of living.'"

A statistical survey of all psychiatric institutions, hospitals, and homes for chronically ill patients was ordered. At Tiergarten 4, three medical experts reviewed the forms returned by institutions throughout Germany, but did not examine any patients or read their medical records. Nevertheless, they had the power to decide life or death.

Patients whom it was decided to kill were transported to six killing centers: Hartheim,

Sonnenstein, Grafeneck, Bernburg, Hadamar, and Brandenburg. The members of the SS in charge of the transports donned white coats to keep up the charade of a medical procedure.

The first killings were by starvation: starvation is passive, simple, and natural. Then injections of lethal doses of sedatives were used. Children were easily "put to sleep." But gassing soon became the preferred method of killing. Fifteen to twenty people were killed in a chamber disguised as a shower. The lethal gas was provided by chemists, and the process was supervised by physicians. Afterward, black smoke billowed from the chimneys as the bodies were burned in adjacent crematoria.

Families of those killed were informed of the transfer. They were assured that their loved ones were being moved in order to receive the best and most modern treatment available. Visits, however, were not possible. The relatives then received condolence letters, falsified death certificates signed by physicians, and urns containing ashes. There were occasional lapses in bureaucratic efficiency, and some families received more than one urn. They soon realized something was amiss.

A few doctors protested. Karl Bonhoeffer, a leading psychiatrist, worked with his son Dietrich, a pastor who actively opposed the regime, to contact church groups, urging them not to turn patients in church-run institutions over to the SS. (Dietrich Bonhoeffer was executed by the SS just before the end of the war.) A few physicians refused to fill out the requisite forms. Only one psychiatrist, Professor Gottfried Ewald of the University of Göttingen, openly opposed the killing.

Doctors did not become killers overnight. The transformation took time and required a veneer of scientific justification. As early as 1895, a widely used German medical textbook made a claim for "the right to death." In 1920, a physician and a prominent jurist argued that destroying "life unworthy of life" is a therapeutic treatment and a compassionate act completely consistent with medical ethics.

Soon after the Nazis came to power, the Bavarian Minister of Health proposed that psychopaths, the mentally retarded, and other "inferior" people be isolated and killed. "This policy has already been initiated at our concentration camps," he noted. A year later, mental institutions throughout the Reich were instructed to "neglect" their patients by withholding food and medical treatment.

Pseudo-scientific rationalizations for the killing of the "unworthy" were bolstered by economic considerations. According to bureaucratic calculations, state funds that went to the care of criminals and the insane could be put to better use, for example by loans to newly married couples. Incurably sick children were seen as a burden for the healthy body of the *Volk*, the German people. In a time of war, it was not difficult to lose sight of the absolute value of human life. Hitler understood this. Wartime, he said, "was the best time for the elimination of the incurably ill."

The murder of the handicapped was a prefiguration of the Holocaust. The killing centers to which the handicapped were transported were the antecedents of the death camps. The organized transportation of the handicapped fore-shadowed mass deportation. Some of the physicians who became specialists in the technology of cold-blooded murder in the late 1930s later staffed the death camps. All their moral, professional, and ethical inhibitions had long been lost.

During the German euthanasia program, psychiatrists were able to save some patients, at least temporarily, but only if the psychiatrists cooperated in sending others to their death. In the Jewish communities of the territories later conquered by the Nazis, *Judenrat* leaders, Jews appointed by the Germans to take charge of the ghettos, had to make similar choices.

Gas chambers were first developed at the handicapped killing centers. So was the use of burning to dispose of dead bodies. In the death camps the technology was taken to a new level: thousands could be killed at one time and their bodies burned within hours.

The Roman Catholic Church, which had not taken a stand on the Jewish question, protested the "mercy killing." Count von Galen, the Bishop of Münster, openly challenged the regime, arguing that it was the duty of Christians to oppose the taking of human life even if this were to cost them their own lives. It seemed to have an effect.

On August 24, 1941, almost two years after the euthanasia program was initiated, it appeared to cease. In fact, it had gone underground. The killing did not end; mass murder was just beginning. Physicians trained in the medical killing centers went on to grander tasks. Irmfried Eberl, a doctor whose career began in the T-4 program, became the commandant of Treblinka, where killing of a magnitude as yet unimagined would take place.

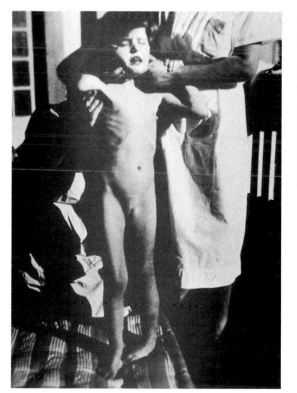

A mentally disabled girl photographed shortly before her murder. **Germany.** *Archiv Ernst Klee, Frankfurt, Germany.*

THE

HOLOCAUST

IN WESTERN EUROPE

The fate of Jews in Western Europe differed from country to country. Three major factors determined what happened to Jews in the lands between the Rhine and the Atlantic: the degree of control exercised by the Nazis in the conquered country; the history of Jews in the region; and the behavior of the local population. Despite local distinctions, anti-Jewish policy followed a familiar scenario. The pattern set by Germany toward its own Jews between 1933 and 1939, and toward Austrian Jews in 1938, became the model imposed swiftly on occupied countries.

First, Jews were categorized; then civil liberties were restricted and property confiscated. Next, Jews were dismissed from universities and civil service jobs, which often included school teaching, and were barred from the professions. Jewish businesses were taken over and Aryanized. Jews were then isolated, forced to wear the Jewish star and forbidden to use public facilities.

Finally, Jews were assembled, first in large cities and then in transit camps. From 1942 on, they were deported from these transit camps to the death camps in the east.

France: The German army invaded France on May 17, 1940. An armistice signed in June divided the country. Part was ruled by Germany and Italy, and part remained under nominal French control, ruled by the Vichy government, whose leaders were German puppets.

Of the 350,000 Jews living in France when the Nazis invaded, half were recent émigrés from Germany or refugees escaping nazism, not French citizens. Half of the French Jews lived in Paris; the rest were scattered among hundreds of cities, towns, and villages throughout the country, especially after the Nazi invasion.

German resources were stretched thin in France, with only three battalions of German police (some three thousand men) in the occupation zone. In order to carry out their anti-Jewish plans, the Germans needed French cooperation. They had little trouble finding it.

During the first two years of Nazi occupation, the Vichy government aggressively implemented anti-Jewish legislation defining, isolating, and impoverishing the Jews. By 1941, thousands of French Jews were penniless refugees. At the same time that the ghettos of Poland were being emptied in the summer of 1942, deportations of Jews from France began. The French police were indispensable to the operation. In six months, 42,500 Jews were shipped eastward to Auschwitz from the transit camp in Drancy. A third of them were from the unoccupied zone ruled by the Vichy government. By the war's end, 77,000 Jews from France were killed in concentration camps — 20 percent of French Jewry.

Belgium: At the time of the Nazi invasion on May 10, 1940, there were about 66,000 Jews living in Belgium, most of them in the cities of Antwerp and Brussels. Only one in ten was a Belgian citizen; the others were immigrants and refugees. Within a few months of the occupation, anti-Jewish legislation was promulgated. Jews were defined according to the Nuremberg Laws categorization. In the next two years, eighteen anti-Jewish measures were imposed. Property was confiscated, Jews were forbidden to attend public schools, prevented from leaving the country, and forced to wear yellow stars. From the summer of 1942 to mid-1944, 26,500 Jews were deported to Auschwitz via the Mechelen transit camp.

Norway: There were nineteen hundred Jews in the Norwegian population of three million. About one thousand lived in Oslo and about three hundred in Trondheim. Norway's Minister-President Vidkun Quisling, the Nazi collaborator whose name has become synonymous with betraying one's country, cooperated fully with the Reich commissar in dealing with the Jews. An inventory of real estate and commercial holdings was made, property was confiscated, and passports stamped with the letter J. Eight hundred Jews were deported to Auschwitz, and the rest evaded arrest by slipping into Sweden. Norway was *judenrein* — without Jews.

Luxembourg: When the Nazis invaded on May 9, 1940, there were forty-five hundred Jews in Luxembourg, three thousand natives and fifteen hundred refugees from Germany.

Arrest of Jews by French police and German officers. Paris, France, August 20, 1941.
Bibliotheque Historique de la Ville de Paris, France.

A decree of September 1, 1941, required Jews thoughout the Reich to wear a yellow Star of David badge whenever they appeared in public; children under the age of six were exempted. The same decree forbade Jews to leave their cities of residence without written permission from the police. In various countries, the Jewish star took different forms. *USHMM.*

TOP:
Jewish women in Paris, forced to wear yellow stars. Paris, France, c. 1940. *Bibliotheque Historique de la Ville de Paris, France. Photographer: André Zucca.*

On the morning of
February 12, 1941, the
German occupation
government encircled
the Jewish quarter of
Amsterdam with a
barbed-wire fence.
Eventually, most Dutch
Jews were confined
within it. Amsterdam,
Netherlands, 1941(?).
*Rijksinstituut voor
Oorlogsdokumentatie,
Amsterdam, Netherlands.*

About a thousand were evacuated by
retreating French troops. The small Jewish
community in the tiny duchy was ghettoized.
Jews were forced to wear armbands, their
property was expropriated, and they were
assigned to forced labor. About twenty-five
hundred escaped to France and Portugal. Eight
hundred were deported to Lódź in Poland, and
then to the death camp at Chelmno. Others
were sent to Theresienstadt and Auschwitz. Only
four hundred — fewer than one in ten —
survived in Luxembourg.

The Netherlands: There were 140,000 Jews
living in Holland when the Nazis invaded on
May 10, 1940. Under the occupation, a civil
administration controlled by the Germans ran
the country. Anti-Jewish laws were quickly
applied. Jewish enterprises were registered
with the civilian authorities, and a census of
Jews was taken. By 1941, Jewish children
could no longer attend public schools. Jews
were barred from public places, and curfews
were imposed. Jews could shop only during
specified hours, could not visit libraries or
museums, or leave their homes in the evening.
On May 2, 1942, Jews were forced to wear
the yellow star.

In October 1942, deportations to the east
began. In the next two years 110,000 Jews
were sent to the death camps, where fewer
than 5 percent survived. By 1945, three out
of four Dutch Jews were dead, despite efforts
by religious and political groups to hide
Jews.

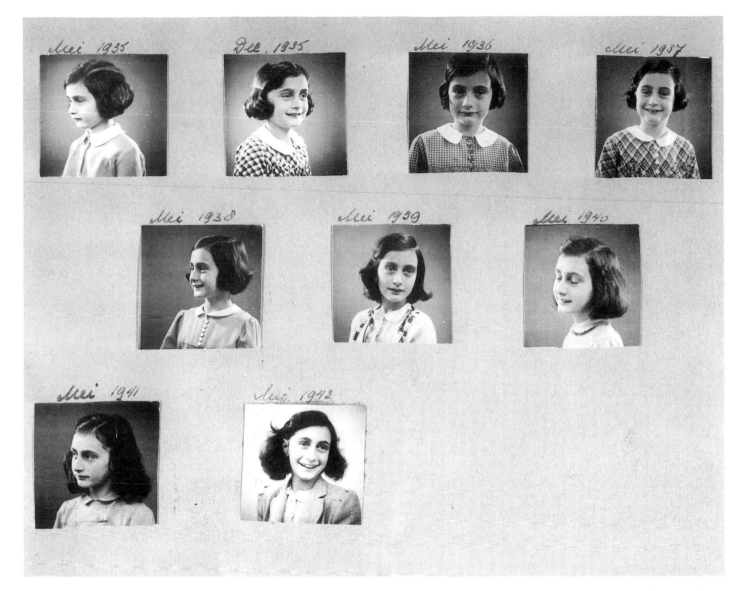

Mei 1935 Dec. 1935 Mei 1936 Mei 1937

Mei 1938 Mei 1939 Mei 1940

Mei 1941 Aug. 1942

Anne Frank. Amsterdam, Netherlands, 1935–1942. *Anne Frank Stichting, Amsterdam, Netherlands.*

ANNE FRANK

Anne Frank is the most famous child to die in the Holocaust. Yet her fate was no different from that of tens of thousands of other Jewish children in Western Europe.

Anne was born in Germany on June 12, 1929. Her parents fled to Amsterdam soon after Hitler came to power. When the Nazis invaded Amsterdam in 1940, Anne's childhood ended a month shy of her twelfth birthday. She had to stop going to school and was forced to wear the yellow star. Her father was no longer allowed to own his business.

On June 5, 1942, Anne's older sister Margot received a summons to report for forced labor. The Frank family immediately went into hiding at a vacant annex of Otto Frank's office, where they were joined by Fritz Pfeffer (whose anxiety and sense of isolation were recorded by Anne in her diary) and the van Pels family (called the van Damms in the diary). The van Pels' son, Peter, two years Anne's senior, is a major figure in the diary, their tentative adolescent friendship and romance painstakingly chronicled and analyzed by Anne. For two years, the eight people hid in a tiny attic. Their only contacts with the outside world were daily visits from one of the four Dutch people who brought them food and supplies.

Anne was given the diary by her father on

her thirteenth birthday, just when the family went into hiding. In her first entry she wrote: "I hope I will be able to confide in you completely as I have never been able to do in anyone before, and I hope that you will be a great support and comfort to me." She called the diary Kitty. Anne understood what would happen if the attic were discovered. On October 9, 1942, she wrote:

Our many Jewish friends are being taken away by the dozen. These people are treated by the Gestapo without a shred of decency, being loaded into cattle trucks and sent to Westerbork. . . . It is impossible to escape; most of the people in the camp are branded as inmates by their shaven heads. . . . If it is as bad as this in Holland, whatever will it be like in the distant and barbarous regions they are sent to? We assume that most of them are murdered. The English radio speaks of their being gassed.

Anne knew she was born to be a writer. On May 11, 1944, she wrote: "I want to publish a book entitled *The Annex* after the war. Whether I shall succeed or not, I cannot say, but my diary will be a great help."

Like all adolescents, Anne wrestled with the conflict between her ideals and the real world around her, although the real world she knew was framed by terror. On July 15, 1944, just after she turned fifteen, she wrote:

That's the difficulty in these times: ideals, dreams, and cherished hopes rise within us, only to meet the horrible truth and be shattered.

It's really a wonder that I haven't dropped all my ideals because they seem so absurd and impossible to carry out. Yet, I keep them, because in spite of everything, I still believe that people are really good at heart. I simply can't build up my hopes on a foundation consisting of confusion, misery, and death.

By September, Anne was in Auschwitz. Hope died at Auschwitz; so too innocence.

On August 4, 1944, the Security Service received an anonymous call informing them of the hiding place. During the arrest that followed, Anne's diary was thrown on the floor of the attic. It was found and saved by Miep Gies, a Dutch woman who had helped the Franks. Anne and her family were taken to the Westerbork transport camp. From there they were sent to Auschwitz on September 3, part of the last transport to leave the camp.

All new arrivals at Auschwitz were "selected" for work or death according to their physical appearance. Hermann van Pels, Peter's father, was sent to the gas chamber. Anne, Margot, and their mother, Edith, were sent to the women's camp as workers. Edith died at Auschwitz early in January 1945. Anne and Margot were sent on death marches to Bergen-Belsen, where they died of typhus in March, only four weeks before the liberation of the camp. Peter left Auschwitz on a death march and arrived in Mauthausen in weakened condition. He died shortly before the camp's liberation in May.

Of the eight who lived in the attic, only Otto Frank survived. His daughter's diary was returned to him after the war. Anne survives through the diary. *The Diary of Anne Frank* has been printed in hundreds of editions in dozens of languages and has sold more than twenty million copies. The diary was made into a play that ran on Broadway and has been performed tens of thousands of times by professional, amateur, and school groups. It was also made into a successful movie seen by millions of people throughout the world.

What accounts for the power of the *Diary*? Anne captivates us with her wit and her sensibility. It is easy to identify with the teenager whose life, even in hiding, epitomizes the struggle of adolescents everywhere as they grow to adulthood. One moment Anne is in despair, the next she is filled with hope. She can also laugh at herself and see her parents for what they are, even as she rebels. Her dreams, her fears, and her doubts are universal. On this level alone, the *Diary* stands as a marvelous example of the literary genre known as *Bildungsroman* — a story of growing up.

But because we know that Anne did not survive, that this life of enormous potential was snuffed out in the Holocaust, the *Diary* has a poignancy that is at once unbearable and transfiguring. Through this attractive young woman the Holocaust is made real: Anne Frank has become for our time the emblem of lost possibility.

GHETTOS, 1940–1944

Millions of Jews lived in Eastern Europe, most of them concentrated in cities and towns where they made up a substantial part of the population. The 24,000 Jews of Kielce were more than one-third of that Polish city's residents. One in four residents of Kovno, Lithuania (40,000), and Krakow, Poland (60,000), were Jews. In the Byelorussian capital of Minsk, with 240,000 residents, there were 80,000 Jews. In Radom, Poland, 30,000 Jews were also one-third of the total population. After the division of Poland between Germany and the Soviet Union following the 1939 invasion, more than two million Polish Jews came under the control of the Reich.

In Poland, ghettos were formed soon after the Nazi invasion. They endured until the policy of annihilation was firmly in place and the instruments of destruction — the killing centers — were established. In the Soviet Union and those areas of Poland that had been annexed by the Soviet Union in 1939, ghettos were formed after the Nazi invasion of June 1941, following the first wave of mass murder in which mobile killing squads rounded up and killed hundreds of thousands of Jews. The Vilna ghetto in Lithuania followed the murders at Ponar, and the Riga ghetto in Latvia was formed after thousands of Jews had been shot in the Bikernieki Forest.

The Jewish ghettos in Poland were set up in haste but with great efficiency. The Piotrovkov Trybunalski ghetto, established in 1940, was the first. Lódź, Warsaw, Lublin, Radom, and Lvov soon followed. By 1942, all the Jews of Poland and the German-controlled territories of the Soviet Union were confined to ghettos, living in hiding, or on the run.

Some ghettos were closed, while others were relatively open. The Warsaw ghetto was surrounded by eleven miles of walls; Krakow, too, was walled; and the Lódź ghetto was sealed, enclosed by wooden fences and barbed wire. Piotrovkov Trybunalski, Radom, Chelm, and Kielce were open ghettos. Poles could go back and forth, and at first Jews had little difficulty leaving. Before the final deportations, however, all ghettos were sealed.

From the German point of view, ghettos — or "Jewish residential quarters," as they were euphemistically called — were captive city-states, holding pens for a subjugated population with no rights. Jewish labor was to be exploited, goods and property were confiscated.

Moving large numbers of widely dispersed people into ghettos was a chaotic and unnerving process. In Lódź, where an area already housing 62,000 Jews was designated as the ghetto, an additional 100,000 Jews were crowded into the quarter from other sections of the city. Bus lines had to be rerouted. To avoid the disruption of the city's main transportation lines, two streets were fenced off so trolleys could pass through. Polish passengers rode through the center of the Lódź ghetto on streets that Jews could cross only by way of crowded wooden bridges overhead.

In Warsaw, the decree establishing the ghetto was announced on October 12, 1940 — Yom Kippur, the Jewish Day of Atonement. Moving schedules were posted on billboards. Whole neighborhoods were evacuated. While Jews were forced out of Polish residential neighborhoods, Poles were also evicted from the area that would be the ghetto. During the last two weeks of October 1940, according to German figures, 113,000 Christian Poles and 138,000 Jews had to be relocated, taking with them whatever belongings they could pile on a wagon. All abandoned property was confiscated. In every Polish city, the ghettos were overcrowded. The Warsaw ghetto, which occupied only 2.4 percent of the city's land, contained 30 percent of the city's population. Israel Gutman, a survivor of the Warsaw ghetto and its preeminent historian, wrote:

The closed ghetto cut the Jews off completely from the population at large. This separation prevented the Jews from coming into contact with non-Jews and left them in a state of isolation, insulation, and choking congestion. In one stroke the livelihoods of workers who had been integrated into the production process of the city and self-employed craftsmen whose businesses were outside the confines of the ghetto were wiped out.

Ghetto life was one of squalor, hunger, disease, and despair. Rooms and apartments were overcrowded, with ten or fifteen people typically living in space previously occupied by four. Daily calorie allotments, even with smuggling, seldom exceeded 1,100. Without smugglers who brought in food, starvation would have been rampant. The smugglers' motto — "Eat and drink, for tomorrow we die" — was only too apt.

There were serious public health problems. Epidemic diseases were a threat; typhus, the most dreaded. Dead bodies were often left on the street until the burial society came. Beggars were everywhere. Perhaps most unbearable was the uncertainty of life. Ghetto residents never knew what tomorrow would bring.

Governance of the ghetto rested with the *Judenrat* (Jewish Council), Nazi-appointed officials charged with controlling its municipal life. The Jewish Council was appointed before the ghetto was formed. Self-chosen or singled out for appointment, they served as go-betweens, representing Jewish interests to their German masters and passing on German demands to desperate Jewish residents. They labored to deliver a modicum of municipal services — sanitation, food, jobs, welfare, heat, water, and police. To provide these services, they taxed those who still had some resources and worked those who had none. They practiced the time-honored traditions of their people honed by centuries of exile and persecution. Decrees were evaded or circumvented. They tried to outwit the enemy and alleviate the awful conditions of the ghetto, at least temporarily.

In the ghetto, life went on. Families adjusted to new realities, living in constant fear of humiliation, labor conscription, and deportation. Survival was a daily challenge, a struggle for the bare necessities of food, warmth, sanitation, shelter, and clothing. Clandestine schools educated the young. Religious services were held even when they were outlawed. Cultural life continued with theater and music, poetry and art offering a temporary respite from squalor.

The word *ghetto* was originally the name of the Jewish quarter in Venice. (In Italian the word means foundry: the area had been the site of a cannon foundry.) Ghettos were

Street scene from the early Warsaw ghetto. Warsaw, Poland, c. 1940. *Bundesarchiv, Koblenz, Germany.*

Moving into the ghetto. Oftentimes, tens of thousands of people would have to move into the ghetto area at one time. They would take the apartments forcibly vacated by the native population. Drogobych, USSR [Ukraine], October 1942. *Ullstein Bilderdienst, Berlin, Germany.*

traditionally permanent places of Jewish residence, but in Poland the ghettos were viewed by the Nazis as a transitional measure. "I shall determine at which time and with what means the ghetto, and thereby the city of Lódź, will be cleansed of Jews," boasted Hans Biebow, the Nazi official who ran the Lódź ghetto. "In the end . . . we must burn out this bubonic plague."

In the summer of 1942, the Nazis began liquidating the ghettos of Eastern Europe. Within eighteen months, almost all of the ghettos of Poland were emptied, and the death camps of Sobibór, Treblinka, and Belzec could be closed. By the summer of 1944, more than two million Jews had been transported to concentration camps and there were no ghettos left in Eastern Europe.

THE WARSAW GHETTO

Before the war, Warsaw had been a cosmopolitan city and the largest center of Jewish life in Europe. Warsaw's Jewish population was 375,000, almost 30 percent of the city's total. Only New York City was home to more Jews.

The Warsaw Jewish Council appointed by the Germans served as a quasi-governmental authority to provide for the needs of more than 400,000 residents living in constantly deteriorating conditions. It was also responsible for conscripting workers to meet the German demands for forced labor. The *Judenrat* was headed by Adam Czerniaków, a sixty-year-old engineer from a cultured Polish background, who had long been involved with Jewish life and had been a member of the Jewish Community Council of Warsaw. The Germans instructed him to appoint a twenty-four-member council and serve as its chairman. Czerniaków appointed former members of the Community Council as well as members of the Jewish Citizens Committee, which had been created during the first days of the siege of Warsaw.

The *Judenrat* evolved into a multilayered municipality with a series of departments, including a Jewish police force. The *Judenrat* struggled in vain to serve two masters: the Nazis, who viewed the council as an instrument of their policies; and the Jews, whose ever-increasing needs they unsuccessfully tried to meet.

By the summer of 1940, tens of thousands of conscripted ghetto residents worked for the Germans for long hours, low pay, often under sadistic supervisors. On November 16, 1940, the ghetto was sealed and conditions worsened dramatically. The Nazis practiced what sociologists call "clean violence" — death by starvation.

The Germans allocated food supplies for all residents of Warsaw according to a carefully calculated schedule of priority; Jews were at the bottom of the scale. Deaths from starvation and disease became ordinary events in the ghetto. During 1941, 43,000 inhabitants — more than one in ten — died inside the ghetto. Daily life was an unending struggle for survival. Smuggling was necessary simply to keep people alive.

Smugglers were forced to be innovative and adaptive. Their methods constantly changed. At first, they moved goods back and forth past inattentive guards. Transfer points were established between two houses attached back-to-back that straddled the ghetto border. Boundary lines were changed and barbed-wire fences erected, but smuggling continued. Smugglers managed to find breaches in the

Adam Czerniaków, chairman of the Warsaw ghetto *Judenrat*. Warsaw, Poland, 1939–1942. *Yad Vashem, Jerusalem, Israel.*

wall. Holes were made and easily covered up by bricks, which were removed at night, allowing goods to be moved swiftly into the ghetto. Jewish policemen and their Polish counterparts found smuggling a source of personal revenue — no serious smuggling effort could succeed without bribery. Every conceivable scheme was exploited. Even carts carrying the dead to the cemeteries outside the ghetto did not come back empty. Children became quite adept at smuggling. With survival at stake, dangerous missions were undertaken.

An informal structure of governance and culture developed parallel to the *Judenrat*. A political underground created a clandestine press that published bulletins, manifestos, and newspapers. Cultural life went on; concerts, theatrical programs, and poetry readings found an audience. Education and religion endured. Synagogue services were held, and schools for children as well as adult-education classes continued. Youth movements and urban training communes carried out their work camouflaged as soup kitchens. Cells of the Jewish underground were disguised as agricultural workers' groups. Historians led by Emmanuel Ringelblum painstakingly documented ghetto life, believing that the historical records of a doomed community must be preserved.

Ringelblum was an active force within the Warsaw ghetto. A university-trained historian, Ringelblum had worked for more than a decade with the American Jewish Joint Distribution Committee in Poland. He was sent by the JDC to deal with refugees stranded on the Polish border in 1938. In the ghetto, he worked at the Institute for Social Self-Help, which ran soup kitchens. At night the kitchens became clubs for the political underground. Ringelblum kept a daily chronicle of events in Poland and spearheaded efforts by historians to create an archive of the ghetto and of events throughout Poland. Scientific papers were commissioned. Among them was a study of the effects of starvation. Ringelblum personally read every item that was added to the archive and published a bulletin that gave his colleagues in the underground, who heard only fragmentary reports, a clearer picture of the full scope of

Jews being taken out for forced labor in the Warsaw ghetto. Warsaw, Poland, 1941. *Bundesarchiv, Koblenz, Germany.*

what was happening to the Jews of Poland.

The eminent educator Janusz Korczak (Henryk Goldszmit), the Mr. Rogers of Polish radio, ran an orphanage. He was Poland's most famous children's advocate, a Jewish physician who wrote under the pseudonym Korczak. During the years between World War I and II, he moved easily between the liberal circle of Polish society that was gradually opening to Jews and those in the Jewish community who wanted to play a wider role in Polish life. Korczak's children's books, in which the central figure was the benevolent King Matt, a heroic boy-king who sought to bring reforms to his people, brought him

Corpses taken to a burial site in the Warsaw ghetto. Cart after cart was emptied in the huge grave. Warsaw, Poland, September 19, 1941. In 1941, one out of every ten residents of the Warsaw ghetto died from disease, starvation, cold, or despair. *Photo: Heinz Joest. Collection of Gunther Schwarberg, Hamburg, Germany.*

renown, as did his weekly radio program. He developed a popular and respected children's newspaper, written by young people, that appeared as an insert in a Polish newspaper. But the center of Korczak's life was the orphanage he directed, in which he put his educational methods to the test.

When the ghetto was formed in 1940, the orphanage had to be relocated into crowded quarters at 33 Chlodna Street, which were ample by ghetto standards. Korczak moved the group of children as though they were a theatrical troupe "in a kind of parade." It was a prelude of things to come. For the next two years, the old doctor, as he was known, used all his connections, energy, and ability to help his orphans survive in dignity, to feed them, clothe them, sustain and educate them. Korczak resisted overtures from friends to escape the ghetto and seek safety on the Aryan side. He would not leave without his children.

During the summer of 1942, more than 300,000 Jews were rounded up in the ghetto, marched to the Umschlagplatz transit point, and transported in cattle cars to Treblinka, some sixty miles away. The task of rounding up Jews for deportation fell to the Jewish police, who, together with a two-hundred-man force of SS Latvian soldiers and German police, systematically laid siege to the ghetto block by block, street by street, and finally building by building.

Adam Czerniaków was instructed to preside over the destruction of his people. In the middle of July, when rumors about the scope of deportation swept the city, he sought some reassurance from the Germans. At first he was told that all but 120,000 Jews would be deported. He then learned that his request for the exemption of children and orphans had been denied.

On July 23, the ninth day of the Hebrew

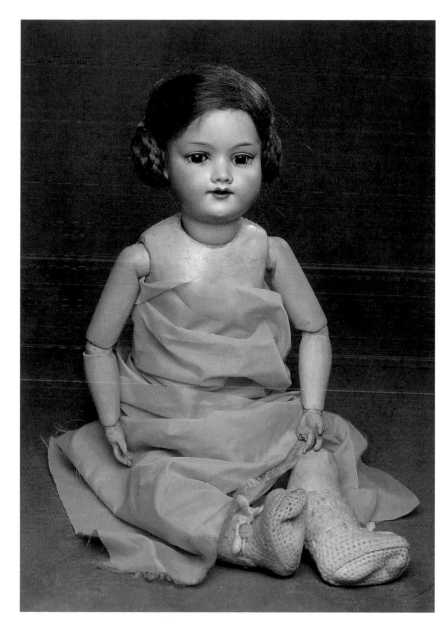

month of Av, the anniversary of the destruction of the first and second Temples in Jerusalem in 586 B.C.E. and 70 C.E., Czerniaków concluded the ninth book of his diary. That evening he swallowed cyanide. His last words were a tragic confession of failure: "The SS wants me to kill children with my own hands." It was something he could not do. The order for deportation appeared without Czerniaków's signature.

Even in death, Czerniaków was a controversial figure. Those close to him saw his suicide as an act of personal courage that expressed his integrity and sense of public responsibility. Those active in the ghetto's militant underground were less charitable. Emmanuel Ringelblum, the chronicler of the Warsaw ghetto, wrote: "Suicide of Czerniaków — too late, a sign of weakness — should have called for resistance — a weak man."

In the early days of the deportations, a decision was made by the underground, the Jewish Fighting Forces, that the time was not yet ripe for resistance. Their reasoning was that the fate of those deported was uncertain — at least in the minds of most ghetto residents. There was too little support for a final stand. The fighters were not trained. No weapons had been secured. But as the deportations continued, those who remained became increasingly angry that they had not resisted the Germans or even struck against the Jewish police. A Jewish fighting organization was formed by the Zionists, but did not yet fight, during those fateful days.

On August 6, 1942, the Nazis struck against the children's institutions in the ghetto. Korczak may have suspected that deportation meant death. He lined his children up in rows of four. The orphans were clutching flasks of water and their favorite books and toys. One hundred and ninety-two children and ten adults were counted off by the Nazis. Korczak stood at the head of his wards, a child holding each hand. One child carried the flag of King Matt, with the star of David set against a white field on the other side.

They marched through the ghetto to the Umschlagplatz, where they joined thousands

A wooden butterfly on wheels made in Theresienstadt by an unknown prisoner. Theresienstadt inmates sent toys secretly home to their children. *On loan from the Terezín Memorial, Czechoslovakia. Photo USHMM.*

of people waiting in the broiling August sun. There was no shade, shelter, water, or sanitary facilities. There were none of the cries and screams usually heard when people were forced to board the trains. The orphans walked quietly in their rows of four. One eyewitness recalls: "This was no march to the train cars, but rather a mute protest against the murderous regime . . . a process the like of which no human eye had ever witnessed."

Korczak was with his children to the end. All were gassed at Treblinka.

THE LÓDŹ GHETTO

Lódź was the industrial center of prewar Poland. More than one in three of its population of 665,000 were Jews. On September 8, 1939, the Germans captured the city and made it part of the territory annexed to the Reich, known as the Wartagau. Lódź was renamed Litzmannstadt in honor of the German general who had conquered the city during World War I.

The German occupation force was particularly ferocious in its treatment of the Lódź Jews. In addition to forced labor and confiscation of property, synagogues were blown up. When the ghetto was sealed in April 1940, 164,000 Jews lived in 48,100 rooms, most of them without running water or sewer connections. The Lódź ghetto, unlike the one in Warsaw, could be cut off from the outside world both above and below ground. Lódź, the first Polish ghetto to be sealed, was also the last to remain in existence, operating until 1944.

A Jewish Council, with Mordechai Chaim Rumkowski as chairman, was formed by the Germans to keep order among the starving and desperate population. Unlike the situation in Warsaw, in Lódź the *Judenrat* controlled all aspects of food, work, and shelter. Czerniaków allowed a form of laissez-faire capitalism in Warsaw. In contrast, Rumkowski ran a centralized, autocratic municipality in Lódź. When the rabbinate was abolished, Rumkowski himself performed marriages. His picture appeared on ghetto currency.

Rumkowski developed what he believed to be a long-term strategy for survival — salvation through work. He was determined to save the Jews of Lódź by making them a productive and indispensable work force for the Nazis. "Only one thing can save us," he said: collective acceptance of a productive life. In the midst of squalor, disease, starvation, and the stench of raw sewage, Lódź's Jews got up each morning and went to work, both within the confines of the ghetto and in work details outside.

Conditions deteriorated further when twenty thousand Jews from Germany, Luxembourg, and Czechoslovakia were brought into the ghetto. Five thousand Gypsies were also incarcerated in one section. By 1941, forty thousand workers were employed in ghetto factories run by the council. Lódź was also different from Warsaw and the other ghettos in that there was little private enterprise. No smugglers alleviated hunger — Rumkowski would not permit it. The Lódź ghetto was isolated, separated by barbed wire and open spaces from the rest of the Germanized city. The *Judenrat* ran everything — hospitals, dispensaries, schools, orphanages, even a thriving cultural life.

Yet, despite its impressive productivity and the profits made by ghetto industries, the Nazis were not content to let Lódź remain a working ghetto. During the first five months

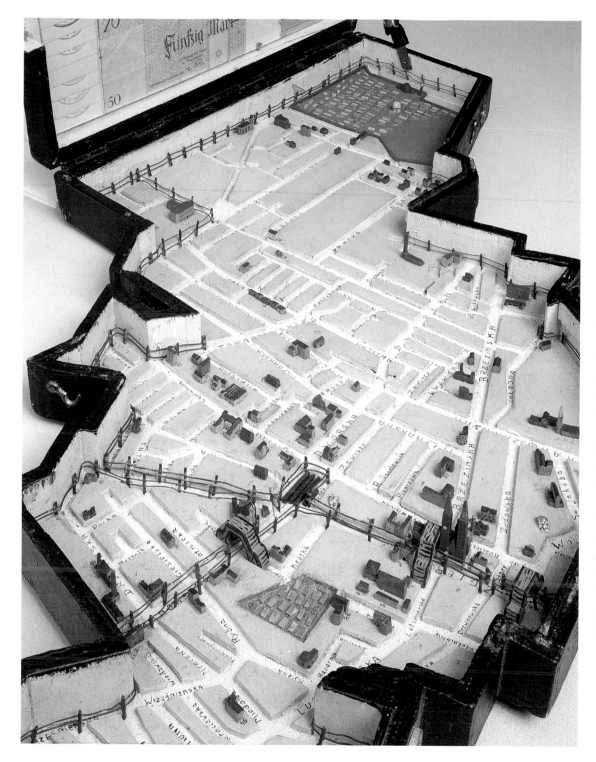

Leon Jacobson model of the Lódź ghetto. Jacobson built this model after he was transferred to Lódź in 1940. The scale is 1:5000. Its shape corresponds to the ghetto wall. The interior shows the location of footbridges, churches, ruined synagogues, factories, and cemeteries. Around the edges is barbed wire made of scrap wood. The inside cover displays official seals from ghetto factories and offices, ghetto money, and a ration card.

In August 1944, Jacobson was deported to Auschwitz along with the remaining ghetto inhabitants. Before his departure, he wrapped the model in tar paper and buried it in the basement of his building, which was later destroyed. After the war, Jacobson's brothers discovered the model in the rubble of the building. They dug it out and gave it to him in Germany. Jacobson later brought the model with him to the United States. *On loan from Leon Jacobson. Photo USHMM.*

of 1942, fifty-five thousand Jews and all five thousand Gypsies were deported and murdered in gas vans at Chelmno. Rumkowski was informed of their fate. More than two thousand patients were deported to Chelmno from Lódź Hospital, including four hundred children and eighty pregnant women. Eighteen patients who tried to escape were shot. Rumkowski acknowledged his responsibility. "I received an uncompromising order and carried it out myself to prevent others from doing it," he said.

In early September 1942, the Nazis demanded that all children and old people be surrendered. Rumkowski complied. "The decree cannot be revoked. It can only be slightly lessened by our carrying it out calmly," he said. In a public speech, he

Ghetto bridge built in Lódź. When the Lódź ghetto was established, the trolley car system could not be rerouted around the ghetto. Three bridges were built. Jews could walk over the bridges that divided the ghetto. Lódź, Poland, 1941.
Bundesarchiv, Koblenz, Germany.

pleaded: "Brothers and sisters, hand them over to me. Fathers and mothers, give me your children."

Rumkowski was consistent. "I must cut off the limbs to save the body itself," he argued. "I must take the children because if not, others will be taken as well." In the next ten days, twenty thousand children and old people were deported to certain death in Chelmno. Many Jews refused to turn over their children. German authorities lost patience, entered the ghetto in force, and carried out the deportations themselves.

For a while it seemed that Rumkowski's strategy had worked. During the period between September 1942 and May 1944, when the other ghettos of Poland were being emptied, there were no further deportations to the extermination camps from Lódź. With 90 percent of its starving residents working,

Lódź now took on the atmosphere not of a ghetto but a slave-labor camp.

But even Lódź did not escape the Final Solution. On June 23, 1944, deportations to Chelmno resumed, with Auschwitz the destination. Of the Lódź Jews, 46,000 died in the ghetto and 145,000 were deported to the gas vans of Chelmno or the gas chambers of Auschwitz / Birkenau. The number of survivors is not known. When Lódź was liberated by Soviet troops in January 1945, only 877 Jews emerged from the ghetto.

Rumkowski himself was deported to Auschwitz in August 1944, where he was murdered. There are three conflicting versions of his death. They may tell us more about what the Jews of Lódź thought ought to have happened than about his actual fate. According to some eyewitness reports, Rumkowski was beaten to death by Jews. In

Jews entering the Lódź
ghetto. Lódź, Poland,
1940–1944. *Jewish
Historical Institute, Warsaw,
Poland.*

Deportation of Jewish
children from an
orphanage to the
Chelmno death camp.
Lódź, Poland, September
1942. *Jewish Historical
Institute, Warsaw, Poland.*

approximately eighty thousand Jews still in the ghetto might have been saved. It can also be asked if it mattered that the Jews of Lódź left the ghetto without knowing their fate. Were the victims entitled to know their fate? What would they have done with such knowledge? Without Rumkowski's urging, would they have been forced to board the trains anyway? Whatever judgment history renders, it is clear that Rumkowski's power was limited. He could not control conditions or initiate policy. Power lay with Hans Biebow and his superiors, with those for whom the Final Solution was the ultimate priority.

TOP:
The Reichsführer SS Heinrich Himmler talks to Mordecai Chaim Rumkowski, the chairman of the *Judenrat* in Lódź. Lódź, Poland, June 5, 1941. *Jüdisches Museum Frankfurt am Main, Frankfurt, Germany.*

BOTTOM:
Deported Jews arriving at the Chelmno death camp where many were gassed in mobile killing vans. Chelmno, Poland. *Jewish Historical Institute, Warsaw, Poland.*

another account, Rumkowski arrived at Auschwitz by train with a letter from Hans Biebow, the German overseer of the Lódź ghetto. He was "invited" to tour the camp by his "hosts." His wagon stopped at the crematorium, where he was burned alive without being gassed. In still another account, the aged Rumkowski, too old to work, was selected for the gas chamber upon his arrival.

Historians have wondered if Rumkowski's strategy could have succeeded. If in the summer of 1944, Soviet troops had not halted their advance on the east bank of the Vistula River, seventy-five miles from Lódź, the

THE JEWISH COUNCILS

The stories of Adam Czerniaków and Mordechai Chaim Rumkowski exemplify the agonizing situation of the German-appointed Jewish Council leaders in the ghettos of Nazi-occupied Eastern Europe. Their daily responsibility was to provide the impossible: adequate food and shelter, heat, medicine, and work to a starving ghetto population. They had to care for the young and sustain the elderly. How could they make life bearable in the conditions of the ghetto? The resources at their disposal were meager; their authority was derived from their German masters. They presided, whether they knew it or not — and some did know — over doomed communities.

In every ghetto, the defining moments that tested the courage and character of the *Judenrat* leaders came when they were asked to provide lists of those to be deported. Once all tactics of bribery, delay, stonewalling, argumentation, and pleading were exhausted, a decision had to be made.

Judenrat leaders found themselves in a quandary. The time-tested strategies for dealing with the enemy were not working. The wisdom of Jewish tradition offered little guidance to this most agonizing question facing Jewish Council leaders. Rabbis who were asked what Jewish teaching mandated turned to a precedent in the Talmud. If idolaters tell Jews: "Give us one of yours and we shall kill him; otherwise we shall kill all of you," all should be killed and not a single soul should be delivered for death. But if the enemy should specify the name of the person to be delivered, there are two different opinions as to what should be done. Some Talmudic authorities permitted the community to deliver a designated person. Maimonides, the great twelfth-century philosopher and legal scholar, would not permit the handing over of even a specified individual unless that person was guilty of a capital crime.

Rabbi Abraham Dubner Cahana-Shapiro was approached at 11:00 P.M. on October 25, 1941, by the deeply divided Jewish Council of Kovno, which asked him whether it could issue a German decree ordering all ghetto inmates, without exception, to report to Demokratu Square at 6:00 A.M. on October 28, 1941, or whether it should refuse to publish the decree in order not to become an accomplice to destruction. The frightened rabbi begged for time to study the question. He spent all night poring over sacred books, searching for wisdom in traditional texts. Approached at six in the morning, he pleaded for just a few more hours. At 11:00 A.M. he responded: communal leaders had to summon the courage, take the responsibility, and save as many lives as possible.

Relying on the same texts and the same inherited wisdom, the Vilna rabbinate ruled that *Judenrat* chairman Jacob Gens must not participate in the deportation of a few, even if the rest of the community were to be saved. Gens proceeded with the deportation despite the rabbinic objections. He was not alone.

In Lódz, Rumkowski cooperated, reasoning that his duty was "to preserve the Jews who remain. The part that can be saved is much larger than the part that must be given away." He told his critics: "You may judge me as you wish." Faced with similar choices, Moshe Merin, of Sosnowicc in Upper Silesia, also complied.

Yet other *Judenrat* leaders would not deliver their people to certain death. Dr. Joseph Parnas, the first Jewish Council president in Lvov, refused to deliver several thousand Jews for deportation. He was shot. Leaders of the

In the past our enemies demanded our soul and the Jew sacrificed his body in sanctifying God's name. Now the enemy demands the body of the Jew. That makes it imperative for the Jew to defend it and protect it.

RABBI YITZHAK NISSENBAUM

council of Bolgoraj, in the Lublin District, were also shot when they refused to surrender their people.

In Warsaw, Rabbi Yitzhak Nissenbaum understood that the circumstances of the beleaguered community had no precedent. He called not for *Kiddush Hashem*, "the sanctification of God's name," or martyrdom, but for *Kiddush Hahaim*, the sanctification of life. "In the past our enemies demanded our soul and the Jew sacrificed his body in sanctifying God's name," Nissenbaum said. "Now the enemy demands the body of the Jew. That makes it imperative for the Jew to defend it and protect it."

When the order was finally given to liquidate the entire ghetto, *Judenrat* leaders faced an even more agonizing decision. Czerniaków swallowed a cyanide pill, leaving the deportation order unsigned. He did not call for resistance. Rumkowski urged the Jews of Lódz to get on the trains in an orderly fashion. Those who came voluntarily could bring luggage, while those who did not were rounded up by the Jewish police.

On October 14, 1942, the entire *Judenrat* of Bereza Kartuska committed suicide rather than participate in the deportation. The leader of the Jewish Council at Nieswiez Magalif marched to his death rather than turn Jews over to the Nazis, saying:

Brothers, I know you had not trust in me, you thought I was going to betray you. In this my last minute, I am with you — I and my family. We are the first ones to go to our death.

Street corner in the Kovno ghetto. Kovno [Kaunas], Lithuania.
Photo: George Kaddish YIVO Institute for Jewish Research, New York.

THE KOVNO GHETTO

Before the war, forty thousand Jews lived in Kovno; they were 25 percent of Kaunas' (the city's Lithuanian name) inhabitants. Renowned for its culture and heritage of religious learning, Kovno was the home of the famed Slobodka Yeshiva, which had for generations produced Jewish intellectuals who became leaders in both religious and secular life.

As a result of the pact between Germany and the Soviet Union that divided Poland and gave the Soviet Union the Baltic states, Kovno came under Soviet rule in 1939. When Germany invaded the Soviet Union in June 1941, antisemitic Lithuanians went on a murderous rampage against Kovno's Jews. (Anti-Soviet sentiment and antisemitism were widespread in Lithuania.) The Germans continued what the Lithuanians had started. Within a month, ten thousand Jews had been killed.

A ghetto was established immediately. In August it was sealed, isolating its population of thirty thousand. Three thousand more Jews were killed in a few months. On October 28, 1941, an additional nine thousand — about a third of those who were left — were taken to Kovno's infamous Ninth Fort, one of a chain built around the city in the nineteenth century, where they were murdered.

Unlike the Jewish Councils of other Eastern European ghettos, which were appointed by the Germans, the Kovno *Judenrat* was elected and supported by the ghetto population. In turn, the council aided all factions in the ghetto, including the underground. In Kovno, the Jewish police directly assisted the partisans. The Kovno *Judenrat* was headed by a prominent physician, Elchanan Elkes, who reluctantly accepted the office when he was drafted by the community.

In 1942, word of the fate of Polish Jews reached Kovno through Irena Adamowicz, a non-Jewish courier for the underground. From then on, the members of the Jewish

Council understood they would lead the battle for survival even without knowing if their efforts could postpone or prevent the day of destruction. Despite the Judenrat's best efforts, only two thousand Jews — 8 percent of the ghetto's original population — survived.

In October 1943, just before his deportation, Dr. Elkes wrote to his children living in England:

I am writing these lines, my dear children, in the vale of tears of Vilijampolé, Kovno Ghetto, where we have been for over two years. We have now heard that in a few days our fate is to be sealed. The Ghetto is to be crushed and torn asunder. Whether we are all to perish, or whether a few of us are to survive, is in God's hands. We fear that only those capable of slave labor will live; the rest, probably, are sentenced to death.

We are left, a few out of many. Out of the 35,000 Jews of Kovno, approximately 17,000 remain; out of a quarter of a million Jews in Lithuania . . . only 25,000 live. . . . The rest were put to death in terrible ways by the followers of the greatest Haman of all times and of all generations. . . .

We are trying to steer our battered ship in furious seas, when waves of decrees and decisions threaten to drown it every day. Through my influence I succeeded, at times, in easing the verdict and in scattering some of the dark clouds that hung over our heads. I bore my duties with head high and an upright countenance. Never did I ask for pity; never did I doubt our rights. I argued our case with total confidence in the justice of our demands. . . .

The Germans killed, slaughtered, and murdered us in complete equanimity. I was there with them. I saw them when they sent thousands of people — men, women, children, infants — to their death, while enjoying their breakfast, and while mocking our martyrs. I saw them coming back from their murderous missions — dirty, stained from head to foot with the blood of our dear ones. There they sat at their table — eating and drinking, listening to light music. They are professional executioners. . . .

I am writing this in an hour when many desperate souls — widows and orphans, threadbare and hungry — are camping on my doorstep, imploring us for help. . . . There is a desert inside me. My soul is scorched. I am naked and empty. There are no words in my mouth.

There is a desert inside me. My soul is scorched. I am naked and empty. There are no words in my mouth.

ELCHANAN ELKES, PHYSICIAN, KOVNO, LITHUANIA

THERESIENSTADT

Theresienstadt was a ghetto, a concentration camp, and a way station for western Jews en route to Auschwitz between 1941 and 1945. The population of Theresienstadt was transient: people were deported to the camp from the west, and then deported from the camp to the east. Of the 144,000 Jews sent to Theresienstadt, 33,000 — almost one in four — died there and 88,000 were deported to Auschwitz or elsewhere. By the war's end, only 19,000 were alive.

Reinhard Heydrich, the head of the SS, established a Jewish camp in Terezin, a Czech town forty miles north of Prague, on November 24, 1941. Called by its German name of Theresienstadt, it soon became the home of Jews from Prague and the German Protectorate. In 1942, the 7,000 non-Jewish Czechs who lived in Terezin were expelled and the Jewish community was isolated in a closed environment.

Czech Jews were joined by elderly German Jews. Dutch and Danish Jews arrived later. In contrast to other ghettos in which the young survived and those unable to work were deported, the population of Theresienstadt grew older as the young were sent east and the elderly and infirm remained.

German Jews arriving in Theresienstadt were unaware of what was in store for them. Some arrived at Theresienstadt with top hats and lace dresses. Some paid for the privilege of going there, innocently asking for rooms with a southern exposure. They were soon left without illusions. Conditions were harsh. At times, 90,000 Jews lived in space vacated by 7,000. Food too was scarce. In 1942, 15,891 people died, more than half the daily average population of the transient ghetto. The death rate was so high that a crematorium was built capable of handling 190 bodies a day — 69,000 a year.

Theresienstadt was the home — and the death place — of some of the most prominent Czech, Austrian, and German artists, writers, scientists, jurists, diplomats, musicians, and professors. The presence of so many secularized Western Jews from the great metropolitan centers of Europe gave rise to a rich cultural life. A lending library circulated more than sixty thousand books. Symphonic music was performed in concert. Theatrical performances and lectures gave spiritual sustenance to a dying community. By day, artists in the ghetto workshops painted what was acceptable to their Nazi overseers; at night, they painted a true picture of camp life, hiding their art behind the ghetto walls.

Fifteen thousand children passed through Theresienstadt. The community saw to it that their education continued with a rigorous daily routine of classes, athletic activities, and art. They painted pictures and wrote poetry. By war's end, only a few hundred of these children survived.

On September 28, 1944, the final deportations began. A month later, only a small crew of Jews remained. As one survivor summed it up: "If Auschwitz was hell, Theresienstadt was the anteroom."

Four hundred and fifty-six Danish Jews were sent to Theresienstadt in the fall of 1943. They were the unlucky ones who had not escaped to Sweden. Unlike other European countries, which quickly lost interest in their deported Jewish citizens, the Danes persisted in their demands for an accounting of their citizens' fate and insisted that the Red Cross visit the ghetto.

To quash rumors about the killing centers, the Nazis permitted the visit. But they arranged an elaborate hoax. In the weeks before the visit, deportations were intensified. The ghetto was beautified. Gardens were planted, houses painted, sidewalks washed, and new barracks built. Turf was laid on the village green. A building was refitted to serve as a social center, concert hall, and synagogue. A monument was even erected to honor dead Jews.

Fearful that any slip of the tongue or crack in the veneer of peaceful village life would

further endanger the beleaguered Jews of Theresienstadt, Paul Eppstein, the head of the Jewish Council of Elders, greeted the guests in black suit and top hat. A band played light music. A café created for the occasion was filled with customers. Goods were displayed in store windows. When the delegation came to the soccer field, a goal was scored on cue. Danish Jews, no more than two or three in a room, were visited in their freshly painted quarters. A children's opera, *Brundibar*, was performed for the guests.

The hoax succeeded so well that a propaganda film showing how well the Jews were living under the benevolent protection of the Third Reich was made at Theresienstadt. When the filming was over, most of the cast, including nearly all of the children, were deported to Auschwitz.

In Theresienstadt, ghetto residents used this hand-cart and others like it to transport heavy loads from one place to another. Such cargo often included bodies of the dead.

The "model ghetto" of Theresienstadt was established to house seemingly privileged Jews from Germany, many of whom were aged. Conditions were harsh and they took a toll on the elderly population. Crematoria were erected to dispose of the dead, who were carried in this cart. *On loan from the Terezín Memorial, Czechoslovakia. Photo USHMM.*

Daily life in Theresienstadt ghetto. Terezín, Czechoslovakia, wartime. *YIVO Institute for Jewish Research, New York.*

Class of children in Theresienstadt ghetto. Probably a staged scene prepared by the Nazis for the Red Cross visit. Terezín, Czechoslovakia, 1944. *Yad Vashem, Jerusalem, Israel.*

DEFIANCE

In the beginning, the inhabitants of the ghettos expected that somehow life would go on. The weight of Jewish history and experience taught that even the worst persecutions ended, so they struggled to carry on a normal life. When schools were closed, clandestine classes were started. In Lódź and in Warsaw, medical training was provided for those expelled from Polish schools by professors barred from teaching at the Aryanized universities. When synagogues were prohibited, prayer houses were formed in private homes and basements. Fifty underground newspapers were published in the Warsaw ghetto alone. Youth groups continued to meet. Political parties still functioned. Soup kitchens became late-night cultural centers. Theater performances were held. Poetry was written, songs were sung.

Ghetto humor was sardonic and defiant. Among the documents found in the archives of the Warsaw ghetto was the following story:

A police officer comes into a Jewish home and wants to confiscate the possessions. The woman cries, pleading that she is a widow and has a child to support. The officer agrees not to take the things, on one condition — that she guess which of his eyes is the artificial one.

"The left one," the woman guesses.

"How did you know?"

"Because that one has the human look."

Shimon Huberband collected the folklore of the ghetto, which used humor to defend against chaos and fight despair. "A teacher asks his pupil, 'Tell me, Moyshe, what would you like to be if you were Hitler's son?' 'An orphan,' the pupil answers." The Jews also used humor to describe their own situation. On life in the ghetto: "We eat as if it were Yom Kippur [the Day of Atonement, a day of fasting], sleep in sukkas [a temporary hut open to the sky without a roof], and dress as if it were Purim [when outlandish costumes are the rule of the day]."

Never Say, written by Hirsh Glik, a young Vilna poet, became the partisan hymn:

Never say, this is the last road for you,
Leaden skies are masking days of blue.
The hour we yearn for is drawing near,
Our step will beat the signal: we are here.

From southern palms, from lands long white
with snow,
We come with all our pain and all our woe,
Wherever seeped our blood into the earth,
Our courage and our strength will have rebirth.

Tomorrow's sun will gild our sad today,
The enemy and yesterday will fade away
But should the dawn delay or sunrise wait too long
Then let all future generations sing this song.

This song was written with our blood and not
with lead,
This is no song of free birds flying overhead,
But a people amid crumbling walls did stand,
They stood and sang this song with rifles held
in hand.

In Theresienstadt, a frail and weakened Rabbi Leo Baeck offered weekly classes in theology. Frieda Brandeis taught hundreds of children to express their pain in drawings. In classes held in the ghetto, children wrote poetry. Eva Pickova, a twelve-year-old child, wrote about fear:

Today the ghetto knows a different fear,
Close in its grip, Death wields an icy scythe.
An evil sickness spreads a terror in its wake,
The victims of its shadows weep and writhe.

Today a father's heartbeat tells his fright,
And mothers bend their heads into their hands
Now children choke and die with typhus here,
A bitter tax is taken from their bands.

My heart still beats inside my breast
While friends depart for other worlds.
Perhaps it's better — who can say? —
Than watching this, to die today?

No, no, my God, we want to live!
Not watch our numbers melt away.
We want to have a better world.
We want to work — we must not die!

Sunset. This watercolor by Helga Pollaková appears without a signature. Helga Pollaková was born on December 11, 1928, and deported to Theresienstadt on May 15, 1943. She was transported to Auschwitz on December 19, 1944. Her fate is unknown. *On loan from the State Jewish Museum in Prague. Photo USHMM.*

But Eva, like Anne Frank, did die. Deported to Auschwitz, she died in December 1943. She never reached her fourteenth birthday.

There were many acts of quiet heroism in the ghetto streets. In Warsaw, house committees served as neighborhood mutual-aid societies. Families survived by sharing scraps of bread. Children smuggled food for their parents. Many individuals resisted the impulse to think only of self-preservation. Gestures of friendship bridged loneliness and sorrow. Moral dignity was preserved by some even to the end.

A crayon drawing signed in pencil "Weidmann, Petr, 2 V 1944, 13½" (May 2, 1944). Petr Weidmann was born on September 1, 1930. He was deported to Theresienstadt from Prague on November 20, 1942. He was transported to Auschwitz on October 4, 1944. He did not survive. *On loan from the State Jewish Museum in Prague. Photo USHMM.*

My camera will be my revenge.

HIRSH KADUSHIN, PHOTOGRAPHIC CHRONICLER, THE KOVNO GHETTO

A neighbor of Hirsh Kadushin (George Kaddish) was murdered by the Lithuanians with his family. As he lay dying, he wrote with his own blood on the kitchen floor *Yiddin Nekamah*, "Jews Revenge." Kovno, Lithuania, June 1941. *Photo: George Kaddish, YIVO Institute for Jewish Research, New York.*

Emmanuel Ringelblum, Warsaw, Poland, before 1939. Ringelblum was a historian and social activist who organized the *Oneg Shabbos* group to document ghetto life. Ringelblum's diary and the archives he gathered are indispensable for understanding life inside the Warsaw ghetto. Hidden on the Aryan side after the final destruction of the ghetto, Ringelblum was shot by the Nazis on March 7, 1944. *Yad Vashem, Jerusalem, Israel.*

CHRONICLES

Documenting the story of the ghettos called for determination and ingenuity. Lódź had for its chroniclers a group of journalists and historians who formally recorded the details of ghetto life from January 1941 until the deportations of July 1944. In Kovno, the Jewish Council commissioned artists to make a visual record of ghetto life. Its secretary, Abraham Golub, assisted by several colleagues, gathered vital information for his diary. Before deportation, he managed to convey his work to a priest, with instructions that it be opened after the annihilation of the last Jew in Lithuania.

Hirsh Kadushin, an engineer by training, became the photographic chronicler of the Kovno ghetto. He began his work after a dying neighbor drew a message on the ground with his blood: *"Yiddin Nekama!"* (Jews Revenge!) Kadushin felt that he had been summoned. "I don't have a gun," he said. "The murderers are gone. My camera will be my revenge." He built a small, clandestine camera and carried it under his clothing. He managed to photograph every aspect of ghetto life. He worked in a hospital where a nurse he worked with bartered film. As the ghetto was being destroyed, Kadushin buried his photographs. He retrieved them after the war and has given them to the United States Holocaust Memorial Museum to stand as a permanent record of life and death in the Kovno ghetto.

The most comprehensive effort to document ghetto life was undertaken by a group of several dozen writers, teachers, rabbis, and historians led by Dr. Emmanuel Ringelblum in a secret operation code-named *Oneg Shabbos* (Joy of the Sabbath). They wrote diaries, collected documents, commissioned papers, and preserved the posters and decrees that comprised the memory of the doomed community. They had no illusions. Their only hope was that the memory of the Warsaw ghetto would endure.

On the eve of destruction, when all seemed lost, the archive was placed in milk cans and some metal boxes and buried deep beneath the streets of Warsaw. One can was found in

The discovery of the Ringelblum Archive, which was hidden in milk cans. The documents are being examined at the Jewish Historical Institute in Warsaw. Warsaw, Poland, December 1950. *Yad Vashem, Jerusalem, Israel.*

Displayed here is the second *Oneg Shabbos* milk can, discovered at Nowolipki Street 68 in Warsaw on December 1, 1950, together with several original documents from the *Oneg Shabbos* archive. These records include copies of several

underground newspapers, public notices by the Jewish Council, and a narrative of deportations from the Warsaw ghetto. *On loan from the Jewish Historical Institute, Warsaw, Poland. Photo USHMM.*

A letter to Yitzhak Gitterman, an *Oneg Shabbos* member and director of the Joint Distribution Committee, pleading for rescue from deportation:

"Dear, dear Gitterman, I beg you most dearly, save me if it is still possible. I have been

taken off the streets and carried away. . . . I want to see my wife and two little children again, whom I have left in the province. Save me as soon as possible. . . ."

The author died in Treblinka death camp. *Photo USHMM.*

1946. It is on display at the Jewish Historical Institute in Warsaw. A second can, on display at the United States Holocaust Memorial Museum, was discovered on December 1, 1950, at Nowolipki 68, Warsaw. Scholars at the Jewish Historical Institute speak of a third milk can. Despite repeated searches for this can and other metal containers, they remain buried in the rubble.

Without these documents, those who were not there would be impoverished in the quest to understand the inner life of the ghetto.

INVASION OF THE SOVIET UNION

On June 22, 1941, the German army invaded the Soviet Union along a two-thousand-mile-long front. Three million German soldiers went into battle against the Reich's former ally. The invasion force, which included Finnish, Romanian, and Hungarian troops, totaled more than one hundred infantry divisions and 3,550 tanks. Despite advance warnings that an attack was coming, Soviet troops were overwhelmed.

The Germans moved swiftly. In a month, the Baltic states of Latvia, Lithuania, and Estonia were captured. The cities of Minsk and Smolensk were also taken. By September, the Ukrainian capital of Kiev had fallen, and the city of Leningrad was under siege. Odessa and Kharkov were captured in October. Hundreds of thousands of Soviet soldiers were captured or killed. In November, the Germans laid siege to Sebastopol, the Black Sea port in the Crimea.

German troops swept to within thirty-seven miles of Moscow by the end of September, forcing the Soviet government to move out of the city. But like Napoleon's army, which also fought on two fronts, Hitler's juggernaut was bedeviled by supply problems, the Russian weather, and unexpected resistance from Soviet troops fighting to defend their homeland. In the north, the German advance was stopped near Leningrad, and on December 6, a Soviet counteroffensive pushed the Germans back at Kalinin. The Germans suffered large numbers of casualties, and their plans for a quick victory were confounded.

In the spring of 1942, the German offensive resumed. By late July, Stalingrad was under siege and major advances were made in the Crimea. In September, the German army entered Stalingrad, where they met ferocious resistance by Soviet troops. But only in the winter of 1942 / 43 did the Soviet army go on the offensive.

The aim of the invasion of the Soviet Union went beyond military conquest. It was, in the words of Heinrich Himmler, "an ideological battle and a struggle of races." In an address designed for German troops, Himmler summed up the Nazi racial demonology in which Slavs and Jews were seen as barely human:

Here in this struggle stands National Socialism: an ideology based on the value of our Germanic, Nordic blood. Here stands a world as we have conceived it: beautiful, decent, socially equal . . . a happy beautiful world full of culture. That is what our Germany is like.

On the other side stands a population of 180 million, a mixture of races whose very names are unpronounceable, and whose physique is such that one can shoot them down without pity and compassion. . . . These people have been welded by the Jews into one religion, one ideology that is called Bolshevism.

When you, my men, fight over there in the East, you are carrying on the same struggle against the same subhumanity, the same inferior races that at one time appeared under the name Huns, another time . . . under the name Magyars, another time under the name Tartars, and still another time under the name Genghis Khan and the Mongols.

It was only logical that killing these inferior peoples to ensure Aryan racial supremacy was permissible, if not essential.

THE MOBILE KILLING SQUADS

The German invasion of the Soviet Union marked a turning point in the Holocaust. In Soviet territory, mass killing became operational policy. Accompanying the army were small units of SS and police called Special Action Squads, or *Einsatzgruppen*. During the invasion of Poland two years earlier, the *Einsatzgruppen* followed the army and rounded up Jews, who were then forced into ghettos. In the Soviet Union, their assignment was simply to kill any Jews they could find in the territory taken by the army. The *Einsatzgruppen* did not operate alone. Order Police battalions and reserve battalions, Waffen SS units, the Higher SS and Police leaders, and stationary Order Police also carried out mass executions.

Jews were only too easy to find. Almost nine out of ten lived in large cities in the path of the army's rapid advance. The mobile killing units moved swiftly, taking the Jewish population by surprise and leaving communities paralyzed and unable to act.

The mass exterminations were well organized. As soon as an area was invaded, the *Einsatzgruppen* went into action. Jews were immediately rounded up, along with Communist party officials, Gypsies, and members of the intelligentsia. Jewish women and children were included in the roundups: the orders called for "total extermination" of the Jewish population. Those rounded up were then marched to the outskirts of the city or town and shot. Their bodies were buried in mass graves — hastily dug ditches filled with bodies piled layer upon layer.

At the Nuremberg trial of war criminals in 1946, one of the *Einsatzgruppen* commanders described a typical massacre:

The Einsatz unit would enter a village or town and order the prominent Jewish citizens to call

About one-quarter of all Jews who perished in the Holocaust were shot by members of the SS mobile killing squads. This man was executed in the presence of members of the German Army, the German Labor Service, and the Hitler Youth. Vinnitsa, Ukraine, 1942. *YIVO Institute for Jewish Research, New York.*

together all Jews for the purpose of "resettlement." They were requested to hand over their valuables and shortly before execution to surrender their outer clothing. They were transported to the place of executions, usually an antitank ditch, in trucks — always only as many as could be executed immediately. . . . Then they were shot, kneeling or standing . . . and the corpses thrown into the ditch.

Local residents could see what was happening, could hear the shots and the cries of the victims. Most of them did nothing to intervene. They, too, were terrified: what happened to the Jews one day might be done to them the next. The Wehrmacht (the German army) and the SS often encouraged the local population to conduct pogroms, particularly in Lithuania and Latvia, where virulent antisemitism was endemic. The killing units had so much to do that auxiliary police comprised of natives were indispensable. Local pro-Nazi collaborators volunteered for this work.

In Piryatin, a small city in the Poltava oblast in the Ukraine, the Germans murdered sixteen hundred Jews on April 6, 1942, the second day of Passover. They were all old men, women, and children who had not been able to flee eastward when the army invaded. The Jews were led out of town on the Greben road to Pirogovskaya Levada, where large pits had been dug. The Jews were stripped of all their clothing and belongings, which were sorted on the spot by the Germans and the local police. They were then forced into the pit five at a time and shot with submachine guns. A survivor remembers:

I saw them do the killing. At 5:00 P.M. they gave the command, "Fill in the pits." Screams and groans were coming from the pits. Suddenly I saw my neighbor Ruderman rise from under the soil. . . . His eyes were bloody and he was screaming: "Finish me off!". . . A murdered woman lay at my feet. A boy of five years crawled out from under her body and began to scream desperately, "Mommy!" That was all I saw, since I fell unconscious.

Three thousand men participated in the *Einsatzgruppen.* The officers of the units that rounded up and murdered Jews were not German criminals but ordinary citizens.

Mass graves of seven thousand Jews murdered in Khmelnitski Proskurov. Ukraine, January 1943. *Museum of the Polish Army, Warsaw, Poland.*

According to Raul Hilberg, they were not hoodlums, perverts, or psychopaths. The great majority were university-educated professional men. They used their skills and training to carry out their assignments in what they believed was a professional manner. In doing so, they became efficient killers.

"I never permitted the shooting of individuals," an *Einsatzgruppen* leader testified, "but ordered that several of the men should shoot at the same time in order to avoid direct personal responsibility." Other group leaders who were not so fastidious "demanded that the victims lie down flat on

Between June 25 and July 8, 1941, thousands of Jews from Kovno were rounded up by Lithuanian militiamen and taken to the "Seventh Fort." Every day Lithuanian guards removed groups of Jews, beat them, raped the women, and then shot them. Kovno, Lithuania, c. June 1941. *Archiv Ernst Klee, Frankfurt, Germany.*

Mass execution in the eastern occupied territories. Poland / Lithuania, c. 1941. *Centre de Documentation Juive Contemporaine, Paris, France.*

Massacre of Jews by Germans and Latvians. This photo was found among the Gestapo papers in the city of Liepaja. Liepaja, Latvia. *Novosti Press Agency—APN, Moscow, USSR.*

the ground to be shot through the nape of the neck. I did not approve of these methods." When asked why, he responded, "It was, psychologically, an immense burden to bear."

A handful of men in the mobile killing units asked to be relieved of their assignment. Permission was granted and no action was taken against them. The rest went along and performed the task with discipline, if not zeal. One officer wrote to his wife and children in October 1942:

I have already told you about the shooting — that I could not say "no" here either. But they've more or less said they finally found a good chap to run the administrative side of things. The last one was by all accounts a coward. That's the way people are judged here. But you can trust your Daddy. He thinks about you all the time and is not shooting immoderately.

The killers drank heavily. Alcohol somehow made the work more bearable. They spoke in euphemisms — of special actions, special treatment, executive measures, cleansing, resettlements, liquidation, finishing off, appropriate treatment. The words *murder* and *killing* were not used.

The killers themselves were marked. "Look at the eyes of the men in this kommando,

how deeply shaken they are," Himmler was told by one commander. "These men are finished for the rest of their lives. What kind of followers are we training here? Either neurotics or savages."

To deal with this problem, a more impersonal method of killing was sought. If the killers could no longer be brought to the victims in order to slaughter them face to face, the victims must be brought to the killers and dispatched in a way that kept the victims at a distance. Thus, a second form of killing was developed: the death camp, where killing was done by gas, and the bodies were then burned.

Before the mobile killing units of various types finished their work, approximately 1.2 million Jews were killed, one by one by one. Their bodies were piled high in mass graves throughout the occupied Soviet territories from the Baltic to the Ukraine. Later, in 1942 and 1943, when the war turned against the Nazis, SS Kommando soldiers returned to the murder sites to unearth the graves and burn the bodies in an attempt to obliterate all traces of the crime.

BABI YAR

On September 19, 1941, the advancing German army captured Kiev, the capital of the Ukraine. Within a week, a number of buildings occupied by German military and civilian authorities were blown up by the NKVD, the Soviet secret police. In retaliation, the Germans proceeded to kill all the Jews of Kiev.

An order was posted throughout the city in both Russian and Ukrainian:

Kikes of the city of Kiev and vicinity! On Monday, September 29, you are to appear by 8:00 A.M. with your possessions, money, documents, valuables and warm clothing at Dorogozhitshaya Street, next to the Jewish cemetery. Failure to appear is punishable by death.

From the cemetery, the Jews were marched to Babi Yar, a ravine only two miles from the center of the city. The Germans forced everyone to remove every item of clothing: men and women, boys and girls, young and old. There were no exceptions. The clothing was gathered and folded neatly in piles. Rings were stripped from the fingers of the naked men and women. The Jews were then shot. The bodies fell into the ravine. The sounds of gunfire could be heard in Kiev.

A truck driver at the scene described what he saw:

One day I was instructed to drive my truck outside the town. . . . It must have been about 10 o'clock. On the way there we overtook Jews carrying luggage marching on foot in the same direction that we were traveling. There were whole families. The further we got out of town the denser the columns became. . . .

I watched what happened when the Jews — men, women, and children — arrived. The Ukrainians led them past a number of different places where one after the other they had to remove their luggage, then their coats, shoes, and overgarments and also underwear. They also had to leave their valuables in a designated place. There was a special pile for each article of clothing. It all happened very quickly. . . . I don't think it was even a minute from the time each Jew took off his coat before he was standing there completely naked. . . .

Once undressed, the Jews were led into the ravine which was about 150 meters long and 30 meters wide and a good 15 meters deep. . . . When they reached the bottom of the ravine they were seized by members of the Schutzpolizei and made to lie down on top of Jews who had already been shot. This all happened very quickly. The corpses were literally in layers. A police marksman came along and shot each Jew in the neck with a submachine gun. . . . I saw these marksmen stand on layers of corpses and shoot one after the other. . . . The marksman would walk across the bodies of the executed Jews to the next Jew, who had meanwhile lain down, and shoot him.

I only saw this scene briefly. . . . I was so shocked by the terrible sight that I could not bear to look for long. . . .

Masses kept on coming from the city to this place, which they apparently entered unsuspectingly, still under the impression that they were being resettled.

Kurt Werner was one of the men in Sonderkommando 4a who did the shooting. He recalled the "complete terror of the Jews when they caught first sight of the bodies as they reached the top edge of the ravine." His work was unpleasant, and most difficult. He spent the whole morning in the ravine: shooting, loading submachine guns, leading Jews to the ravine.

It's almost impossible to imagine what nerves of steel it took to carry out that dirty work down there. It was horrible. . . . That evening we were given schnapps again.

Despite their best efforts, the Sonderkommando left some Jews alive. One survivor, Dina Pronicheva, described her experience to Anatoli Kuznetsov.

Her whole body was buried under the sand but she did not move until it began to cover her mouth. . . . She started to choke and then, scarcely realizing what she was doing, she started to struggle in a state of uncontrolled panic, quite prepared now to be shot rather than to be buried alive. . . .

The Ukrainian policemen up above were apparently tired after a hard day's work, too lazy to shovel the earth in properly. . . . Dina could just make out the nearest side of the sand pit and started slowly . . . making her way across it. . . . There was a little bush at the top which she managed to get a hold of. With a

Soviet POWs shoveling in the Babi Yar ravine where 33,000 Jews were killed on September 29–30, 1941. Kiev, USSR, autumn of 1941. *Hessisches Hauptstaatsarchiv, Wiesbaden, Germany.*

last desperate effort she pulled herself up, and, as she scrambled over the ledge, she heard a whisper which nearly made her jump back.

"Don't be scared, lady! I'm alive too."

It was a small boy in vest and pants who had crawled out as she had done. He was trembling and shivering all over.

In the days between Rosh Hashanah and Yom Kippur, the Jewish High Holiday and the Day of Atonement — Days of Awe — 33,771 Jews were killed at Babi Yar. In the following months, Babi Yar remained in use as an execution site for Gypsies and Soviet prisoners of war. Soviet accounts after the war exaggeratingly speak of 100,000 dead. The true number may never be known.

In August 1943, in the face of the Red Army advance against German troops, the mass graves of Babi Yar were dug up and the bodies burned in an attempt to remove the evidence of mass murder. Paul Blobel, the commander of Sonderkommando 4a, whose troops had slaughtered the Jews of Kiev, returned to Babi Yar. For more than a month, his men and workers conscripted from the ranks of concentration camp inmates dug up the bodies. Bulldozers were required to reopen the mounds. Massive bone-crushing machinery was brought to the scene. The bodies were piled on wooden logs, doused with gas, and ignited. The flames of the pyres were seen in Kiev.

When the work was done, the workers from the concentration camp were killed. Under cover of darkness on September 29, 1943, twenty-five of them escaped. Fifteen survived to tell what they had seen.

For twenty-five years after the war, the Soviet Union barely acknowledged Babi Yar. No memorial marked the site. In 1961, Yevgeny Yevtushenko, then a young Soviet poet, wrote about Babi Yar as an emblem of national shame.

No gravestone stands on Babi Yar;
Only coarse earth heaped roughly on the gash:
Such dread comes over me.

A year later, the poem was set to music by Dmitri Shostakovich in his Thirteenth Symphony. The Soviet prime minister, Nikita Khrushchev, was not happy about the subject of the work (the poem was also a blazing denunciation of the persistence of Russian antisemitism), and no government officials were present at the symphony's first performance.

In 1974, a memorial was finally erected at Babi Yar. Identification of the victims is vague; the word *Jew* was not used. Not until 1991, on the fiftieth anniversary of the Babi Yar massacres, was the identity of its victims revealed on the monument.

HOLOCAUST IN ROMANIA

In 1940, Romania, with a Jewish population of more than 750,000, was home to the third largest Jewish community in Europe. Only Poland and the Soviet Union had more Jews. An ally of France, Romania lost territory to the Soviet Union, Hungary, and Bulgaria after the fall of France. In November 1940, Romania became a partner of Germany. As Romania moved into the German orbit, it adopted an aggressive program of Romanization modeled on Nazi policies of Aryanization. Jews were identified, their assets were confiscated, and they were excluded from commercial life. Soon forty thousand Jewish homes were seized and handed over to Romanian non-Jews.

Supported by the Nazi police organizations — the SS and SD — the right-wing Iron Guard staged a putsch in January 1941. Hitler sided with General Ion Antonescu, the Romanian dictator, in order to ensure the support of the Romanian army for the German invasion of the Soviet Union. Before the unsuccessful takeover attempt was crushed, the Jews of Bucharest were attacked in a Romanian version of *Kristallnacht*. Synagogues were burned, shops demolished, and homes invaded. In a seventy-two-hour period, 120 Jews were killed. Many disappeared. Bodies of Jews were found in slaughterhouses with placards around their necks that said "Kosher meat."

When Germany invaded the Soviet Union in June 1941, the Romanian army was at the side of the Wehrmacht. Romania recaptured

Romanian Jews boarding the death train Iasi-Calarasi. Notice the old man with the cap boarding the train. Iasi, Romania, June 30, 1941. *Süddeutscher Verlag Bilderdienst, Munich, Germany.*

the territories of Bessarabia and Northern Bukovina, which had large Jewish populations. The slaughter began.

Within three days of the invasion, a massive pogrom took place in the northern Romanian town of Iasi. At least eight thousand Jews were killed and thousands were deported in sealed trains. On June 30, 4,332 survivors of the pogrom were loaded on two trains. One was scheduled for Calarasi, some three hundred miles away. The cattle cars simply shuttled back and forth until their human cargo perished from hunger and dehydration in the heat of the Romanian summer. Before the journey was over, 2,544 people died. Somewhere on Romanian soil, the mass graves of these Jewish dead are to be found.

Survivors and victims of the death train Iasi-Calarasi during a stop. The old man with the cap leaves the train. Targu Frumos, Romania, June 30, 1941. *YIVO Institute for Jewish Research, New York.*

In Odessa, the Soviet port on the Black Sea, the Romanian army murdered Jews by burning, as part of a reprisal against Jews and Communists ordered by Antonescu in response to an attack on Romanian headquarters. On October 23, 1941, nineteen thousand Jews were taken to the square at the harbor. Gasoline was poured on them and then set aflame. That afternoon, another twenty thousand Jews were taken to the village of Dalnik. Some were shot. Others were shut in a warehouse, which was then set afire.

Romanian army teams joined *Einsatzgruppen* D in the slaughter of tens of thousands of Jews in the territories of Bukovina and Bessarabia, which had been occupied by Soviet troops in 1940. In some instances, the local Romanian and Ukrainian population were willing participants in the killing.

Those 120,000 Jews who remained in Bessarabia and Bukovina were expelled and forced to go by foot to Transnistria to an area between the Diester and Bug rivers. During this death march, many thousands of Jews died. Many were shot, but hunger, thirst, and exhaustion claimed the lives of many more. During the next three years, seventy thousand Jews perished in Transnistria, victims of famine, disease, cold-blooded murder by the Nazis, and of mayhem. Over 100,000 Ukrainian Jews were slaughtered in Transnistria while under Romanian administration.

As the German military situation deteriorated in 1942 and 1943, Antonescu, suddenly sensitive to the prospect of an Allied victory, was hesitant about deporting the Jews of "old Romania," including the regions of Walachaia, Romanian Moldavia, and the city of Bucharest. He did agree, however, that Romanian Jews living in the Reich could be sent to concentration camps. Antonescu also approved plans for the deportation of Romanian Jews to the death camp at Belzec, although the plans were never carried out. He decided to use Romania's surviving Jews as hostages, valuable commodities to be traded to the Allies for cash. For the moment, Jews were worth more alive than dead. In December 1942, the asking price for a Jew was $1,336. At that price per head, Antonescu was willing to send seventy-five thousand Jews to Palestine. He even repatriated Jewish orphans from Transnistria to increase the number of Jews he could use as bargaining chips.

By war's end, more than 350,000 Romanian Jews were dead. Two-thirds of them had been killed not by the Nazis, but by Romanians and Hungarians. Three hundred thousand more remained alive, waiting to be ransomed. The idea of ransoming Jews for money had a long life in Romania. Even before the fall of Romanian dictator Nicolae Ceausescu in 1989, it was public knowledge in Romania that Jews had been ransomed by the Israeli government. Ceausescu received massive cash payments — reported to be in excess of one billion dollars — for his Jews.

The Wannsee villa where the plan on how to implement the Final Solution was discussed. Wannsee, Germany, 1922. *Ullstein Bilderdienst, Berlin, Germany.*

THE WANNSEE CONFERENCE, 1942 — THE DECISION TO KILL ALL JEWS

When was the decision made to murder all the Jews? Historians disagree as to the date when the Holocaust began and whether the idea of murdering all the Jews took shape slowly over time or was rather a premeditated plan that existed at the very beginning of the Nazi regime.

Did Hitler's desire to rid Germany of the Jews, which he stated so clearly in *Mein Kampf,* lead inexorably to his determination to kill all the Jews in Europe? Virulent antisemitism was the thread that ran through Adolf Hitler's life from his youth. As early as 1919 he wrote: "Rational antisemitism must lead to systematic legal opposition. Its final objective must be the removal of the Jews altogether." In many other instances Hitler outlined his goals and then proceeded to carry them out when the opportunity arose. The policy of genocide, however, seems to have evolved

gradually and in response to circumstances even Hitler could not have anticipated in his early days as a Nazi rabble-rouser.

Until 1939, the basic aim of Nazi policy was the forced emigration of Jews. That policy failed when few countries were willing to offer the Jews a haven even as Nazi territorial expansion brought more and more Jews under the control of the Reich. Between 1933 and 1938, only 150,000 Jews left Germany. When Austria joined the Reich in March 1938, more than 200,000 Jews came with it. With the conquest of Poland a year later, more than two million additional Jews fell within the German orbit. Emigration was not the answer. It simply would not work.

The mass killing of Jews began immediately following the German invasion of the Soviet Union in June 1941. The operations of the mobile killing units had been planned well in advance of the invasion. A decision had been made to kill Jews — but did the policy include all Jews?

By the late summer of 1941, only a few

months into the Soviet campaign, the massive killing centers — the infrastructure that made the Holocaust possible — were in place. They were the result of operational actions carrying out a decision that had already been made.

On December 8, the day after the Japanese attack on Pearl Harbor, the gassing of Jews began in mobile gas vans at Chelmno, a Polish town forty miles west of Lódź. Gas chambers were already under construction at Auschwitz and Belzec. Although the policy of mass extermination was not yet articulated, it was in fact already being carried out.

At the Wannsee Conference of January 20, 1942, a meeting of the officials responsible for coordinating the systematic murder operation, the "Final Solution to the Jewish Problem" was formally enunciated. Wannsee marked a turning point in the war against the Jews.

The conference was called by Reinhard Heydrich, head of the SS Reich Security Main Office. He invited the state secretaries of the most important government ministries to a villa in the affluent Berlin suburb of Wannsee in order to "coordinate without regard to geographic boundaries a Final Solution to the Jewish problem."

Among the agencies represented were the Department of Justice, the Foreign Ministry, the Gestapo, the SS Police, the Race and Resettlement Office, and the office in charge of distributing Jewish property. Also at the meeting was a representative of the General-Government, the Polish occupation administration, whose territory included more than two million Jews. The head of Heydrich's Jewish Office, Adolf Eichmann, had prepared the conference protocols.

The fifteen men seated at the table were considered the Reich's best and brightest. More than half of them held doctorates from German universities. They were well informed about the policy of dealing with the Jews. Each understood that the cooperation of his agency was vital if such an ambitious policy were to succeed.

Heydrich introduced the agenda:

Another possible solution of the [Jewish] problem has now taken the place of emigration, i.e., evacuation of the Jews to the East. . . . Such activities are, however, to be considered as provisional actions, but practical experience is already being collected, which is of greatest importance in relation to the future final solution of the Jewish problem.

The men at the table needed little explanation. They understood that "evacuation to the East" was a euphemism for concentration camps,

> *Rational antisemitism must lead to systematic legal opposition. Its final objective must be the removal of the Jews altogether.*
>
> **ADOLF HITLER**

and that "the Final Solution" was systematic murder. The prototypes had already been tested. For months, the Einsatzgruppen had been hard at work killing hundreds of thousands of Jews in the East. Gas vans had been operating for more than forty days at the Chelmno death camp. A farmhouse at Auschwitz / Birkenau was being converted into a gas chamber. Gas chambers using carbon monoxide from engine exhaust were under construction at the Belzec death camp. Experimentation with Zyklon B had begun at Auschwitz.

During the conversation at Wannsee there was no evasion. "They spoke about methods of killing, about liquidation, about extermination," Eichmann reported. As they talked, butlers served brandy. The course was set and the goal announced. Implementation of the Final Solution would soon take place.

There was no opposition, no qualms of conscience. On the contrary, the members of the coordinating committee were enthusiastic about doing their part. The representative of the General-Government in Poland, Dr. Josef Bühler, welcomed the start of the final solution in its territory. Transportation would present some difficulty. According to the protocol, Bühler said:

> *Jews should be removed . . . as fast as possible, because it is precisely here that the Jew constitutes a substantial danger as carrier of epidemics. . . . Moreover, the majority of the two and one-half million Jews involved were not capable of work.*

Three decades later, at his trial in Jerusalem, Eichmann recalled: "At the end, Heydrich was smoking and drinking brandy in a corner near a stove. We all sat together like comrades . . . not to talk shop, but to rest after long hours of work."

GENOCIDE AS STATE POLICY

Once the decision to kill all the Jews was made and the policy announced to the bureaucracy, the program of systematic slaughter that has become known as the Holocaust reached its maturity. Although there have been many instances of mass murder in human history, the Holocaust was unique.

The Holocaust was intentional and premeditated. Unlike other state policies in modern history that resulted in the death of entire populations — such as the Australian treatment of the Aborigines and the British treatment of Irish peasants, which led to mass death from famine — the murder of the Jews was the goal of Nazi policy from at least 1941 onward.

The Holocaust served no political or territorial purpose. Unlike the Native Americans who were crushed and then forced onto reservations because they stood in the way of western expansion, the Jews posed no territorial threat to the Nazis. Their murder led to no geopolitical benefit, yielded no territorial gain. The killing of Jews was not the means to an end, but a fundamental goal in and of itself.

The Holocaust was total and all encompassing. Unlike the Turkish campaign against the Armenians, when Armenians living in Constantinople and other cities were safe while those living in the eastern regions were victims, every Jew in Europe was targeted by the Nazis. At the Wannsee Conference, Heydrich noted that the Final Solution would have to deal with eleven million Jews, including those in Britain and Ireland. The goal of exterminating all Jews was nothing less than a major realignment of the human species.

The Holocaust was also different from all previous anti-Jewish violence. In the past, attacks on Jews had been episodic, confined to isolated geographic areas, and illegal in that the antisemitic outbursts that took place were often not sanctioned by law. Throughout history, anti-Jewish violence was based on religion, not biology. Jews were killed for what they believed and practiced. Conversion and emigration were possible.

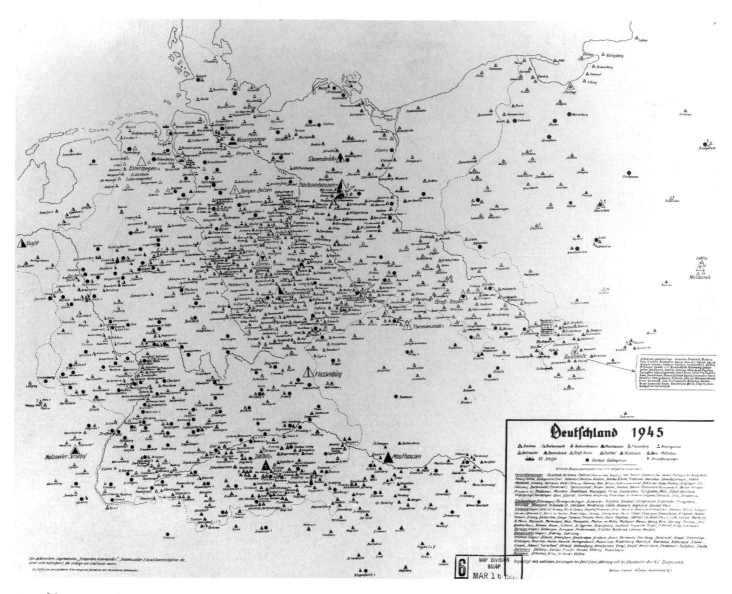

Map of the concentration camps. *Courtesy of the Library of Congress.*

In contrast, nazism was unrelenting. For twelve years, the persecution and then the destruction of the Jewish people was a national priority, even at the cost of rational policy. Jewish workers were killed in spite of an acute labor shortage, and railroad trains were made available to carry Jews to death camps even when every piece of rolling stock was needed to supply German troops on the eastern front. Jews were hunted down throughout Europe, from central Russia to the Spanish border. Above all, the policy of extermination was sanctioned by law, decrees, and official directives. The legal system itself served as the instrument of oppression and death. For example, in September 1942, Justice Minister Thierack turned over jurisdiction for Jews, Gypsies, Poles, Russians,

Ukrainians, Czechs, and asocial Germans to Himmler. He explained his decision in a letter to Martin Bormann: "In doing so, I stand on the principle that the administration of justice can make only a small contribution to the extermination of these peoples."

Nazi Germany became a genocidal state. The goal of annihilation called for participation by every arm of the government. The policy of extermination involved every level of German society and marshaled the entire apparatus of the German bureaucracy. Parish churches and the Interior Ministry supplied the birth records that defined and isolated Jews. The Post Office delivered the notifications of definition, expropriation, denaturalization, and deportation. The Finance Ministry confiscated Jewish wealth and property; German industrial and commercial firms fired Jewish workers, officers, and board members, even disenfranchising Jewish stockholders. The universities refused to admit Jewish students, denied degrees to those already enrolled, and dismissed Jewish faculty. Government transportation bureaus handled the billing arrangements with the railroads for the trains that carried Jews to their death.

The location and operation of the camps were based on calculations of accessibility and cost-effectiveness — the hallmarks of modern business and administrative practice. The killing was done coolly and systematically under the supervision of bureaucrats. German corporations profited handsomely from the industry of death. Pharmaceutical firms tested drugs on camp inmates without any regard for toxic side effects. Companies bid for contracts to build ovens and supply the gas used for extermination. German engineers working for Topf and Sons supplied one camp alone with forty-six ovens capable of burning five hundred bodies an hour.

From the crude violence of the Kristallnacht pogrom in 1938, the murder process escalated to ever more sophisticated levels of bureaucratic management. Murder by mass shooting carried out by the mobile killing units, which was seen as having a dangerously unsettling effect on the perpetrators, gave way to death centers where a small staff could efficiently murder tens of thousands daily without coming directly in contact with the victims. The kind of ingenuity and control of inventory and cost that is prized in modern industrial practice was rationally brought to bear on the process of destruction.

In the eyes of the perpetrators, the Final Solution to the Jewish Problem was Germany's great achievement. In a speech to SS and police leaders in Pozen, Himmler goaded them to greater self-sacrifice. He said:

I also want to talk to you quite frankly on a very grave matter. Among ourselves it should be mentioned quite frankly and yet we will never speak of it publicly. I mean the evacuation of the Jews, the extermination of the Jewish race. . . . Most of you must know what it means when one hundred corpses are lying side by side or five hundred or one thousand. To have stuck it out and at the same time — apart from exceptions caused by human weakness — to have remained decent fellows, that is what has made us hard. This is a page of glory in our history, which has never been written and is never to be written.

SS officers inspect inmates at forced labor. Mauthausen, Austria, c. 1941. *YIVO* Institute for Jewish Research, New York.

In 1942, Hitler boasted:

> In my *Reichstag* speech of September 1, 1939, I have spoken . . . that if Jewry should plot another world war in order to exterminate the Aryan peoples of Europe, it would not be the Aryan peoples which would be exterminated, but Jewry.
>
> At one time, the Jews of Germany laughed about my prophecies. I do not know whether they are still laughing or whether they have already lost all desire to laugh. But right now, I can only repeat: they will stop laughing everywhere, and I shall be right also in that prophecy.

In addition to mass murder, the Holocaust was the perverse perfection of slavery. Next to the extermination camp at Auschwitz / Birkenau, the SS ran a slave-labor camp called Monowitz, or Auschwitz III, which housed profitable industrial operations, most notably I. G. Auschwitz, a division of the giant conglomerate I. G. Farben. In combination with Birkenau, this vast petrochemical complex brought human slavery to its ultimate "perfection" by reducing human beings to consumable raw materials from which all mineral resources were systematically extracted. Every part of the body was recycled to serve the Nazi war economy: gold teeth went to the treasury, hair was used to stuff mattresses, and ashes from the incinerated corpses became fertilizer. Unlike the practitioners of slavery in both the ancient and modern world, the Nazis did not regard the slave as a capital investment but as a commodity to be discarded and easily replaced. As one survivor put it: "They oiled the machines; they did not feed the workers."

The Final Solution was a managerial triumph. There was no budget for the program. With the cooperation of German industry and the ingenuity of the Nazi bureaucrats who harvested material from the dead, the entire killing operation was run in the black.

The Holocaust also represented a quasi-apocalyptic triumph for Nazi ideology. Its motivating sources of fear and hatred were transformed into the fervor of religion and took on the power of a religious crusade. In the Nazi world view, the annihilation of the Jews was essential to the survival and salvation of the German state.

THE WARSAW GHETTO UPRISING, PASSOVER 1943

Between July and September of 1942, approximately three hundred thousand Jews were shipped from Warsaw to Treblinka. Only fifty-five thousand remained in the ghetto. As the deportations went on, despair gave way to a determination to resist. A newly formed group, the Z.O.B. (*Zydowska Organizacja Bojowa*, or Jewish Fighting Organization), slowly took effective control of the ghetto. It issued a proclamation:

> Jewish masses, the hour is drawing near. You must be prepared to resist. Not a single Jew should go to the railroad cars. Those who are unable to put up active resistance should resist passively, should go into hiding. . . . Our slogan must be: All are ready to die as human beings.

On January 9, 1943, Himmler visited the Warsaw ghetto. He ordered the deportation of another eight thousand Jews. The January deportations caught the Jews by surprise. Jews made use of the many hiding places they had created since the July–August deportations. They did not report as ordered. The resistance sprang into action. There were battles in the streets, near the Umschlagplatz (the transit point for deportation), and in buildings. Open battles were costly to Jewish fighters; many were killed. Partisan tactics proved more effective. Dark narrow hallways became dangerous for the Germans. Jewish fighters could strike quickly, then escape across the rooftops. German troops moved cautiously. They would not go down to cellars. The German *Aktion* ended within a few days.

Those who remained believed that resistance had brought the deportations to a halt. Hideouts were fortified and resistance units were strengthened in preparation for the next battle. As one Z.O.B. leader recalled: "We saw ourselves as a Jewish underground whose fate was a tragic one, the first to fight. For our hour had come without any sign of hope or rescue."

The uprising began on April 19, 1943, the second night of Passover, and continued until the final liquidation of the ghetto more than a

Roundup of Jews during the Warsaw ghetto uprising. More than 56,000 Jews surrendered. Warsaw, Poland, April 19–May 16, 1943.
National Archives, Washington, D.C.

month later. The day before, word had been received that a German *Aktion* was imminent. The inhabitants of the ghetto were alerted immediately, and within fifteen minutes Z.O.B. forces were at their positions in cellars they had turned into makeshift fortresses.

At 6:00 A.M. on the nineteenth, Colonel von Sammern launched the *Aktion* with a force of some two thousand men supported by tanks and flame throwers. The Z.O.B. had a small arsenal of hand guns and rifles, a few machine guns, and homemade Molotov cocktails (hand grenades). Von Sammern's troops were routed by 7:30. There were casualties on both sides. The Jewish fighters were exhilarated: the Nazis were suddenly vulnerable to attack. It seemed that the supermen could be forced to retreat. Zivia Lubetkin recalled:

> When the Germans came up to our posts and marched by and we threw those hand grenades and bombs and saw German blood pouring over the streets of Warsaw . . . there was much rejoicing. The tomorrow did not worry us. The rejoicing amongst the Jewish fighters was great and, see the wonder and the miracle, those German heroes retreated, afraid and terrorized from Jewish bombs and hand grenades, home-made.

On April 20, the Germans attacked a factory area where five Z.O.B. squads were stationed. The Jews set off a mine, forcing the Germans to retreat once again. When they reappeared, the Jewish fighters opened fire. This was followed by hand-to-hand combat. The Germans raised a white flag, requesting a fifteen-minute truce. The Jewish response was a volley of fire.

The Germans tightened the siege of the ghetto. Electricity, water, and gas were cut off. Police dogs were brought in to uncover shelters where the fighters were hiding.

On the third day, the tactics shifted. The Germans no longer entered the ghetto in large groups, but roamed through the ghetto in small bands. Resistance forces of men and women also broke into small mobile squads.

The German commander, General Jürgen Stroop, who had taken over command of the operation, decided on a new strategy: the ghetto was to be burned, building by

We saw ourselves as a Jewish underground whose fate was a tragic one, the first to fight. For our hour had come without any sign of hope or rescue.

RESISTANCE LEADER, WARSAW GHETTO

building, street by street. On April 22, he reported:

> The fire that raged all night drove the Jews who, despite all the search operations, were still hiding under roofs, in cellars and other hiding places. Scores of burning Jews jumped from windows or tried to slide down sheets. We took pains to ensure that those Jews, as well as others, were wiped out immediately.

The Germans had planned to liquidate the ghetto in three days. The Jews held out for more than a month. Fighters succeeded in hiding in the sewers, even though the Germans tried first to flood and then to smoke them out with smoke bombs.

The Warsaw ghetto uprising was nothing less than a revolution in Jewish history. Jews had resisted the Nazis with armed force. The significance and symbolic resonance of the uprising went far beyond the numbers of those who fought and died. Those who were part of it fully understood what it meant. On April 23, Mordecai Anielewicz, the twenty-four-year-old commander of the Z.O.B., wrote to Yitzhak Zuckerman, a unit commander:

> What we have experienced cannot be described in words. We are aware of one thing only: what has happened has exceeded our dreams. The Germans ran twice from the ghetto. . . . I have the feeling that great things are happening, that what we have dared is of great importance. . . .
>
> Keep well, my dear. Perhaps we shall meet again. But what really matters is that the dream of my life has become true. Jewish self defense in the Warsaw ghetto has become a fact. Jewish armed resistance and retaliation have become a reality. I have been witness to the magnificent heroic struggle of the Jewish fighters.

I have been witness to the magnificent heroic struggle of the Jewish fighters.

MORDECAI ANIELEWICZ, RESISTANCE LEADER, WARSAW GHETTO

On May 8, the Germans sent gas inside the bunkers at Z.O.B. command headquarters at Mila 18. Aryeh Wilner, a young resistance leader, shouted: "Come, let us destroy ourselves. Let's not fall into their hands alive." The suicides began. Pistols jammed and their owners begged their friends to kill them. But apparently no one dared take the life of a comrade. Someone discovered a hidden exit, but only a few succeeded in escaping. The others suffocated.

As the Germans carried out the plan to set the ghetto aflame, some Jews escaped through the sewers and searched for a hiding place on the Polish side. A survivor reported:

On May 10, 1943, at 9 o'clock in the morning, the lid of the sewer over our heads literally opened and a flood of sunlight streamed into the sewer. At the opening of the sewer, Krzaczek [a member of the Polish resistance] was standing and calling all of us to come out. . . . We started to climb out one after another and at once got on a truck. It was a beautiful spring day and the sun warmed us. Our eyes were blinded by the bright light, as we had not seen daylight for many weeks and had spent the time in complete darkness. The streets were crowded with people, and everybody . . . stood still and watched, while strange beings, hardly recognizable as humans, crawled out of the sewers.

Some aspects of the Warsaw uprising were common to all ghetto insurrections. Resistance came at the end, when all hope for survival was abandoned (and when trust in Jewish Council leadership was lost). More than 300,000 were dead at Treblinka; Czerniaków had committed suicide; the rail cars were at the station. The fighters knew they were bound to lose. There was no longer a choice between life and death, but at stake was the honor of the Jewish people. The choice was to die fighting and to inflict casualties on the enemy.

Jewish fighters faced overwhelmingly superior forces. The German figures reported after the battle, even if they are understated with regard to their losses, reflect the mismatch. Of the Jews captured, seven thousand were shot, seven thousand were transported to the death camp of Treblinka, and fifteen thousand were shipped to Lublin.

Nine rifles, fifty-nine pistols, and several hundred grenades, explosives, and mines were captured. Among the Germans and their collaborators, the losses were sixteen dead and eighty-five wounded. The ghetto was in ruins. Simcha Rottem described the scene:

In the streets, if you can call them that, for nothing was left of the streets, we had to step over heaps of corpses. There was no room to get around them. Beside fighting the Germans, we fought hunger and thirst. We had no contact with the outside world; we were completely isolated.

Yitzhak Zuckerman, known by his nickname Antek, was recognized as a hero for his efforts. His heroism was of little comfort. He told Claude Lanzmann, "I began drinking after the war. It was very difficult. Claude, you asked my impression. If you could lick my heart, it would poison you."

DEPORTATIONS

R ailroads were the essential link to the killing process. Between 1942 and 1945, trains carrying human cargo from every corner of Nazi-occupied Europe rolled into death camps carefully situated along major Polish rail lines. The Reichsbahn, the German railroad, was one of the largest organizations in the Third Reich. It had 1.4 million workers, of whom 500,000 were civil servants, who kept the system in operation. During the Holocaust, their job was to allocate personnel, obtain freight cars, coordinate train schedules, keep the tracks open, drive locomotives, and clean cars.

As the supply lines needed for a two-front war lengthened, there was a chronic shortage of trains. The railroad system was stretched thin even in its efforts to provision the army. Allied bombing raids on the major European rail lines disrupted traffic, but the trains carrying Jews continued to roll. Transports were given additional cars, more Jews were crammed into fewer trains, indirect routes were taken so the human traffic could keep moving.

Arrival of Hungarian
Jews in Auschwitz.
Auschwitz, Poland,
spring of 1944. More
than 437,000
Hungarian Jews were
deported to Auschwitz
between May 14 and
July 8, 1944. *Yad Vashem,
Jerusalem, Israel.*

Women and children
from a Hungarian
transport. Auschwitz,
Poland, spring of 1944.
Yad Vashem, Jerusalem, Israel.

A fifteen-ton freight car of the "Karlsruhe" model, one of several types that were used to deport Jews. Its cramped interior would have held eighty to one hundred people. Deportation trains usually carried between one thousand and two thousand people, whose crushing weight slowed the speed of travel to only thirty miles per hour or so. The snail's pace of deportation trains greatly prolonged the ordeal. *Donated by the Polish State Railways. Photo USHMM.*

The transport of Jews, and their destination, was no secret to the Reichsbahn workers. At Auschwitz alone there were forty-four parallel tracks at the train station, more than twice the number of New York's Pennsylvania Station. A special railroad spur was built to run directly to the exit ramp at Birkenau, whose chimneys were clearly visible from the trains. No railway man resigned and none protested. Raul Hilberg commented that they did their work well: no Jew was left alive for lack of transport.

Jews were ticketed as people, although they were transported to the death camps as cattle, mainly in freight cars. The SS used travel agents to book one-way passage to the camp at a rate of four *Pfennige* (pennies) per kilometer of track they would travel. Children under ten rode for half fare; those under four rode free. A group rate of half the usual third-class charge was introduced for deportations of more than four hundred people. The Reichsbahn did not charge for the

trains that returned empty. Indeed, the SS was offered a credit for one-way passenger transport. Tickets for the guards had to be paid in advance. Reichsbahn employees used the same forms and procedures to book tourists going on vacation as they did to send Jews to Auschwitz.

There were, in general, three forms of deportation. First, Jews were deported from towns and cities to transit camps or ghettos. Then they were deported from smaller ghettos to larger ones. From 1942 on, they were deported to one of the six major killing centers: Auschwitz / Birkenau, Majdanek, Chelmno, Treblinka, Belzec, and Sobibór.

Deportations were sometimes complex mass operations involving elaborate logistics. During the summer of 1942, approximately 300,000 Jews from the Warsaw ghetto were transported to Treblinka in a six-week period. Between May 15 and July 9, 1944, 434,351 Jews from fifty-five Hungarian localities were deported to Auschwitz in 147 trains. Most were gassed at Birkenau soon after they arrived. The railway system was stretched to its limits to keep up with the demand of the camp, where as many as 12,000 people a day were being gassed.

In some areas, deportations were gradual. First the elderly were taken from the ghetto, then those who could not work or had no work permits. Later, children and those without influence or family connections were removed. Selections were made in the ghetto by the German-controlled Jewish Councils. In the end, however, all Jews were deported from the ghettos.

The Nazis made a disciplined effort to disguise their intentions from their victims. They often employed euphemism and doublespeak to avoid speaking directly about murder. Deportation was called "resettlement in the East." Anxious victims were told that they were being sent to labor camps. They were encouraged to pack their belongings and take them along. The ruse often worked. Even as late as the spring of 1944, many Hungarian Jews had not heard of Auschwitz.

The train trip was often long. From Hungary, the trip took days; from Greece, more than a week. In the summer, the sealed cattle cars were suffocatingly hot; unheated,

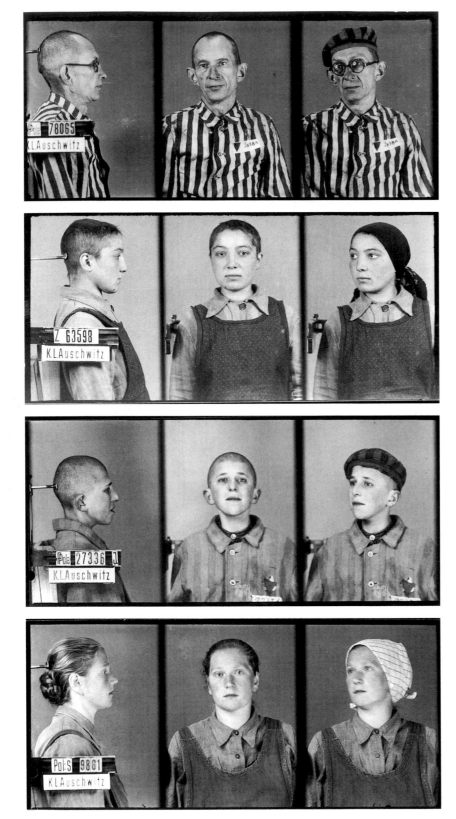

Mug shots of prisoners registered for concentration camps. Most Jews who entered the death camps were immediately sent to their death and no registration forms were required, no prisoner identification photographs were taken. *State Museum of Auschwitz, Oświęcim, Poland.*

> Now, in this hour of decision, we said to each other things that are never said among the living. . . . Everybody said farewell to life through his neighbor. . . .

PRIMO LEVI

they were freezing cold in winter. The SS made few provisions for food or water; the most they provided was a bucket for bodily needs. Crowded passengers were often forced to sit in feces and urine. The stench was overwhelming. When the doors were open upon arrival, grateful passengers thought that the worst of the ordeal was behind them. They were disoriented and exhausted.

Primo Levi recalls that train trip to hell:

We suffered from thirst and cold: at every stop we clamored for water, or even a handful of snow, but we were rarely heard; the soldiers of the escort drove off anybody who tried to approach the convoy. Two young mothers, nursing their children, groaned night and day, begging for water. . . . The hours of darkness were nightmares without end. . . .

Next to me, crushed against me for the whole journey, there had been a woman. We had known each other for many years, and the misfortune had struck us together, but we knew little of each other. Now, in this hour of decision, we said to each other things that are never said among the living. . . . Everybody said farewell to life through his neighbor. . . .

The climax came suddenly. The door opened with a crash, and the dark echoed with outlandish orders in that curt, barbaric barking of Germans in command. . . .

A vast platform appeared before us, lit up by reflectors. A little beyond it, a row of lorries. . . . A dozen SS men . . . began to interrogate us. . . . "How old? Healthy or ill?" And on the basis of the reply they pointed in two different directions.

Rudolf Vrba, who escaped from Auschwitz on April 7, 1944, bringing vital and accurate information to the attention of the West, recalls the arrival of prisoners at the ramp:

Selection of Hungarian Jews on the Auschwitz ramp. Auschwitz, Poland, spring of 1944.
Yad Vashem, Jerusalem, Israel.

There was a place called the ramp where the trains with the Jews were coming in. They were coming in day and night, and sometimes one per day and sometimes five per day, from all sorts of places in the world.

I worked there from August 18, 1942 to June 7, 1943. I saw those transports rolling one after another, and I have seen at least two hundred of them in this position. I have seen it so many times that it became a routine.

Constantly, people from the heart of Europe were disappearing, and they were arriving to the same place with the same ignorance of the fate of the previous transport.

And the people in this mass . . . I knew that within a couple of hours after they arrived there, ninety percent would be gassed.

HIDING

There were three ways out of the ghetto: death inside the walls, escape, or deportation to a death camp.

The ghetto itself was an instrument of slow, passive murder. People lived under intolerable conditions, packed into overcrowded quarters with little or no sanitary facilities. Disease was epidemic. Starvation, cold, and long hours of grueling work weakened many to the point of death. More than one in ten inhabitants of the Warsaw ghetto died there in 1941. In Theresienstadt, death claimed more than one in two residents in 1942. Every day, death carts collected corpses to be cremated or buried in mass graves. Emmanuel Ringelblum wrote of Warsaw in the spring of 1942:

Death lurks in every chink, every little crack. There have been cases of everyone living in an apartment being fearfully tortured because someone opened a shutter. One of the tortures is to have the culprit strip naked and then roll down a pile of coke [the coal used for heating]. The pain is excruciating and every part of the body bleeds. . . . The Germans driving prisoners in trucks to the Pawia Street prison beat passers-by on the street mercilessly. The Gestapo agent sitting in the back of the car leans out the window, reaches along the narrow Karmelicka Street, and slashes passers-by on with a long lead-tipped stick. He overturns rickshas, and beats the ricksha drivers.

Escape was possible only for a few if there were a way out, the financial resources to survive, and a place to go. Some escaped through gaps in the wall or by tunneling underneath it. Others slipped away from work brigades when they were on the Aryan side of the city. In Warsaw, the sewers were a vital link between the ghetto and the Polish side. Smuggling, hiding, underground operations, even preparing for the resistance — all depended on the sewers. In the end, when the Nazis completely demolished the ghetto, the only way of escape was through the sewers. In Łódź, where there were no sewers, the isolation of the ghetto was complete. A girl in the Łódź ghetto wrote in her diary:

When we look at the fence separating us from the rest of the world, our souls like birds in a cage, yearn to be free. . . . How I envy the birds that fly to freedom. . . . Will I ever live in better times? After the war will I be with my parents and friends? Will I live to eat bread and rye flour until I'm full?

Some Jews who escaped the ghetto took refuge in the forests bordering Vilna, Minsk, and Kovno. Others found hiding places on the Aryan side of the wall. It was possible, though dangerous, to live among the Poles while pretending to be a Polish Catholic. Some Jews found Poles willing to hide them as a gesture of solidarity, an act of resistance, or even a business proposition. For some, hiding was only a temporary reprieve. Rose Brunswic recalled walking along the Vistula River after her escape from the Warsaw ghetto:

I thought, it doesn't matter to me if I get caught. . . . Should I jump into the river and finish up with myself. I didn't know how to swim. I thought suicide would be the best thing. I wouldn't fall into German hands. I would do it myself. And along came this man Jan Majetski and he said, "You know, it's almost curfew. What are you doing here?" He realized I was Jewish. . . . He said, "I am the director of the Polish Refugee camp. . . . I can give you a little room and you can stay there, but not for long."

As the hunt for Jews intensified, Jan turned to Rose and said: "I can't keep you any longer. We have to part." Rose did fall into German hands, but, with false identity papers in hand, she was able to pass as a Pole.

Those who hid lived in constant fear of betrayal and discovery. Poles who hid Jews were subject to death if they were discovered. Informers who turned in Jews and their rescuers received rewards. The true identity of a Jew attempting to pass as a Pole could be given away at any moment by a gesture, a slip of the tongue, an accent, circumcision. There was always a chance of being recognized by former neighbors, classmates, and friends. Jews who were discovered in hiding were sent directly to the camps or shot on the spot. Gangs of blackmailers threatened Jews and the Poles who hid them. Thus, the Germans did not always have to expend their own resources and personnel to uncover those in hiding.

Life in hiding was perilous. Abraham Malnick described his escape from the Kovno ghetto:

I went to try to find a place to hide. It's like a rat looking for some place to hide. I didn't know where to go, and I didn't know where they would find us. I saw a little shed. You see the ghetto was made where farmers used to live . . . farmer country. There was a shed with a cellar inside where they kept hay. So I opened the barn and I saw through a trap door in the bottom. So I pushed away the hay in the side and as I was trying to go inside two mothers with little babies came to me and said, "Please help me. Please help us." I said, "What are you doing? I know what I'm doing." They said, "Please let me go in with you in that basement . . . in that hole." I said, "Come down." I didn't care. And I put hay on the trap, and I just went down. And it was dark, but I could see through that crack in the door, in that little trap door.

The Germans came, the police, and they start banging houses: Raus, raus, raus, Juden raus. I didn't know what was going on. And he opened . . . the German opened the door, flinging the door wide open and he comes in and he starts shaking around all that hay and straw and he's standing on top of that door. The door is almost collapsed, and I'm trying to hold up the door. . . .

He looked around and looked around, and took his bayonet . . . I could see all that . . . and shoveled around in all that hay and he walked . . . back and forth. As soon as he walked out, one baby started to cry. So I said, "Please. Please. Help us. Help us." So, she stopped. The baby stopped crying.

I was only 15 years old, and I could see the German all day long going back and forth. The other baby started crying. So the mother urinated in her hand and gave the baby a drink to keep quiet.

They came in and looked but didn't step on the door again. Another guard came and they joked and they had a good time going back and forth. At 4 or 5 o'clock, the whistle blew. And a German truck picked them all up, at the post over there. And I made sure and seen them off and walked to the first and looked around.

I told the mothers to come out. And one baby was dead. She . . . the mother . . . the mother choked her own baby. And one baby is still alive because the mother she urinated and she got a drink but the other baby from, from fear, the mother choked her own baby, choked her own child . . . choked her own child.

For those who could not escape and did not die within the ghetto walls, the last way out of the ghetto was deportation. The Nazi euphemism, resettlement in the east, was a one-way passage to death.

Razor parts confiscated by the Nazis from prisoners who arrived at Auschwitz. *On loan from the State Museum of Auschwitz-Birkenau. Photo USHMM*

RESETTLEMENT IN THE EAST

Concentration camps served three major purposes. At first, they were penal colonies; later, large camps were established to supply labor for special projects; and finally, the camps were used for "liquidation," or murder. Throughout the duration of the war, the concentration camp universe expanded rapidly to meet the demands of war production and the policy of genocide.

There were more than nine thousand camps scattered throughout German-occupied Europe. They included transit camps, prisoner-of-war camps, private industrial camps, work-education camps, foreign labor camps, police detention camps, even camps for children whose parents had been sent to slave-labor camps. More than three hundred camps were for women only.

By mid-1942, within a few months of the Wannsee Conference, six camps served as killing centers where the victims were gassed: Treblinka, Sobibór, Belzec, Chelmno, Auschwitz / Birkenau, and Majdanek. The last two also doubled as slave-labor and penal camps.

Deportees arrived at Auschwitz and Birkenau expecting resettlement elsewhere, so it was natural for them to bring along articles of daily living: suitcases, toothbrushes, mirrors, can openers, umbrellas, and the like. But these were false expectations, encouraged by Nazi deceptions. SS guards immediately confiscated the belongings of all newcomers. The deceptions continued into the gas chambers, where most Jewish deportees lost their lives within hours of their arrival.

Tea strainers, potato peelers, can openers. *On loan from the State Museum of Auschwitz-Birkenau. Photo USHMM.*

Cutlery. *On loan from the State Museum of Auschwitz-Birkenau. Photo USHMM.*

Scissors. *On loan from the State Museum of Auschwitz-Birkenau. Photo USHMM.*

Toothbrushes. *On loan from the State Museum of Auschwitz-Birkenau. Photo USHMM.*

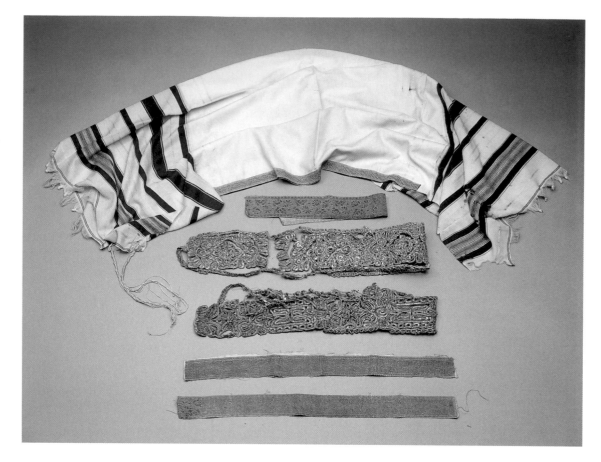

Nazis also confiscated sacred objects that belonged to their victims. This prayer shawl (*tallit*) was taken from one of the male Jews arriving in Auschwitz/Birkenau. The crown of the *tallit* is called an *atara*. Some were made of silver or gold lace. *On loan from the State Museum of Auschwitz, Oświęcim, Poland. Photo USHMM.*

In 1942, the concentration camps held 100,000 inmates. Their population grew geometrically: to 224,000 in 1943, and 524,000 in 1944. By January 1945, the concentration camps held 714,000 inmates, of whom more than 200,000 were women.

More than three million people — mostly Jews — were murdered in these camps, some by starvation and exhaustion, disease, shootings, and beatings. But many more were killed by gassing.

IMPLEMENTING THE FINAL SOLUTION

The Final Solution was implemented in stages, although the various forms of killing overlapped as primitive methods gave way to what was considered state-of-the-art technology. Killing by bullets was followed by gassing in mobile killing vans, which were in turn supplanted by stationary gas chambers of much greater capacity.

Stage I: The mobile killing units, or *Einsatzgruppen*, began their work in June 1941. But the mass shootings were inefficient and psychologically burdensome to the killers. It became desirable to send the victims to the killers. Thus, killing centers were created at strategic railway junctions near the main Jewish population centers of Poland.

Stage II: Mobile gas vans were used at Chelmno beginning in December 1941. The main drawback of the vans was their limited capacity. They could not handle large numbers of victims. They were also slow. The excruciating suffering of the victims, who died by asphyxiation, was of little concern to the SS, but the task of unloading the vans after each use was time consuming and "unpleasant." Dying took so long that the anguished victims could not control their bowels and left a mess. One eyewitness reported:

The back door of the van would be open. The Jews were made to get inside the van. This job was done by three Poles, who I believe were sentenced to death. The Poles hit the Jews with whips if they did not get into the gas-van fast enough. . . . The driver then switched on the engine, crawled under the van and connected a pipe from the exhaust to the inside of the van. The exhaust fumes now poured into the inside of the truck so that the people inside were suffocated. After about ten minutes, when there were no further signs of life from the Jews, the van set off toward the camp in the woods where the bodies were then burned.

Stage III: Stationary gas chambers were in operation beginning in March 1942. Within a few months they were established at all the killing centers except Chelmno, which continued to operate with what was then obsolete technology. Two types of gas were used for killing: carbon monoxide and hydrocyanic acid, which was the agent of choice at Auschwitz / Birkenau. The gas chambers had a much larger capacity than the vans and could handle hundreds of victims at a time. They were more reliable. According to Rudolf Höss, the commandant of Auschwitz, "the head of the Kommando [at Chelmno] told me that this method, however, was very unreliable, as the gas buildup was very irregular and often insufficient for killing." At the height of the Hungarian deportations of August 1944, as many as twelve thousand Jews were gassed in one day at Auschwitz.

KILLING CENTERS

Each of the killing centers — Auschwitz / Birkenau, Majdanek, Chelmno, Sobibór, Belzec, and Treblinka — was located on a main railroad line in Poland. In each of them, killing was by gas, either carbon monoxide or Zyklon B. German scientists searching for the cheapest and most efficient means of extermination had experimented with a variety of gases before they discovered that the insecticide Zyklon B could kill two thousand people in less than thirty minutes. Whichever method was used, the results were the same.

Chelmno: Three hermetically sealed trucks were initially used at Chelmno. About fifty to seventy people were loaded in each van. A detachable exhaust pipe from the engine was

connected to the compartment. Over the next thirty-seven months, beginning in December 1941, more than 150,000 Jews were murdered at Chelmno. Most were from the Wartaland region of central Poland, but Chelmno's dead also included five thousand Gypsies deported from Lódź, some Poles, Soviet prisoners of war, and eighty-eight children from Lidice, the Czechoslovakian village destroyed in retaliation for the assassination near Prague of Reinhard Heydrich.

Treblinka: During the fourteen months of Treblinka's operation, which began in July 1942, between 750,000 and 870,000 Jews were murdered by a staff of 150. Thirty of them were SS personnel, all veterans of the euthanasia program in Germany, supported by 120 Ukrainians. There were fewer than one hundred known survivors of Treblinka.

Sobibór: Between 200,000 and 250,000 Jews were murdered in carbon monoxide gas chambers during the sixteen months of Sobibór's existence. In October 1943, a revolt was staged by some of the last prisoners in the camp. During the battle, some three hundred escaped. At the end of the war, there were only fifty known survivors of Sobibór.

Belzec: Between March and December 1942, between 550,000 and 600,000 Jews and several thousand Gypsies were murdered in the gas chambers of Belzec. Less than a handful of those taken to Belzec survived. Only one, Rudolf Reder, told of what he had seen.

From August up to the end of November 1942, I was in the death camp. It was the period of the mass gassing of the Jews. The few of my friends of suffering who had succeeded in surviving there a longer time told me that in that period there was the largest number of transports of death. They came every day, without interruption, three times daily. Each train numbered fifty cars, with hundreds of people in each

General view of the Birkenau (Auschwitz II) concentration camp. Auschwitz, Poland, February 1945. *Sovfoto, New York.*

one of them. When the transports arrived at night, the victims of Belzec waited in closed cars until 6 o'clock in the morning. Sometimes the transports were larger and more frequent. Jews arrived from everywhere — and only Jews. Never were there any other transports. Belzec served only to kill Jews.

Majdanek: Majdanek was located in a suburb of Lublin along the main highway linking Lublin, Zamosc, and Chelm. Nearly 500,000 people from twenty-eight countries and representing fifty-four ethnic groups passed through Majdanek. According to Polish sources about 360,000 — more than 60 percent, many of them Poles — died from starvation, exhaustion, disease, and beatings. Seven gas chambers were employed, as were the camp's two wooden gallows.

Birkenau: Birkenau (Auschwitz II) was the largest and deadliest of all the Nazi death camps. More than 1,100,000 people were murdered there, most in the gas chambers. Tens of thousands of Poles, nineteen thousand Gypsies, and twelve thousand Soviet prisoners of war were also among those who were slaughtered at Birkenau. One million one hundred thousand were Jews.

OPPOSITE:
Selection of Hungarian Jews in Auschwitz. Auschwitz, Poland, spring of 1944. *Yad Vashem, Jerusalem, Israel.*

WHO SHALL LIVE AND WHO SHALL DIE

At the entrance to each of the death camps — the reception area — the dead were removed from the trains and the living divided according to their ability to walk. Those able to walk were sent on; people unable to walk were taken away. Those who could walk then faced the first *Selektion.* An SS officer pointed to the left or to the right. Old people, pregnant women, young children, and the infirm were immediately condemned to death. Segregated by sex, they surrendered their valuables and removed their clothes before entering the gas chambers. The Nazis tried to deceive arriving prisoners until the end: the gas chambers were labeled showers.

Toby Stern describes arriving at Auschwitz with her baby:

We were so happy they opened the cars. We came down. They started to hit us. Go there, go there, go there. Everybody wanted to be with the families, we shouldn't lose each other. We should be together. And a man ran . . . to me. He said, "Give away the child [to] an older lady." So I asked him why. I told my brother, "Booda, go and ask why should I give away the baby." . . . He disappeared. . . . Then a second guy came. And he said, "Give away the baby." . . . I used to live with my mother, so I gave the baby to my

125

Flow Chart for "Operation Reinhard," Auschwitz, and Majdanek

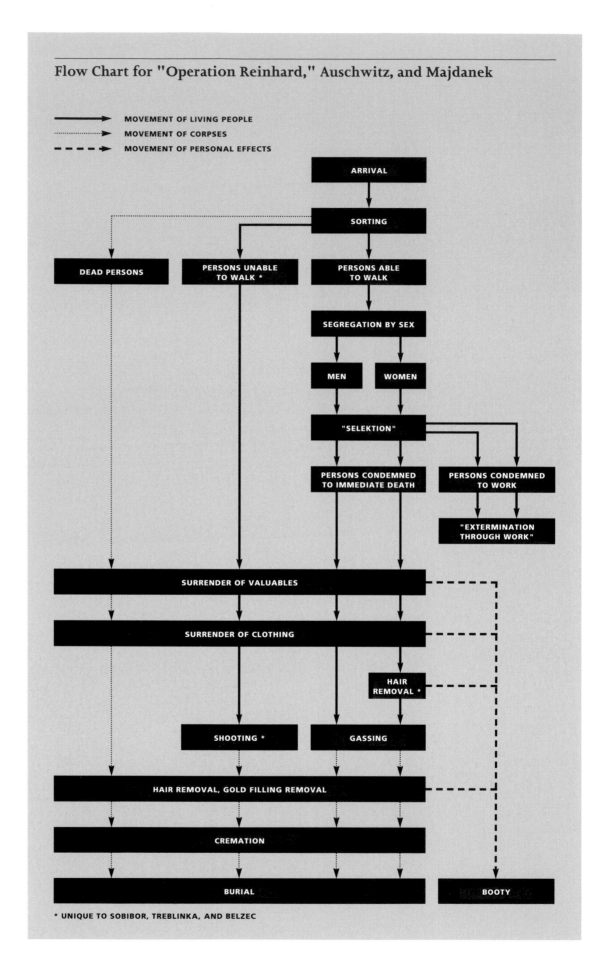

→ MOVEMENT OF LIVING PEOPLE
⋯▷ MOVEMENT OF CORPSES
‑ ‑ ‑▶ MOVEMENT OF PERSONAL EFFECTS

ARRIVAL

SORTING

DEAD PERSONS

PERSONS UNABLE TO WALK *

PERSONS ABLE TO WALK

SEGREGATION BY SEX

MEN   **WOMEN**

"SELEKTION"

PERSONS CONDEMNED TO IMMEDIATE DEATH

PERSONS CONDEMNED TO WORK

"EXTERMINATION THROUGH WORK"

SURRENDER OF VALUABLES

SURRENDER OF CLOTHING

HAIR REMOVAL *

SHOOTING *   **GASSING**

HAIR REMOVAL, GOLD FILLING REMOVAL

CREMATION

BURIAL   **BOOTY**

* UNIQUE TO SOBIBOR, TREBLINKA, AND BELZEC

126

mother. *And I hear right now how he cried, "Mommy, I want to go with you. I don't want to stay with Bubby."*

Those selected for work were registered and branded and sheared. Their hair was shaved and their arms tattooed with a number. Uniforms were issued. Their ordeal as inmates was just beginning. They would face additional "selections" in the future. The officer in charge of the "selection" was a physician. His "expert opinion" was required to determine who would live and who would die. The most infamous of all of them, Dr. Josef Mengele, who also oversaw some of the cruelest quasi-medical experiments conducted on inmates, was often to be found at the ramp in Birkenau.

The inmate who survived the first selection lived in constant fear of future selections. Fritzie Fritshall recounted her experience:

Selection. We needed to get undressed every day. And we needed to run — not walk — in front of SS officers. We needed to show that we still had strength left. . . . I recall some women, as the hair grew back, they were beginning to get gray hair. And they would take a little piece of coal from one of the pot-bellied stoves that was in a barrack. And they would use coal to color their hair with, so that they would look a little younger. One grayed at the age of maybe eighteen or nineteen under those conditions. If one had a scar, a pimple, if one didn't run fast enough, if one didn't look right for whatever reason to the particular person that was doing the selection. . . . They would stand there with a stick . . . [to the right or to the left] as you ran by them. One never knew if they were in the good line or the bad line. One line would go to the gas chambers. The other line would go back to the camp and to the barracks, to live another day. We knew the trains were coming in. . . . And we knew many of the barracks were being emptied out, day in and day out, to make room for the new people that were coming in. We never knew when our turn would come next. So one always lived in fear and one always tried to get through these selections for one more day.

At Belzec, Sobibór, and Treblinka, all but a few were dead within hours. At Auschwitz and Majdanek, which were also slave-labor camps, one could hope for a reprieve. Still, the vast majority were killed shortly after arrival. The process can be demonstrated in a simple chart. The language of the chart is taken from the ordinary workplace, for indeed the killing centers were factories of death.

PRISONERS OF THE CAMPS

A mosaic of victims who were incarcerated in the concentration camps includes Soviet prisoners of war, political prisoners, common criminals, Gypsies, and homosexuals.

Soviet Prisoners of War: From the time of the German invasion of the Soviet Union in June 1941 to the end of World War II in May 1945, as many as 3.3 million Soviet prisoners of war died at the hands of the Nazis as a result of mass executions, brutal mistreatment, intentional starvation, and lack of clothing or shelter. Most were killed during the first year. The German army, which had custody of some prisoners of war, was responsible for virtually all of these deaths. The comparative figures for death rates among

In the Mauthausen concentration camp inmate number 1469 lies murdered at the base of the quarry. Many inmates were pushed by the SS guards to their deaths down the steps leading from the quarry. *American Jewish Archives, Cincinnati, Ohio.*

127

prisoners of war is instructive: a large percentage of all Soviet POWs died during their incarceration by the Nazis as opposed to 3.6 percent of Anglo-American POWs in German custody. After 1942, when the POWs became essential to the Nazi war economy, the death rate decreased. By 1943, half a million Soviet POWs were working as slaves. Many were sent to concentration camps.

The fate of Soviet POWs was doubly tragic. They were disgraced at home. Stalin believed that no Soviet soldier should have ever allowed himself to be taken prisoner. The Russian soldier was supposed to fight to the death; anyone choosing to become a prisoner was to be automatically excluded from the Soviet community.

Gypsies: Throughout Nazi-occupied Europe, Gypsies (Roma and Sinti) were interned, and then deported to slave-labor and death camps. The fate of the Gypsies closely paralleled that of the Jews. Gypsies were singled out according to their purported racial identity as defined by Nazi ideology and so-called racial science. They were despised because of their social status. The existence of Gypsies was also seen as a threat to Aryan blood purity. What the Germans most feared was the mixing of Gypsy and German blood. While German Jews of mixed blood might escape deportation, Gypsies of mixed blood were hunted down relentlessly. Tens of thousands were killed by the *Einsatzgruppen* and collaborators in the east; more were deported and killed in camps.

Twenty thousand Gypsies were registered as inmates of Auschwitz / Birkenau. Thousands more were incarcerated in Bergen-Belsen, Buchenwald, Dachau, Mauthausen, and Ravensbrück. Five thousand Gypsies were transported from Lódź to the killing center of Chelmno, where they were gassed in mobile killing vans. In concentration camps, only Jews and Gypsies were without any legal protection. There was no need to account for the dead, to give a reason or a cause.

At Birkenau, a special camp was built to house Gypsy inmates, who continued to live in family units. Gypsy children were subjected to brutal and inhumane "medical experiments" by Dr. Mengele and his staff. On July 31, 1944, the Gypsy camp at Auschwitz was

"liquidated." All its men, women, and children were sent to the gas chambers.

Unlike the Jews who documented their tragedy and whose survivors kept diaries and wrote memoirs, took part in oral history projects, and conserved documents, Gypsies have an oral tradition. Only a few books have been written on their experience in the Holocaust. Therefore, the magnitude of Gypsy dead cannot be currently known. Somewhere between 20 and 50 percent of the entire population of European Gypsies was killed by the Nazis.

Political prisoners, Jehovah's Witnesses, and homosexuals were sent to concentration camps not to die, but as punishment and in order to change their behavior. Nevertheless, many of them died during their imprisonment in the harsh environment of the camps.

Political Prisoners: Political dissidents were the first to be incarcerated in concentration camps. Beginning in 1933, political opponents of the Nazi regime were sent to Dachau

TOP:
Deportation of German Gypsies. Hohenasperg, Germany, May 18, 1940.
Bundesarchiv, Koblenz, Germany.

BOTTOM:
Gypsy children in Belzec concentration camp. Belzec, Poland, c. 1940. *Archives of Mechanical Documentation, Warsaw, Poland.*

and other camps in Germany. In the early years, almost all concentration camp inmates were people considered politically offensive, although by 1942 Jews comprised the overwhelming majority of prisoners. Communists, Social Democrats, and trade-unionists were marked by the red triangles they wore. Bound by political ties, they were the most organized of all prisoner groups. Some were active in the underground and resistance.

Jehovah's Witnesses: The civil disobedience of the Jehovah's Witnesses, and their refusal to accept the authority of the Nazi regime or to stop proselytizing, infuriated the Nazis, even though the Witnesses were a tiny minority of the German population. In the camps, the Witnesses, who wore purple triangles, were protected by other members of their sectarian community. In a sense, the Witnesses remained in the camps by choice, since they would be freed if they renounced their faith. Few did. Instead, they met, prayed, and sought to convert others. The Nazis did not plan their extermination; nevertheless, more than one in three Witnesses died in concentration camps.

Homosexuals: In the occupied territories, homosexuality was not a particular focus of Nazi animus, merely an indication of Slavic inferiority. Only German homosexuals were persecuted. Their sexual orientation was seen as a threat to breeding the Aryan "master race." Since their status as Aryans was never in question, they were not targeted for systematic murder. In the camps, homosexuals were identified by pink triangles. (The pink triangle was adopted as an emblem of the gay rights movement decades later.) They were subjected to harsh treatment designed as a form of behavioristic conditioning based on the notion of learning through aversion. Homosexuals in the camps were often mistreated by other inmates.

SLAVE LABOR

As the tide of war turned against Germany after 1942, the concentration camps, which had been established primarily to carry out Nazi racial policies, became an indispensable part of the war economy. Forced labor was essential to

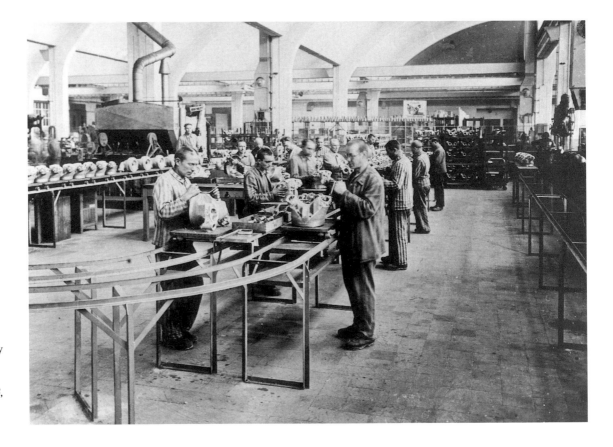

For hundreds of German firms, concentration camps were a source of inexpensive labor. The assembly line at the Bavarian Motor Works (BMW) aircraft engine factory in Allach was manned almost entirely by prisoners. Allach, Germany, 1940–1944. *Bayerische Motorenwerke AG, Historisches Archiv, Munich, Germany.*

the war effort. Estimates vary as to the number of foreign workers pressed into service by the Reich. The number of forced laborers certainly exceeded seven million. Some earned salaries and received standard benefits. Those considered lesser races were paid less and fed less. More than one and one-half million foreign workers were also concentration camp inmates.

In the camps, working conditions were brutal. Slaves often worked eleven-hour shifts, with a minimum amount of sleep and almost no provision of food or warmth. Some of the most respected German corporations had no scruples about using concentration camp slave labor. The well-known companies that lined up to receive workers included Flick, I. G. Farben, BMW, Siemens, Messerschmitt, Daimler-Benz, and Krupp. The decision to use slave labor was entirely voluntary.

Growing labor shortages in Germany placed some restraints on the way the SS treated prisoners. In 1942, Soviet POWs were put to work rather than starved to death. There were some efforts to hold down the mortality rate. For a while, Himmler even considered the idea of using rather than destroying Jewish labor. But nothing, not even the consideration of economic utility, could impede the Final Solution. No Jewish laborer was indispensable.

Treatment that was "considerate" according to SS standards still led to a mortality rate that reveals the reality of life in the labor camps: in 1943, 8,491 deaths were recorded in the Mauthausen concentration camp system among an average population of 21,100.

Unlike the conditions of slavery in the Americas, where the slave was a valuable resource, and master and slave often sustained some kind of personal relationship, the Nazis regarded the slave not as a capital investment but as an easily replaceable waste product.

The decision to operate a slave-labor enterprise was not made by Nazi bureaucrats at Auschwitz or in Berlin, but by corporate executives sitting in their home offices. Major capital expenditures were committed to investments designed to yield significant profits. I. G. Farben, Germany's largest industrial complex, invested more than 700 million Reichsmarks in a vast petrochemical

Women at forced labor in the Ravensbrück concentration camp. Ravensbrück, Germany. *Süddeutscher Verlag Bilderdienst, Munich, Germany.*

You couldn't cry in Auschwitz. You cried, you died. If you showed even more weakness than you already had, you didn't survive the day.

MICHAEL VOGEL, AUSCHWITZ SURVIVOR

complex at Auschwitz III, where human slavery was brought to its ultimate perfection. Slaves were literally worked to death. In the periodic process of "selection," those who could no longer work were eliminated in the gas chambers nearby at Birkenau.

At Auschwitz, some work was useless, but the ability to work was essential to survival. Fritzie Fritshall recalled work as a test of endurance and as defiance.

They would line us up every morning and they would take us outside; and we would carry huge rocks from one side to another. One day we would come and we would take these huge rocks from this side and we would carry them to that side. The next day, they would bring us back; and we would take these same huge rocks, and we would carry them from that side back to this side. Now you need to know we were

The Mauthausen quarry had 186 steps. The inmates of the "penal brigade" were marched up and forced to carry large blocks of stone. Mauthausen, Austria, 1942. *Rijksinstituut voor Oorlogsdokumentatie, Amsterdam, Netherlands.*

Soviet POWs exhausted by hard labor. This photograph was taken on September 21, 1944, five days before their execution. *National Archives, Washington, D.C.*

undernourished. We were all weak. And to carry a big rock like that was a lot of weight and a lot of work. By the time they took us back to the barracks at night we could barely crawl. But we needed to show that we could still walk, and we were strong enough to give one more day.

Slave laborers clearly understood their situation. Michael Vogel recalled his experience:

Another thing was to see when you went to work, when you went to slave labor, who was no longer there. Who's left. And it became like an animal. Oh, I'm living another day, or he's no longer. And you know the worst part, that you couldn't cry for it. You couldn't cry in Auschwitz. You cried, you died. If you showed even more weakness than you already had, you didn't survive the day.

AUSCHWITZ

Auschwitz was the largest and most highly organized of the Nazi death camps. More people were killed there than at any other camp. It was actually three camps in one: a concentration camp, a killing center, and a complex of slave-labor camps. Auschwitz and its satellite camps were in a closed zone of some nineteen square miles guarded by up to six thousand men in twelve companies of SS Death's Head units. (Death's Head personnel, who had been in charge of concentration camps since 1934, wore a skull-and-bones insignia on their uniforms.)

The three major units of Auschwitz were Auschwitz I, a concentration camp; Auschwitz II (Birkenau), the killing center; and Auschwitz III (Buna-Monowitz), the slave-labor complex.

The concentration camp of Auschwitz, located in the Polish town of Oświęcim, was opened in June 1940 with a transport of 728 Polish prisoners who were held in what originally had been an Austrian military barracks. Its purpose was the incarceration of political prisoners, and that remained the primary role of Auschwitz I throughout the war. Yet, over the next four and a half years, Auschwitz I and its burgeoning subcamps became the hub of a huge operation resulting in the murder of more than 1,250,000 prisoners — more than 90 percent of them Jews — and the employment of hundreds of thousands of slave laborers.

A sign over the entrance of Auschwitz read *Arbeit Macht Frei* (Work Liberates). In fact, within the camp and its subcamps, inmates who were not immediately murdered were worked and starved to death. Fritzie Fritshall arrived at Auschwitz when she was just fifteen. Her most vivid recollection was the smell.

How does one describe the walking into Auschwitz, the smell? And someone pointing out to you that those are gas chambers, that your parents went up in smoke. When I asked, "When will I see my mother?" several hours after I came into the camp, I was shown the smoke. This is how I found out where she went.

Auschwitz I has been described as like a garrison, with "two- and three-story red brick buildings arranged in monotonous rows." Its streets were cobblestone. Block 11 housed political prisoners. Its basement windows were barred; its upper windows, sealed. No one was to see what took place within this block, which was the site of the first experiments with gas. A few feet across the courtyard was Block 10, the site of medical experimentation. (The worst of the forced sterilization, hypothermia experiments, and pseudo-scientific research on infants, twins, and dwarfs were conducted at Birkenau.) Between the two blocks was the Black Wall, the site of many executions.

Sterilization experiments were carried out in Auschwitz by an air force physician, Dr. Horst Schumann. If enemies of the state could not reproduce, genocide would be but a matter of time. The elimination of the unwanted could be more passive and less bloody. Two to three times a week, groups of thirty prisoners — male and female — were brought in to have their testicles or ovaries irradiated with X rays. Schumann varied the dosage. As a rule, prisoners subjected to these experiments were sent back to work, even though they suffered from serious burns and swelling. The results of sterilization experiments by means of X-ray irradiation proved disappointing. Surgical castration was more dependable and time-efficient. Nevertheless, Schumann continued his experiments.

In November 1943, Dr. Josef Mengele became the chief physician of Birkenau. Mengele wanted to "prove" the superiority of the Nordic race. His first experiments were performed on Gypsy children supplied to him from the so-called kindergarten. Before long, he expanded his interest to twins, dwarfs, and persons with abnormalities.

Mengele subjected his experimental group to all possible medical analyses that could be performed while they were still alive. The tests he conducted were painful, exhausting, and traumatic for the frightened and hungry children who made up the bulk of his subjects.

The twins and the crippled persons designated for experiments were photographed, their jaws and teeth cast in plaster molds. On Mengele's instructions, an inmate painter made comparative drawings of the shapes of heads, auricles, noses, mouths, hands, and legs of the twins.

When the research was completed, some subjects were killed by phenol injections and their organs were autopsied and analyzed. Scientifically interesting anatomical specimens were preserved and shipped out to the Institute in Berlin-Dahlem for further research.

On that day he left Auschwitz, January 17, 1945, Mengele took with him the documentation of his experiments. He still imagined that they would bring him scientific honor.

Elie Wiesel has argued that only those who were there can ever know what it was like to live even for one day at Auschwitz. Fritzie Fritshall tells why:

How do I describe fear? How do I describe hunger to someone that has probably had breakfast and lunch today? Or even if you're dieting, or even if you're fasting for a day. I think hunger is when the pit of your stomach hurts. When you would sell your soul for a potato or a slice of bread. How do I describe living with lice in your clothes, on your body? The stink. The fear. The selections. The "appells." The being told when to go to a toilet, not when you needed to use it. The using of the morning coffee to wash

your face with. Mengele. And mostly, mostly death and the gas chambers.

By the summer of 1941, Auschwitz was no longer adequate to handle its assigned tasks. Auschwitz II–Birkenau was built on farmland surrounded by beautiful birch trees. Birkenau was divided into nine subunits, each isolated from the others by electrically charged barbed-wire fences. A network of canals thirteen miles in length surrounded the camp. Chains of guard posts, two-thirds of a mile out from the fences, and patrolled by dogs, provided yet another line of security.

Michael Vogel, then a nineteen-year-old Czech Jew, recalled the ordeal of roll call.

During roll call they would kill many of us. Kill us for the simple reason that someone did it in their pants. They soiled their pants, soiled their uniform. Poor guy couldn't hold it in. Dysentery was something very common. After two weeks at Auschwitz your eyes would swell up from water, your whole face would be blown up. Your legs would puff because of malnutrition and hygiene. And then you became a skeleton.

The wooden barracks at Birkenau were built to hold forty-eight horses; they housed humans — eight hundred people. Alice Lok recalls that:

Six people slept on a plank of wood, on top of us another layer. and if one of us had to turn, all the others had to turn because it was so narrow. One cover, no pillow, no mattress.

Other blocks housed between four hundred and five hundred people with neither a lavatory nor a washbowl. Prisoners would relieve themselves in a bucket, and when the bucket was filled it had to be emptied in the lavatory. Primo Levi has written of the indignity:

It is our task to shuffle to the latrine with the bucket which knocks against our bare calves, disgustingly warm; it is full beyond all reasonable limit, and inevitably with the shaking some of the content overflows on our feet so however repugnant this duty may be, it is always preferable that we, and not our neighbor, be ordered to do it.

Auschwitz inmates sorting the luggage after the arrival of Hungarian Jews. Auschwitz, Poland, spring of 1944. *Yad Vashem, Jerusalem, Israel.*

Hairbrushes, hand brushes, shoe daubers. *On loan from the State Museum of Auschwitz-Birkenau. Photo USHMM.*

Prisoners ate their
minimal rations from
bowls such as these,
which were found in
Auschwitz
concentration camp.
*Donated by the State Museum
of Auschwitz, Oświęcim,
Poland.* Photo USHMM.

The latrine, serving two hundred and fifty
people at a time, was a wooden hut 30 by
130 feet, with rows of holes sunk through a
concrete floor. It was filled in the morning by
prisoners routinely suffering from dysentery
as a result of camp food. Lilly Appelbaum
Malnik was sixteen when she arrived at
Auschwitz. She described the conditions in
the toilet:

> In Auschwitz we had a barrack which was nothing
> but a toilet. One long toilet . . . a plank with two
> holes, one opposite the other. Two rows . . . And one
> person would walk right in the middle of those holes
> with a whip in their hand. God forbid if you missed
> the hole. They would hit us.

Until 1943, the only drinking water was
provided by one tap in the camp lavatory.

Buna was the site of a slave labor complex,
the heart of the major industrial projects
sponsored by I. G. Farben. Auschwitz was
surrounded by forty-five satellite camps
scattered throughout upper Silesia and
southwestern Poland. Each developed its own
economic nexus of industries and corporate
investors. These camps relied on what
appeared to be an unending supply of cheap
labor. Workers died by the thousands only to
be replaced by those new arrivals who
survived the first selections.

Only a small remnant of those who entered
Auschwitz survived. Those who lived in
Auschwitz had a variety of experiences. Some
were political prisoners, others were slave
laborers. Some worked as *Sonderkommando,*

feeding the crematoria. The Jewish inmates who made up the *Sonderkommando* were given better food while they did their gruesome work. But they, too, were expendable and were sent in turn to the gas chambers, then replaced by new inmates.

All lived and worked in the shadow of death. For some prisoners living in the presence of death became too much. They lost hope. They gave up. They became *Musselmäner*, the walking dead. Cecile Klein described her sister's despair and the effort it took to sustain her.

My sister just didn't want to live. She refused to eat. She became very depressed. Each day I would force open her mouth. We would get one day a piece of margarine with the bread, and one day a piece of wurst, so I would change the wurst for margarine so that I could push the margarine in her mouth . . . it should melt, that she should swallow.

We were surrounded by electrified wires. She only wanted we should go and kill ourselves. She would say she doesn't want to live, she wants to go to the wires. I always told her, "You tell me when you want to go," because this way I felt I have control and I can talk her out of it.

Each time she would say, "Let's go today," I would

always tell her, "Not today. Look, today it's too warm. Why don't we wait?" Then it was very cold. "Let's wait. We always have time to kill ourselves." But I wanted very much to live. I had a lot of zest and a lot of life in me; and also, I felt that somebody must remain alive to tell all this. Because just like we didn't know, we thought nobody else knew in this world. And this is how I kept her.

MURDER BY GAS

Crematorium II consisted of three elements: an underground undressing room 107 feet long, 25 feet wide, almost 9 feet high; the gas chamber; and a cremation facility on the ground level.

Rudof Höss, the Commandant of Auschwitz, later described what happened:

In the undressing room, prisoners of the Sonderkommando, detailed for this purpose, would tell them in their own language that they were going to be bathed and deloused, that they must leave the clothes neatly together and above all remember

Clandestine photo of women being herded to the gas chambers of Crematorium V in Auschwitz / Birkenau. Auschwitz, Poland, August 1944. *State Museum of Auschwitz, Oświęcim, Poland.*

In the gas chambers of Auschwitz / Birkenau and Majdanek, the Nazis killed Jews and other victims with prussic acid gas, better known by its commercial name, "Zyklon B." Zyklon B was a common and highly poisonous insecticide; indeed, most concentration camps used the gas to kill rats and insects. Starting in September 1941, the SS began using it to kill human beings. Gassings continued until January 1945.

The gas was contained in chalky pellets. These are from Majdanek concentration camp. The Zyklon B canister is from Auschwitz. *On loan from the State Museum of Auschwitz, Oświęcim, Poland; State Museum of Majdanek, Lublin, Poland; KZ-Gedenkstätte Sachsenhausen, Germany. Photo USHMM.*

LEFT:
Each gas chamber was fitted with an airtight metal door. These doors were bolted shut before gas entered the chamber inside. From the outside, SS guards could observe the killing through a small peephole. This is a casting of the door to the gas chamber at Majdanek. *Photo USHMM.*

ABOVE:
A photograph of the inside of a Majdanek gas chamber. The blue stain is a chemical remnant of Zyklon B. *Photo USHMM.*

where they put them, so that they would be able to find them again quickly after delousing.

The deception of the prisoners continued. Signs at the entranceway said, "To the baths and disinfecting rooms." Notices were posted: "Cleanliness brings freedom!" "One louse can kill you." People were, in the words of Filip Müller, a survivor of the *Sonderkommando*, "invited to hang up their clothes as well as their shoes, tied together by their laces."

Höss told what happened next.

The women went in first with their children, followed by the men who were always fewer in number. This part of the operation went smoothly, for the prisoners of the special detachment would claim those who betrayed any anxiety or who had some inkling of their fate. As an additional precaution, these prisoners of the special detachment and an SS man always remained in the chamber until the last moment.

The door would now be quickly screwed up and the gas immediately discharged by waiting disinfectors through vents in the ceilings of the gas chamber down a shaft that led to the floor. This ensured the rapid distribution of the gas. It could be observed through the peephole in the door that those standing nearest the vents were killed at once. It can be said that about one third died straight away. The remainder staggered and began to scream and struggle for air. The screaming soon changed to the death rattle and in a few minutes all lay still. After 20 minutes at the latest no movement could be discerned.

Sixteen-year-old Alice Lok of Hungary was one of the very few survivors who actually entered a gas chamber and emerged. She described her experience.

And then there were selections again and again and again. One day they said to us, "You will get winter clothes. Go. March up." They selected a bunch of children. The Blockältester [block supervisor] selected the children. And she kind of told us stories, because, of course, the SS wouldn't tell where you are going. But she said, "You will get warm clothes. Don't be afraid. Just go. Warm clothes." And I said to Edith, "Don't worry. I will come back and bring you some warm clothes. I will just snitch another one extra for you."

They took us to a shower. They said it will be a disinfection first, but instead of a shower or a disinfection, it was a different place. There was a window, and outside was written: "Bathhouse." They took away our clothes. They asked us to put our shoes together, tie our shoe laces together, and put our clothes down, and we will get it back after they disinfected. But it turned out that the shower did not work, that it was really the gas.

I know only that it was dark, that the Germans were terribly nervous, that when we came out they were very angry. They threw some clothes, not our own clothes, back to us. Nothing was, of course, disinfected or warm or anything. We couldn't understand the chaos, their anger, their bewilderment, their shouting, "This never happened before!" and marching us angrily back to the barrack. And the realization came only after; when we came back, and this Blockältester couldn't believe that we are alive. And she looked at us and she started to scream, "How could it happen? Why are you back? You're not supposed to be back." I think that was the only time in Auschwitz that the gas did not work.

When the gas did work, the *Sonderkommando* was sent in to haul out the bodies. Gold teeth were extracted, women's hair was shaved. Elevators transported ten to fifteen corpses at a time from the gas chambers to the ovens one floor above. David Luebke wrote: "Crematorium II contained five furnaces each with three muffles. A single muffle could incinerate 3–5 corpses at once. The maximum capacity at any given moment was between 45 and 75 bodies."

Four gas chamber installations were erected in Birkenau. They were built to resemble shower rooms. Each had the capacity to kill some six thousand people a day.

When Soviet troops entered Birkenau on January 27, 1945, they found 358,000 men's suits, 837,000 women's outfits, and more than 15,400 pounds of hair packed into paper bags — the remains of what had been confiscated and shorn from inmates.

There were 405,000 registered prisoners at Auschwitz. The vast majority of those who passed through its gates, however, were never registered. They were sent directly to the gas chambers of Birkenau. Only those sent to work were tattooed on the left forearm.

This is a scale model of "Crematorium II," one of four killing installations inside Auschwitz / Birkenau. The process of killing was the same in all four. The model was sculpted by Mieczysław Stobierski, based on contemporary documents and the trial testimonies of SS guards. A similar model is on display in the State Museum of Auschwitz in Poland.

Victims arrived in Crematorium II through a stairway leading down to the undressing room. Here, SS guards told them to surrender their valuables and undress for delousing showers. Victims were told to remember where they had left their clothing. Posters bearing slogans such as *Cleanliness Brings Freedom* and *One Louse Can Kill* were designed to misrepresent the showers as hygienic. Most victims were deceived. The undressing room in Crematorium II could accommodate about a thousand people.

Once the victims had stripped nude, the guards herded them into an underground gas chamber. Women and children — who were normally the majority — always went in first. Fake shower heads in the ceiling were intended to fool victims into believing that they were about to shower. As soon as the chamber had been filled, sealed, and locked, SS guards poured in Zyklon B pellets through special vents in the roof. The pellets fell to the floor, releasing their deadly gas. Most victims died quickly. After about twenty minutes, ventilating machines sucked out the poisonous air.

When all were dead, their bodies were pillaged and burned.

Under SS guard, prisoners hauled the corpses into an adjacent room, where gold teeth and fillings were removed and hair was shaved off the heads of dead women. Finally, a freight elevator lifted the corpses to an incineration room on the ground floor. The bodies were stuffed into ovens, three or four at a time. Crematorium II had fifteen ovens, which could burn between forty-five and seventy-five corpses at once, and about one thousand people in one day. *USHMM.*

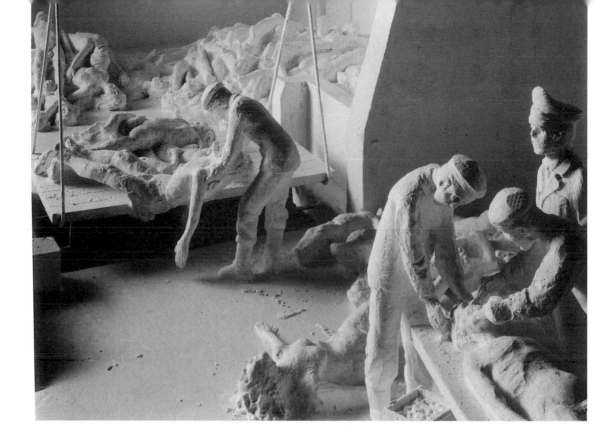

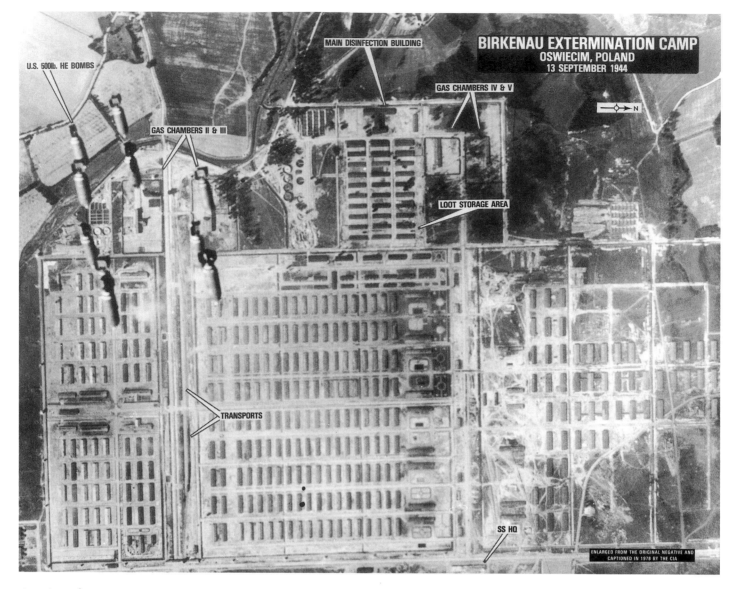

MAIN DISINFECTION BUILDING

BIRKENAU EXTERMINATION CAMP
OSWIECIM, POLAND
13 SEPTEMBER 1944

GAS CHAMBERS IV & V

U.S. 500lb. HE BOMBS

GAS CHAMBERS II & III

→ N

LOOT STORAGE AREA

TRANSPORTS

SS HQ

ENLARGED FROM THE ORIGINAL NEGATIVE AND
CAPTIONED IN 1978 BY THE CIA

American planes
bombing Buna factory.
September 13, 1944,
Auschwitz, Poland. *Dino
Brugioni / National Archives,
Washington, D.C.*

WHY WASN'T AUSCHWITZ BOMBED?

During the spring and summer of 1944, hundreds of thousands of Hungarian Jews were deported to Auschwitz / Birkenau. As many as ten thousand people a day were killed in its gas chambers. Jewish leaders in Budapest and Slovakia, American Jewish organizations, and the U.S. government's War Refugee Board all urged the Allies to intervene. Their requests, though made independently, called for the same action: Auschwitz must be bombed. At the very least, the railway lines leading to the death camp must be knocked out.

These repeated requests were denied. The Americans gave several reasons: Auschwitz was not within the range of Allied bombers; military resources could not be diverted from the war effort; bombing Auschwitz might provoke even more vindictive German action.

In fact, as early as May 1944, the United States Army Air Force had the capability to strike Auschwitz at will. The rail lines from Hungary were also well within range. On July 7, 1944, American bombers flew over the railway lines to Auschwitz. On August 20, 127 Flying Fortresses, with an escort of 100 Mustang fighter craft, dropped 1,336 five-hundred-pound bombs on a factory less than five miles east of Auschwitz. The death camp remained untouched.

In August, Assistant Secretary of War John J. McCloy wrote to Leon Kubowitzki of the World Jewish Congress, noting that the War

144

Refugee Board had asked if it was possible to bomb Auschwitz:

After a study, it became apparent that such an operation could be executed only by the diversion of considerable air support . . . now engaged in decisive operations elsewhere and would . . . be of such doubtful efficacy that it would not warrant the use of our resources. There has been considerable opinion to the effect that such an effort, even if practicable, might provoke even more vindictive action by the Germans.

McCloy was less than candid: there had been no study on bombing Auschwitz. Instead, the War Department had decided in January that army units would not be "employed for the purpose of rescuing victims of enemy oppression" unless a rescue opportunity arose in the course of routine military operations. In February, an internal U.S. War Department memo stated: "We must constantly bear in mind that the most effective relief which can be given the victims of enemy persecution is to insure the speedy defeat of the Axis."

The defeat of the Axis came fifteen months later, too late for those murdered in 1944 and 1945. Bombing Auschwitz could have significantly slowed the killing process and saved innumerable lives. By 1944, American government officials were fully informed about the operations of the killing center. As for McCloy's stated fear of provoking Nazi retaliation, how much more vindictive could the Nazis have become?

Elie Wiesel, an Auschwitz survivor, recalls the hope of an Allied attack:

Then we began to hear the airplanes. Almost at once the barracks began to shake. "They're bombing Buna," someone shouted. [Buna was the German synthetic rubber factory at Auschwitz III that relied on slave labor.] I thought of my father. But I was glad all the same. To see the whole works go up in fire — what revenge! . . . We were not afraid. And yet, if a bomb had fallen on the blocks it alone would have claimed hundreds of victims on the spot. But we were no longer afraid of death; at any rate not of that death. Every bomb that exploded filled us with joy and gave us new confidence in life.

FACE-TO-FACE WITH DEATH: SHOES

urvivors of the concentration camps spoke of their shoes. Primo Levi wrote:

Death begins with the shoes; for most of us, they show themselves to be instruments of torture, which after a few hours of marching cause painful sores which become fatally infected. Whoever has them is forced to walk as if he was dragging a convict's chain. . . . He arrives last everywhere, and everywhere he receives blows. He cannot escape if they run after him; his feet swell and the more they swell, the more the friction with the wood and the cloth of the shoes becomes insupportable.

Viktor Frankl, the doctor who later pioneered logotherapy, basing his healing on the idea that a sense of purpose and meaning is central to the healing process, wrote:

Like nearly all the camp inmates, I was suffering from edema. My legs were so swollen and the skin on them so tightly stretched that I could scarcely bend my knees. I had to leave my shoes unlaced in order to make them fit my swollen feet. There would not have been space for socks even if I had any. . . . So my partly bare feet were always wet and my shoes always full of snow. . . . Every single step became real torture.

I Saw a Mountain

*I saw a mountain
Higher than Mt. Blanc
And more Holy than the Mountain of Sinai.
Not in a dream. It was real.
On this world this mountain stood.
Such a mountain I saw — of Jewish shoes in
    Majdanek.
Such a mountain — such a mountain I saw.
And suddenly, a strange thing happened.
The mountain moved. . . .
And the thousands of shoes arranged themselves
By size — by pairs — and in rows — and moved.*

*Hear! Hear the march.
Hear the shuffle of shoes left behind — that which
    remained.
From small, from large, from each and every one.*

The "Final Solution" was not only systematic murder, but systematic plunder. Before Jews were gassed at Belzec, Sobibór, Treblinka, Chełmno, Majdanek, and and Auschwitz / Birkenau, the SS confiscated all their belongings. First to go were money and other valuables; clothes were next. This mass pillage yielded mountains of clothing. Auschwitz / Birkenau and Majdanek together generated nearly 300,000 pairs of shoes, which were distributed among German settlers in Poland and among the inmates of other concentration camps. All in all, the "Final Solution" produced over 2,000 freight carloads of stolen goods. These shoes were confiscated from prisoners in Majdanek. *On loan from the State Museum of Majdanek, Lublin, Poland. Photo USHMM.*

Prisoners sort shoes taken from Hungarian Jews. Auschwitz, Poland, 1944. *Yad Vashem, Jerusalem, Israel.*

During the first day of internment in a concentration camp, those inmates who were not immediately sent to the gas chamber had their heads shaved and their bodies disinfected. Buchenwald, Germany. *American Jewish Joint Distribution Committee, New York.*

Make way for the rows — for the pairs,
For the generations — for the years.
The shoe army — it moves and moves.

"We are the shoes, we are the last witnesses.
We are shoes from grandchildren and grandfathers.
From Prague, Paris and Amsterdam.
And because we are only made of stuff and leather
And not of blood and flesh, each one of us avoided
    the hellfire.
We shoes — that used to go strolling in the market
Or with the bride and groom to the chuppah,
We shoes from simple Jews, from butchers and
    carpenters,
From crocheted booties of babies just beginning to
    walk and go
On happy occasions, weddings, and even until
    the time
Of giving birth, to a dance, to exciting places
    to life . . .
Or quietly — to a funeral.
Unceasingly we go. We tramp.
The hangman never had the chance to snatch us
    into his
Sack of loot — now we go to him.
Let everyone hear the steps, which flow as tears,
The steps that measure out the judgment."

I saw a mountain
Higher than Mt. Blanc
And more Holy than the Mountain of Sinai.

— Moses Schulstein, translated by Mindele Wajsman and Bea Stadtler

---

TATTOOING AND SHEARING

For those who survived the first selection, the introduction to life inside the death camp was the humiliation of being shorn and tattooed. Inmates remember this process with great bitterness. Michael Jacobs recalled his arrival at Auschwitz as a teenager:

As you stretched out your arm, they gave you a number. . . . And as they gave me my tattoo number, B-4990, the SS man came to me, and he says to me, "Do you know what this number's all about?" I said, "No, sir." "Okay, let me tell you now. You are being dehumanized."

*And as they gave me my tattoo number, . . . the SS man
came to me, and he says to me, "Do you know what this
number's all about?" I said, "No, sir." "Okay, let me tell
you now. You are being dehumanized."*

MICHAEL JACOBS, AUSCHWITZ SURVIVOR

Lilly Malnick was sixteen when she arrived at Auschwitz:

They tattooed me and they told us, from now on, this is [your] name. My name is A-5143. Your name is your number. And the . . . discouragement that I felt . . . I felt like I was not a human person anymore. They had shaved our heads and I felt so ashamed and also when they told us to undress, . . . they made us feel like animals. The men were walking around and laughing and looking at us. You take a girl who was never exposed to a man and you stay there naked. . . . I wanted the ground to open and I should go in it.

For most, the taking of the hair was followed almost at once by death. A member of the *Sonderkommando*, the special unit of prisoners assigned to work in the gas chamber area, described the arrival of a transport:

A big transport came in from Hungary. Beautiful people with beautiful long hair. . . . The music started playing, the women were singing. [At the entrance to Auschwitz, a small orchestra of pretty young women played light music to lull the suspicions of new arrivals.] And we knew right away what's going to happen to them. Beautiful people. All dressed up so nice with jewelry and everything.
It didn't take long. They took their clothes, they cut their hair, they put everything on a pile. . . . Some of them they had such beautiful long hair. They must have taken maybe two or three hundreds of them. They cut their hair and took everything away. . . . In the morning, instead for us to go to work, we had to clean up the bodies.

What happened to the hair?
Until August 1942, hair was not used. As the mass murder of Jews moved into high gear, camp commandants were informed that "human hair will be processed into felt to be used in industry, and thread will be spun out of them." In particular, "the combed-out and cut-off women's hair will be used to make socks for submarine crews, and to manufacture felt stockings for railroad workers." It was also used for hair cloth, the ignition mechanism of bombs, ropes and cords for ships, and as stuffing for mattresses. The commandants were required to submit monthly reports on the amount of hair collected.

Hair was delivered to the German firms Alex Zink Filzfabrik AG in Roth, near Nuremberg; Paul Reinmann in Mieroszow, in the Sudeten (Freidland Bez. Breslau); and Farberei Forst AG, in Forst on the Luzycka Nysa (Neisse) River. One kilogram (2.2 pounds) of hair was worth one-half Reichsmark ($1.09).

Hair was stored in crematoria building lofts at Auschwitz, where it could be dried by heat from the ovens and chimneys before it was shipped. In 1961, former prisoner Karol Bienias described this particular job:

We cleaned the women's hair of pins and other objects, and then combed it with our hands and packed it into sacks for shipment. We loaded one shipment of 1,500 kilograms [3,300 pounds] of hair at the train station in Auschwitz. Faulty sorting was punished by flogging.

BODY DISPOSAL

Cleaning up the bodies and disposing of them was a huge job. At first the dead of Auschwitz II were buried in lime pits, but the mass graves were soon packed to overflowing. As they decomposed, the buried corpses bloated, causing the earth to rise and ooze, and polluting the groundwater. The bodies had to be exhumed and incinerated on vast pyres, then the ashes reburied.

The process later became more sophisticated. Ovens designed and guaranteed by

TOP:
Hungarian Jewish women shorn shortly after their arrival in Auschwitz. Auschwitz, Poland, May 1944. *Yad Vashem, Jerusalem, Israel.*

FAR LEFT:
Hair of women prisoners prepared for shipment to Germany. Auschwitz, Poland, January 1945. *National Archives, Washington, D.C.*

LEFT:
Human hair shorn from prisoners in Auschwitz/Birkenau. *Currently on display at the State Museum of Auschwitz. Photo USHMM.*

The ovens of Birkenau were subjected to heavy use and often broke down under the strain. On these occasions, the corpses were burned in open pits. This clandestine photo was taken during such a pyre. Auschwitz, Poland, August 1944 (during the gassing of Hungarian Jews deported between May and July). *State Museum of Auschwitz, Oświęcim, Poland.*

Topf and Company were built for cremation. At Birkenau, the Nazis installed two crematoria with five triple furnaces, and three with two double furnaces. Before cremation, the *Sonderkommando* checked to make sure that the deceased had not concealed valuables in their body cavities.

Some bodies were disposed of while the victim was still alive. Fourteen-year-old Shony Alex Braun described his work for the special units that operated in the vicinity of the gas chambers.

My job for the Sonderkommando was to go around the camp and pick up dead or nearly dead bodies, put them on a cart and push them up to the crematories where another group of people, Sonderkommandos, would take over and they would shove them into the oven. Some of these people were far from being dead. They were just helpless, very ill or dehydrated, they just didn't have any more power even to stand. So they fell. On one occasion, I

went to the kapo [prisoner foreman] and I said, "This man is not dead!" I got such a terrible slap in the face that I made a somersault. And he says, "You were not supposed to think or say anything! Your job is to pick them up and put them on a cart and shove them up to the crematorium, just as you were told."

According to a study by Auschwitz historian Andrzej Strzelcki, ashes and bones from ovens of Auschwitz crematoria were crushed with wooden mortars, then buried in pits or sunk in the Sola and Vistula rivers or in ponds near Birkenau. They were also used as fill in the terrain and as fertilizer for camp fields.

The SS conserved their limited resources. The fat that dripped from the bodies burned in pits or on pyres was collected in ditches dug for that purpose near the incineration sites, then used as fuel for the fires that burned the bodies. This practice was especially common during rainy weather. From time to time, the bodies of new arrivals were thrown into the crematoria with the bodies of emaciated veteran prisoners because the body fat from the healthier new arrivals made the burning process more efficient.

The engagement of German society in the killing process was widespread. Business firms competed for contracts and received goods including gold and hair. They asked for more.

The universities were also involved. In 1940, a graduate student at Breslau University wrote a Ph.D. dissertation "On the Possibilities of Recycling Gold from the Mouths of the Dead." His discussion of removal proved far from theoretical. The SS soon took steps to implement his teaching. On September 23, 1940, Reichsführer-SS Heinrich Himmler ordered the removal of dental gold from the mouths of prisoners who died in concentration camps. Beginning in 1942, the work of the killing centers yielded large quantities of precious metals. Estimates in 1944 were as high as 10 to 12 kilograms (22 to 26.4 pounds) of gold a month. In the summer of 1944, at the peak of the extermination process, at least forty prisoners were employed at this "dental" labor.

Crematoria were designed to accommodate this function in Birkenau (Crematoria II and III) and provide for a gold workshop

("*Goldarb*"). The planners envisioned a facility for melting the gold and platinum teeth and recasting the metal into ingots.

The first shipments of dental gold reached the Reichsbank in November 1942. Not all precious metals were shipped to the SS dental service and the Reichsbank. In many cases, this "illegal" gold found its way into the hands of the SS camp personnel.

There is no reliable evidence that human fat was used to manufacture soap, or that human skin was treated to make lamp shades, book bindings, purses, or similar objects in Auschwitz. But human bodies were used for experiments conducted by SS doctors. Eighty Auschwitz prisoners were killed in the Natzweiler-Struthof concentration camp in 1943 so their bodies could be preserved in the Anatomy Institute of the Reich University in Strasbourg for eventual inclusion in a collection of human skeletons.

THE FINAL DAYS OF A SHTETL

Jews had lived in the Lithuanian town of Ejszyszki (pronounced A-shish-key) for nine hundred years. In 1939, Ejszyszki's three thousand Jews constituted the majority of the town's population. They were murdered in two days, September 25 and 26, 1941, by German *Einsatzgruppen* and their Lithuanian collaborators. The murder of these three thousand people was but a speck in the vast panorama of slaughter, the two days only a moment in the fourteen hundred days of the Holocaust. And Ejszyszki was only one of more than 4,950 cities, towns, villages, hamlets, and shtetls whose Jews were systematically murdered during the Holocaust.

There was nothing special about the murders in this shtetl. In September 1941,

Atara Zimmerman, Ejszyszok, August 31, 1930. Atara, with mother and siblings, joined father and other family members in America. Family who remained in Ejszyszok were murdered. *Photo by Alte Katz; The Yaffa Eliach Shtetl Collection.*

they were part of the routine rampages of the mobile killing units. But Ejszyszki is unique because the names of its victims are known and because their faces can be seen not in piles of corpses, as evidence of a murderous crime, but as they were captured by four shtetl photographers before the Holocaust. These pictures preserve the texture of a world destroyed, a time when the marketplace of Ejszyszki was crowded with Jews, when the chants of the pious could be heard in its synagogues, and when the young studied the Torah in its schools.

For twelve years, Professor Yaffa Eliach, a child survivor of the town, gathered the photographs from survivors and their families on three continents, researching each picture and recording each name.

Ejszyszki was occupied by Wehrmacht troops within forty-eight hours of the German invasion of the Soviet Union. The typical pattern was followed. A Jewish Council was formed by lot, and men were conscripted for slave labor. When news of killings in Lithuania reached the town, Rabbi Shimon Rozowsky issued a call for resistance. He tried to organize for self-defense, but few listened to him.

In September, on the eve of Rosh Hashanah, the Jewish New Year, Jews were ordered to surrender all valuables. It was announced that those who refused would be killed. The next morning, all Jews were ordered to assemble in the main synagogue and its two study houses. Those who failed to report were shot on the spot. Another thousand Jews from the neighboring towns of Valkininkas and Salcininkai were rounded up and brought to Ejszyszki. For two days, the four thousand Jews were held in the synagogue and study houses without food, water, or sanitary facilities.

On the third day, the killing began. The men were taken out of the synagogue and marched to the marketplace, with Rabbi Rozowsky and Cantor Tobolski leading the way chanting the *Viddui*, the final confession.

At 8:00 A.M., the Lithuanian chief of police, Ostrovskas, dressed for the occasion in a white apron and gloves, chose 250 men, all of them young and healthy, and marched them off to an unknown destination. By four in the

Feigele Blacher (second from right), Hayya-Sarah Dugaczinski, and friends from Ejszyszok and Vilna near the bridge on the outskirts of Vilna Street, January 1, 1935. *Photo by Ben Zion Szrejder; The Yaffa Eliach Shtetl Collection.*

OPPOSITE:
Zipporah Sonenson survived the Holocaust. After liberation, on October 20, 1944, Zipporah and her infant son were murdered in Ejszyszki. *Photo by her father Yitzhak Uri Katz, 1926; The Yaffa Eliach Shtetl Collection.*

afternoon, all the men of Ejszyszki had been shot to death in the old Jewish cemetery. Rabbi Rozowsky, the last to die, was forced to watch the slaughter of his people.

The next day, the women and children were taken to the marketplace in the same manner. They were shot near the Christian cemetery.

There are no Jews in Ejszyszki today. Its synagogue is a sports complex; its study house a theater. Its victims lie buried in a mass grave unnamed and unnoticed. Their memorial reads: "Victims of Fascism 1941–1944."

Yitzhak Katzenelson lived in Warsaw and died in Auschwitz in 1944. He wrote "The Song of the Murdered Jewish People" shortly before his death. Its last lines are an epitaph for a destroyed people.

Never will the voice of Torah be heard from yeshivot,
synagogues and pale students . . .
Masters of Talmud and Codes, small Jews with great
hands, high foreheads, bright eyes — all gone.

Never will a Jewish mother cradle a baby. Jews will
not die or be born.
Never will plaintive songs of Jewish poets be sung.
All's gone, gone. . . .
Woe unto me, nobody is left . . . There was a people
and it is no more. There was a people and it
is . . . Gone . . .

ABOVE:

Peretz Kaleko Alufi and sister Rachel at the outskirts of Mill Street. Peretz was among the shtetl's most popular Hebrew teachers. Rachel was the founder of "Gani," the first Hebrew kindergarten in Ejszyszok. *Photo by Yitzhak Uri Katz, mid-1920s; The Yaffa Eliach Shtetl Collection.*

ABOVE, LEFT:

On the right, Hannah Ginzberg and daughter Freeda with friend Batia Kiuchefski, Vilna, 1930. Hannah survived in Siberia. Freeda died from typhus. Batia Kiuchefski, her husband, and children were murdered in Ponar, Vilna. *The Yaffa Eliach Shtetl Collection.*

153

THE LAST CHAPTER

RESCUE

Whoever [shall] save a single life, saves an entire world.
— The Talmud

Throughout the Holocaust, the process of isolating, rounding up, transporting, and killing Jews depended on the collaboration of local populations. During the height of *Einsatzgruppen* activities in Eastern Europe, pogroms were even initiated by native groups who had behind them a long tradition of antisemitism and virulent Jew-baiting. In both the East and West, collaborators turned in Jews who had managed to avoid arrest or who had escaped from incarceration. Many others who were not active collaborators acquiesced in what they saw happening around them, shrugging their shoulders, telling themselves it was none of their business.

Others were indifferent or remained neutral, aiding neither the Nazis nor their victims. Or so they thought. But indifference only served the Nazi cause. The Nazis depended on the lack of concern shown by Allied nations, who by 1942 were fully informed of the scope of Nazi violence. The Roman Catholic Church, which had vigorously protested the Nazi euthanasia policy, did not speak out against the killing of Jews. The Church was in a position to know what was happening. There were tens of thousands of priests in cities, towns, and villages throughout Europe. They saw houses emptied, villagers deported; they heard confessions. They were unusually well informed. The Vatican was among the first to know of the genocidal programs. Authoritative information on the killing was sent to the Vatican by its own diplomats in March 1942.

Nor is the record of the United States government unsullied. Professor David Wyman, a grandson of two Protestant ministers who has written extensively on American refugee policy, has described the record of the American Department of State as "the abandonment of the Jews," a verdict fully supported by the extensive archival evidence he cited.

In the circumstances of the Holocaust, and given the imbalance of force between perpetrators and victims, neutrality was a charade. In the face of Nazi power, to be neutral was, in fact, to support the killers.

But collaboration and indifference to the murder of the Jews is not the whole story. Throughout Nazi-occupied Europe, thousands of individuals risked their own lives to help Jews. Rescue took many forms. Some rescuers acted on their own; others worked in cooperation with family, neighbors, and friends. Entire communities took the responsibility of sheltering Jews, and, in the case of Denmark, an entire nation rallied to prevent the deportation of its Jewish citizens.

What motivated the rescuers? Some sympathized with the Jews. Others were actually antisemitic, but could not sanction murder or genocide. Some were bound to those they saved by ties of friendship and personal loyalty, while others went out of their way to help total strangers. Some were impelled by their political beliefs or religious values. For some rescuers, the decision to help was the result of the ethical judgment that life must be preserved in the face of death. For others, there was no choice: what they did was natural and instinctive.

Many rescuers felt they were simply acting out of elemental human decency. They later insisted that they were not heroes, that they never thought of themselves as doing anything special or extraordinary.

Marion van Binsbergen Pritchard, now a psychoanalyst in Vermont, described her "decision" to join the rescue effort as a schoolgirl in the Netherlands:

One morning on my way to school, I passed by a small Jewish children's home. The Germans were loading the children who ranged in age from babies to eight-year-olds. They were upset and crying. When they did not move fast enough, the Nazis picked them up by an arm, a leg, the hair, and threw them into the trucks. To watch grown men treat small children that way — I could not believe my eyes. Two women coming down the street tried to interfere physically. The Germans heaved them into the truck, too. I just sat there on my bicycle and that was the moment I decided that if there was anything I could do to thwart such atrocities, I would do it.

Van Binsbergen obtained Aryan identity cards for Jewish students, located hiding places, and helped Jews move into them. She supplied food, clothing, and the all-important ration cards. She registered Jewish babies as gentiles and helped provide medical care. She did not regard her acts as heroic.

It did not occur to me to do anything other than I did. After what I had seen outside the children's home, I could not have done anything else. I think you have a responsibility to behave decently. We all have memories of times we should have done something and didn't. And it gets in the way of the rest of your life.

Her parents imbued her with a strong conviction that "we are our brother's keepers," van Binsbergen said. "When you truly believe that, you have to behave in that way in order to be able to live with yourself."

What difference did the rescuers make? The Nazis' "Final Solution to the Jewish Problem" was meant to be a single, universal policy. Yet across Europe, the varying success in implementing the Final Solution depended both on the Nazi attitude toward a particular occupied country and the attitude of the native population toward their Jews. In Latvia, Lithuania, and Poland, nine out of ten Jews were killed. In Denmark, nine out of ten were saved. A crucial difference was the behavior of ordinary citizens toward their neighbors.

When citizens stood by and did nothing, Jews were murdered. When citizens took it upon themselves to act as rescuers, Jews had a chance. Speaking at a conference on the rescuers in 1984, Elie Wiesel said:

Remember that it is easy to save human lives. One did not need to be crazy to feel pity for an abandoned child. It was enough to open a door, to throw a piece of bread, a shirt, a coin; it was enough to feel compassion. . . . In those times, one climbed to the summit of humanity by simply remaining human.

In those times, one climbed to the summit of humanity by simply remaining human.

ELIE WIESEL

SAVING THE JEWS OF DENMARK

Of all the countries of Nazi-occupied Europe, only Denmark rescued virtually all its Jews. With their long tradition of tolerance toward the Jews, the Danes regarded the Jewish question as a Danish problem rather than one of an isolated minority. Danish Jews were accepted and respected. They were regarded as Danes like any others. Denmark was invaded and occupied in 1940. Danes were considered as Aryans by the Germans. Their languages were related, and the ties between the two countries had been close. At first, the Danes were allowed to run the country without a great deal of interference, and Danish Jews were not persecuted. But by 1943, even they were no longer exempt from the Final Solution. Plans for the deportation of Jews were leaked to Danish political leaders by their German sources.

On September 17, 1943, a list of Jews was confiscated from the Jewish community. It was clear that trouble was coming. On September 28, a German naval attaché, Georg Ferdinand Duckwitz, alerted a leader of the Danish Social Democratic party that an *Aktion* was imminent. The warning was taken seriously, and the Danish response was quick. Fishermen, farmers, businessmen, taxi drivers, doctors, and clergyman joined in a well-coordinated clandestine effort to spirit the Jews out of the country before they could be deported.

The planned deportation of the Jews came at a time when the Danish resistance was divided over the use of violence as a tactic against the occupation. Jørgen Keller, an advocate of nonviolence, recalled: "Now all those who were in favor of passive resistance were ready to prove that their morality was of the same quality as those who were willing to sacrifice their lives." It was an opportunity, he wrote, "to protect your younger brother with your own body. The opportunity was seized by many people who had been living in an ethical conflict with themselves for several months."

On the eve of the Jewish New Year, synagogue services were canceled, and the rabbi told his anxious community to go into hiding. Jews left Copenhagen and other cities by train, car, taxi, and on foot. Hiding places were found in homes, hospitals, and churches in coastal towns and their nearby farms. Then the Jews were to leave Denmark by sea. The Lutheran Bishop of Copenhagen, H. Fuglsang-Damgaard, openly urged Danes to protect the Jews, proclaiming: "We shall fight for the cause that our Jewish brothers and sisters may preserve the same freedom which we ourselves evaluate more highly than life. . . . We must obey God before we obey man."

Money had to be raised to rent fishing boats at a cost of between one thousand and ten thousand kroner per boat. Many individual Jews were able to pay for boats themselves, and the Jewish community obtained a loan using its assets as collateral, which was repaid after the war. Many Danes spontaneously offered to help. Leo Goldberger recalled that his father did not have enough money to pay for passage on a fishing boat. In despair, he boarded a train back to Copenhagen from the coast.

As luck would have it, on the train a woman whom he knew only slightly recognized him and inquired about his agitated facial expressions. He confided our plight. Without a moment's hesitation the lady promised she would take care of everything. . . . True to her word, she met my father later in the day. . . . The money would be forthcoming from a pastor Henry Rasmussen. The sum was a fairly large one—about 25,000 Danish crowns, 5,000 per person [for his family of five], which was more than my father's annual salary. Though it was ostensibly a loan, the pastor refused repayment after the war.

The equivalent of more than $600,000 was spent in the rescue effort. Scores of Danish fishermen risked their lives to save Jews whose lives were threatened.

In October 1943, 7,220 Jews left Denmark on the fishing boats. Danish police came to the help of the rescuers; coast guard vessels acted as escorts. For two weeks, the boats ferried them across the narrow strait separating Denmark from Sweden. In Sweden, which had maintained its neutrality during the war, the Jews could find a haven. In 1943, German troops were in retreat on several fronts — from El Alamein in North Africa, to Stalingrad in the east. Allied troops were advancing on Italy. The Swedish government, which could see that the defeat of Germany was only a matter of time, offered sanctuary to the Jews despite its official neutrality, with the full realization that Germany would regard this action as hostile.

More than 90 percent of the Jews in Denmark escaped deportation to Nazi concentration camps. Only two groups could not get out. The first included those unable to care for themselves: people with disabilities and the elderly. The second consisted of those who could not provide for themselves: the poor. The Jewish community had secured its property and funds before the escape, which could be done legally. But the community had not organized itself to protect human lives because such actions would have required acting outside the framework of Danish law. Leni Yahil, the historian of the Danish rescue, said: "The community as . . . a society sharing a common fate disintegrated. Only the family unit remained intact." Yet, when the deportations took place, there were only 464 Jews left in Denmark. They were transported to "the model ghetto" Theresienstadt.

Historians have wondered what made the Danish experience unique in Europe. According to popular legend, King Christian X served as a noble example by publicly wearing the yellow star as a sign that he identified with the Jews. He is supposed to have worn it prominently on his regular morning horseback rides through the center of Copenhagen. But although the king did express solidarity with the Jews and publicly spoke against deportation, he never actually donned the yellow star.

Danes at every level of society, from fishermen to high government officials, have said they did nothing special. They simply treated Jews as the neighbors they were, and one does not allow the enemy who occupies one's country to deport neighbors. The explanation for their behavior may well be as simple as that.

Jørgen Keller said: "Many of us came from the organized resistance, but others came spontaneously when they were needed. National independence and democracy were our common goals, but the persecution of Jews added a new and overwhelming dimension to our fight against Hitler, human rights."

Keller was later asked if the Jews should feel grateful to their rescuers. "I am not sure that the Danish resistance movement would have gained the strength which it actually did had it not been for the inspiration we received from the Jews," he said. "Jews don't owe us gratitude; rather, we owe each other mutual friendship."

Jews in Denmark had long been treated as nothing more or less than Danish citizens. The Danish people resisted German pressure to divide their nation between Jews and non-Jews, regarding Nazi behavior toward Jews in Denmark as an affront to the entire nation. Even Hitler treated Denmark with respect, and German occupation policies there were more benign than in any other occupied country. The country's democratic institutions were still in place on the eve of the deportations, and at the moment of crisis the Danish people were united in their determination that their nation not be divided.

The Danish rescue effort did not end in October 1943. Refugee property was carefully protected. Homes and their contents were inventoried, and businesses were placed in trusts. Torah scrolls and holy objects were stored in churches and returned intact to the Jewish community after the war. Non-Jewish relatives who remained behind were supported. The Danish government was persistent in its inquiries about its citizens who were deported to Theresienstadt. Packages were sent. In an attempt to alleviate Danish concerns, the Germans allowed a special Red Cross visit to the camp in 1944, even though what the visitors saw was a hoax. Danish Jews were the first prisoners to return home after liberation. Of the 464 Jews deported, only fifty-one perished.

LE CHAMBON-SUR-LIGNON: A CITY OF REFUGE

During the Holocaust, Le Chambon-sur-Lignon, a village in the south of France not far from Lyon, became a place of refuge for five thousand Jews, many of them children. Most of the people in Le Chambon were Huguenots, French Protestants. Huguenots had been persecuted in France following their emergence as dissenters from Roman Catholicism in the seventeenth century, and as a group remained conscious of their position as outsiders in French society.

From the fall of France in June 1940 until November 1942, when Germany took over the entire country, the Lyon region was part of the unoccupied zone of France ruled by the collaborationist Vichy government. The Protestant pastor of Le Chambon, André Trocmé, was instrumental in building a network of people in Le Chambon and its neighboring villages who sheltered Jews in their homes and farmhouses. Local Roman Catholic convents and monasteries also participated in the rescue effort.

The leaders were known as *responsables* — those who are accountable. They were motivated by their religious beliefs as well as humanitarian feelings. Trocmé preached the ethics of the Good Samaritan: "You shall love the Lord your God with all your heart, with all your strength, with all your mind; and your neighbor as yourself."

Resistance in Le Chambon began with a few small steps. At first, Trocmé urged village students to refuse to salute the flag of Vichy France. He refused to sign an oath of unconditional loyalty to Pétain, the head of the Vichy government. Church bells were silenced.

Trocmé's example inspired the young. When French police deported stateless Jews from Paris, the students of Le Chambon delivered a protest letter to a visiting minister of state:

If our comrades whose only fault is to be born in another religion received the order to let themselves be deported or even examined, they would disobey the orders received and we would try to hide them as best we can.

The transformation of Le Chambon into a place of refuge began with a simple act. Magda Trocmé, the pastor's wife, recalled how it happened:

A woman knocked at my door one evening and she said she was a German Jew coming from northern France, and that she was in danger. She heard that in Le Chambon somebody could help her. Could she come into my house? I said, "Naturally, come in, come in." Lots of snow. She had a little pair of shoes, nothing.

Throughout Le Chambon, welcome was natural. Solidarity with the refugee was seen as routine, nothing more than the correct and expected mode of behavior. Years later, when Philip Hallie interviewed the citizens of Le Chambon, they shrugged aside praise for what they had done. He paraphrased their response:

How can you call us "good"? We were doing what had to be done. Who else could help them? And what has all this to do with goodness? Things had to be done, and we happened to be there to do them. You must understand that it was the most natural thing in the world to help these people.

There was another town whose residents united to rescue Jews. In Nieuwlande, a town in the northeast part of Holland, a network of 250 residents was engaged in providing sanctuary for hundreds of Jews from 1942 to 1944. Rescue was a joint communal effort.

Like the villagers of Le Chambon, the citizens of Nieuwlande were religious. Members of the Christian Reformed Church, they were a minority in Holland, where the majority religion is Dutch Reformed. They had an old tradition of revolt against sacrilegious tyranny as well as a powerful teaching of ethical responsibility. Arnold Douwes, one of the most active rescuers, said of his fellow townsmen, "Everyone helped. We didn't have any Dutch Nazis here."

The resistance in Nieuwlande included two Jewish boys who wrote cards, papers, and cartoons ridiculing the Germans. One cartoon showed a woman carrying packages, holding the hand of a child walking behind her. The message was from the Christian Bible: "Never forget to be hospitable, for by hospitality some have entertained angels unaware." The other side of the card said: "Help the people in hiding and buy this card for more than you can afford."

ŻEGOTA

Żegota, the Polish code name for the Council to Aid the Jews, was initiated by a few Poles motivated by their Roman Catholic or Social Democratic values. As Żegota's activities gained momentum, the London-based Polish government-in-exile recognized their work. Żegota helped Jews by providing them with safe hiding places, money, or false identity papers. Some Żegota participants were opposed to the Nazis' murder of the Jews because of their own religious beliefs, others because of friendships with Jews. Some assisted Jews through spontaneous acts of human decency. Some of the Poles who participated were known antisemites, but could not condone mass murder. Because in Poland the punishment for helping Jews was death, all participants in Żegota put their families at risk as well as themselves. Żegota was unpopular among the general Polish population, whose antagonism toward Jews was long-standing and widespread. Given the setting, efforts by Poles to save Jews were all the more remarkable.

WAR REFUGEE BOARD: SO LITTLE SO LATE

The United States began its belated rescue efforts only in January 1944, when Secretary of Treasury Henry Morgenthau presented President Roosevelt with decisive new evidence of governmental inaction that Roosevelt knew would be politically explosive if it became public.

For more than seventeen months, the United States had known of the plan to annihilate the Jews of Europe. Yet little had been done. On August 8, 1942, Dr. Gerhart Riegner, the World Jewish Congress representative in Bern, Switzerland, sent a secret cable through secure channels to the State Department and to Rabbi Stephen S. Wise, president of the World Jewish Congress, informing them

that there has been and is being considered in Hitler's headquarters a plan to exterminate all Jews from Germany and German controlled areas in Europe after they have been concentrated in the east. The number involved is said to be between three and a half and four millions and the object to permanently settle the Jewish question in Europe.

The information had reached Riegner through intermediaries from a highly placed German industrialist, Eduard Schulte, general manager of the Georg von Giesche Mining Company, who was in a position to know what was happening. In fact, the cable was an understatement. A decision to annihilate the Jews of Europe had been made during the first months of 1941. In January 1942, the plan was announced to the participants at the Wannsee Conference. Eleven million Jews were on the list presented by Heydrich. In the spring and summer of 1942, the death camps were opened. Three weeks before Riegner sent his telegram, deportations from Warsaw to Treblinka had begun.

Instead of passing on the cable to Rabbi Wise, the State Department held on to the information until Wise, who had received news of the cable from British sources, inquired about it. Only then was the leader of American Jewry informed of its content. He was asked not to make the information public until it could be confirmed by additional sources. Confirming information was forthcoming in the fall of 1942 and the early winter of 1943, when the ghettos of Poland were being emptied and the death camps were in full operation.

But Wise did not know that, early in February 1943, the State Department tried to shut down the channel through which it would have received information about the Jews. After yet another Riegner telegram, Undersecretary of State Sumner Welles sent the following cable to American consulates in neutral countries:

Telegram 354, February 10
[in reference to] Your 482, January 21

In the future we would suggest that you do not accept reports submitted to you to be transmitted to private persons in the United States unless such action is advisable because of extraordinary circumstances.

Such private messages circumvent neutral countries' censorship and it is felt that by sending them we risk the possibility that steps would necessarily be taken by the neutral countries to curtail or forbid our means of communication for confidential official matter.

HULL [Secretary of State Cordell Hull]
(SW) [Sumner Welles]

Telegram 354 shut down the secret channel of communication and signaled to American embassies abroad that the State Department was uninterested in information concerning the Jews. Eleven months later, it was the key that unraveled the State Department's policy of acquiescence. In the interim, the State Department *appeared* to be doing something. Together with Great Britain, another fruitless refugee conference was convened at Bermuda in April 1943.

News of the Final Solution came from other sources as well. In October 1942, Jan Karski, a secret courier for the Polish government-in-exile, met with Jewish leaders in Warsaw. He listened to their plea: that preventing the physical extermination of the Jews must become part of the Allied war strategy. Public appeals must be made to the German people to pressure their government to stop the extermination. The full facts regarding the murder of European Jews — concentration and extermination camps, ghettos, crime statistics — must be revealed to the public, the Jewish leaders pleaded. Finally, the German nation must be held responsible if the exterminations continued.

Jewish leaders in Warsaw made bold demands. They urged that German cities be bombed, with direct public announcements that the bombing was in retaliation for the extermination of Jews. They demanded that Jewish leaders in London, Samuel Zygelbojm of the Bund and Dr. Ignacy Szwarcbard of the Zionists, be "solemnly charged to make all efforts [so as] to make the Polish government formally forward these demands at Allied councils."

Karski himself pressed this program in meetings with English and American leaders. In London, he met with four members of the British War Cabinet, including Foreign

Minister Anthony Eden. In July 1943, Karski was sent to Washington, where he met with President Roosevelt, Secretary of State Hull, Secretary of War Henry Stimson, Attorney General Francis Biddle, OSS Chief William Donovan (the OSS, or Office of Strategic Services, was the forerunner of the CIA), and Justice Felix Frankfurter as well as with Jewish leaders such as Rabbi Wise, and Nahum Goldman, president of the American Jewish Congress.

Karski also briefed prominent journalists in an effort to convey the severity of the situation. "The Lord assigned me a role," Karski said, "to speak and write during the war, when — as it seemed to me — it might help. It did not."

From October 1943 until the end of the war, I delivered 200 lectures in the United States from coast to coast, from Rhode Island to Florida. In all of them, I spoke about the Jewish tragedy. Every lecture was reviewed by the local press.

Then came my articles on what the Jews demanded, on what I saw in the Warsaw Ghetto. . . . These were published in the New York Times, American Mercury, La France Libre, Harper's Bazaar, Herald Tribune. Many of them were illustrated.

Then in 1944, still during the war, I published a book, Story of a Secret State. Its central theme

Meeting of the War Refugee Board: Secretary of State Cordell Hull, Secretary of the Treasury Henry Morgenthau, Jr., Secretary of War Henry Stimson, and John Pehle, Director of the War Refugee Board. Washington, D.C., March 21, 1944. *Franklin Delano Roosevelt Library, Hyde Park, New York.*

was my visits to the *Warsaw Ghetto* and *Belzec*. The book became a Book-of-the-Month Club selection. It was published simultaneously also in Great Britain, Sweden, Switzerland, France.

Months after Roosevelt met with Karski, a year and a half after the Riegner telegram, and only when President Roosevelt grasped the potential political consequences of inaction, did American policy change.

On January 13, 1944, Secretary of the Treasury Morgenthau received a memo from his general counsel, Randolph Paul, entitled "Report to the Secretary on the Acquiescence of This Government in the Murder of the Jews." The memo charged that State Department officials

have used Governmental machinery to prevent the rescue of these Jews.
have taken steps designed to prevent these [rescue] programs [of private organizations] from being put into effect.
. . . in their official capacity have gone so far as to surreptitiously attempt to stop obtaining of information concerning the murder of the Jewish population of Europe.
They have tried to cover up their guilt by:
(a) concealment and misrepresentation
(b) the giving of false and misleading explanations for their failures to act and their attempts to prevent action; and
(c) the issuance of false and misleading statements concerning the "action" which they have taken to date.

The memo was the result of a discovery by a young Treasury Department lawyer, Josiah DuBois, that the State Department had withheld information about the murder of the Jews from the Treasury. Late one Friday afternoon in December, DuBois was invited to the State Department by a friend, a junior Foreign Service officer named Donald Hiss (the brother of Alger Hiss). Hiss showed DuBois the full text of Telegram 354 of February 10, 1943, which shut down the communication channel through which information about the Final Solution had been received. The uncut version of the cable revealed that four seemingly innocuous words — "Your 482, January 21" — had been

What we did was little enough. It was late. Late and little, I would say.

JOHN PEHLE, WAR REFUGEE BOARD

excised from the copy of Telegram 354 sent to the Treasury. To the untutored, the missing words were a seemingly innocent omission. To Josiah DuBois, they were the key to unraveling a mystery. The four words referred to a January 21, 1943, cable sent through State Department secret channels to Riegner and to Rabbi Stephen S. Wise conveying information about Nazi plans to exterminate Jews.

For the next three weeks, the young Treasury Department lawyer dictated to his secretary by day and wrote at home at night. Even on Christmas Day, DuBois went back to the office and worked to unlock a consistent, systematic pattern of deception and delay by high-ranking State Department officials. As a junior government official, DuBois wrote a memo that was not to bear his signature but that of his superior. DuBois made very serious charges. "I fully recognize the graveness of this statement," he noted. "I make [these charges] only after having most carefully weighed the shocking facts which have come to my attention during the last months." His memo was completed by January 13, 1944, and was signed by Randolph Paul, Treasury's general counsel.

Morgenthau, the son of a prominent Jewish family whose father had served as the American ambassador to Turkey during the massacres of Armenians in World War I, read the report with mounting rage. He condensed it from eighteen to nine pages and changed the title simply to "Personal Report to the President" — adding some comments of his own and sharply pointing out the possible political repercussions if the facts were to become known in an election year. In 1944, Roosevelt was preparing to run for an unprecedented fourth term.

On Sunday morning, January 16, 1944, Morgenthau went to the White House to see Roosevelt. The president read the report, but no copy was left at the White House. Morgenthau presented a proposal for actively involving the United States in the business of rescue. Within days of the meeting, Roosevelt established the War Refugee Board. It was charged with implementing an American policy of rescue. The members of the board were the secretaries of State, Treasury, and War. All funds for the board's work had to come from private sources.

Under the direction of John Pehle, another young Treasury Department lawyer who had worked with DuBois and Paul to expose the State Department cover-up of the Final Solution, the War Refugee Board set out to try to find a haven for Jews. The board lobbied the White House to elicit statements from Roosevelt condemning the murder of Jews, drew up plans for postwar war-crimes trials, and argued for the bombing of Auschwitz. Through its European operatives, one of whom was the Swedish diplomat Raoul Wallenberg, the War Refugee Board played a crucial role in saving perhaps as many as 200,000 Jews.

Yet when John Pehle viewed the work of the WRB from the perspective of twelve years of American efforts, he commented: "What we did was little enough. It was late. Late and little, I would say." Eight years after the Nuremberg Race Laws, five years after *Kristallnacht*, and at a time when Nazi-occupied Europe was dotted with death camps, concentration camps, and slave-labor camps, rescue efforts by the United States government finally began. Until then, American policy toward the Jews was constrained by antisemitism within the State Department, domestic nativistic sentiment (perceived or real), the relative powerlessness and disunity of American Jews, and a 1941 decision that absolute priority should be given to the war effort. Its premise was that the only way to save the refugees was to win the war.

Raoul Wallenberg in his office at the Swedish legation in Budapest. Budapest, Hungary, November 26, 1944.
Photo: Tom Veres, New York.

WALLENBERG AND HIS FELLOW RESCUERS: BUDAPEST, 1944

In March 1944, Germany occupied its ally Hungary. The deportation of Hungarian Jews began a few weeks later. Between May 14 and July 8, 437,402 Jews were deported to Auschwitz. It took 148 trains to carry them. When the deportations were suspended in the face of the advancing Russian army, only the 200,000 Jews of Budapest remained in Hungary.

In January, President Roosevelt had established the War Refugee Board in response to revelations that the United States government had covered up its knowledge of the murder of Jews and actively prevented efforts that might have rescued them. From its inception, the new board had sought international help in an attempt to protect Hungarian Jews. Overtures were made to neutral countries, the Vatican, and the International Red Cross. The Vatican and the Swiss tried to be helpful. Sweden answered the call.

Raoul Wallenberg was chosen to lead the rescue operation. He was a Swedish aristocrat, the scion of a distinguished banking family, and an architect who had been trained at the University of Michigan. He knew Jews. He

had served in the Haifa branch of the family
bank. Wallenberg was given a diplomatic
passport, a large sum of money, and carte
blanche to use whatever methods he wished,
however unorthodox, to rescue Jews.

Wallenberg arrived in Budapest on July 9,
1944. By that date, deportations had been
halted, the Russian army was advancing, and
Himmler was apparently extending peace
feelers to the West. With the defeat of
Germany imminent, the Nazi puppet regime
in Hungary was eager to polish its image in
the international community and fearful
about its position after the inevitable Allied
victory. However, Adolf Eichmann pressed for
continued deportations.

Wallenberg arrived in Budapest and
immediately began issuing Jews with
impressive-looking passports bearing the
Swedish seal. The first batch of five thousand
was only the beginning. Other neutral missions
followed Wallenberg's lead. Carl Lutz, an
American-educated Swiss diplomat, led the
effort for Switzerland. Wallenberg set up hospitals, nurseries, and soup kitchens for the Jews
of Budapest. He worked closely with local Jews

and the Jewish youth movements in Budapest.

In November, Eichmann organized a series
of forced marches. He ordered the roundup
of all Jewish men between the ages of sixteen
and sixty. Many Jews went into hiding. A large
group of Jews was marched to the Austrian
border in the first of a series of death
marches. Wallenberg reacted immediately. He
seemed to be everywhere. He issued
thousands of Swedish safe passes, pursued
convoys carrying Jews, and roamed through
the city, badgering German and Hungarian
officers to release Jews in their custody.

When threats did not work, he offered
bribes, or even stood between Jews and their
captors, saying they would have to take him
first. When Jews had no authentic
identification papers, Wallenberg came up
with forged papers or driver's licenses.
Anything that looked like an official paper,
document, or list of names was flourished by
an imperious Wallenberg with an air of
authority that intimidated even Nazi officials.
Wallenberg did not back down in the face of
personal danger. Eichmann made threatening
noises, saying, "Accidents do happen, even to

a neutral diplomat." Wallenberg's car was rammed.

Another rescuer in Budapest was Giorgio Perlasca, an Italian businessman, who posed as a Spanish diplomat and who worked with the Zionist underground. Without any authorization or authority, Perlasca offered Spanish safe passes to Jews and established children's houses. He explained his motivation: "I simply cannot understand why a man can be persecuted because he is a different religion than mine."

When the Soviet Army entered Budapest on January 16, 1945, 100,000 Jews were still alive. Many, if not most of them, owed their lives to Wallenberg and his colleagues. At that moment, Wallenberg's struggle seemed to be over. He should have been able to look forward to returning home in honor. He approached Soviet officials with a plan for the postwar rehabilitation of Hungarian Jews.

On January 17, 1945, Wallenberg was seen by Dr. Ernö Petö, one of his closest collaborators, in the company of Soviet soldiers. He said: "I do not know whether I am a guest of the Soviets or their prisoner." He was never seen as a free man again.

For ten years, the Soviet Union denied that Wallenberg was in their custody. But after the death of Stalin and the thaw of the Khrushchev years, the Soviet Union formally announced that Wallenberg had been arrested. They produced a death certificate to substantiate their claim that he had died of a heart attack in 1947.

Yet up until the 1980s, there were occasional reports from former political prisoners who said they had seen an aging Swede in various Soviet prisons. In 1991, on the eve of the collapse of the Soviet Union, Mikhail Gorbachev presented the Wallenberg family with Wallenberg's diplomatic passport. Perhaps in the aftermath of the dismantling of the Soviet Union we will finally learn Wallenberg's fate.

In 1981, the United States Congress gave Raoul Wallenberg honorary citizenship, an honor previously accorded only to Winston Churchill.

THE FATE OF BULGARIAN AND ITALIAN JEWS

Bulgaria was an ally of Germany, having joined the Axis in return for the promise of receiving territory. After participating in the attack on Yugoslavia and Greece, Bulgaria acquired Macedonia and Thrace. As Bulgaria moved further within the German orbit, legislation was enacted that restricted Jewish rights. Like Denmark, and unlike Hungary or Romania, Bulgaria did not have much antisemitism before the war. Passage of the anti-Jewish laws was protested by writers, doctors, lawyers, political leaders, and even the Holy Synod, the leadership of the Bulgarian Eastern Orthodox Church. This spontaneous public outcry heralded future opposition to Nazi persecution of Jews.

When the Germans pressed the Bulgarian government to deport Jews in 1943, a secret agreement was reached by which at first only the Jews of Thrace and Macedonia would be deported. Later, Bulgarian Jews would be targeted. In March, twelve thousand Jews from Thrace, Macedonia, and eastern Serbia were sent to Treblinka. But the attempt to deport Bulgarian Jews met with stiff resistance. Again writers and artists, jurists and parliamentarians protested. Even the Jewish community felt secure enough to hold public demonstrations. The government, mindful of public opinion and the collapsing German war effort, postponed the deportation.

Still, persecution of Jews intensified. The Jews of Sofia were expelled to the provinces, and Jewish men between the ages of twenty and sixty were sent to slave-labor camps. But there were no deportations to death camps outside Bulgaria. At the end of the war, fifty thousand Bulgarian Jews remained alive.

Why were Bulgarian Jews saved? The reasons are still obscure. The Communists credited resistance by Communist cadres. According to one widely held explanation, King Boris personally gave the order to block the deportation. He knew that the Bulgarian people would not tolerate deportation of their fellow citizens.

The Jews of Finland came through the war without a loss. When pressed by Himmler in

full participants in Italian culture and society, prominent in professional and intellectual life. In 1920, the president of the highest court in Italy was a Jew, and in the 1930s, 8 percent of all Italian professors were Jewish.

Fascist Italy, ruled by Benito Mussolini, was an ally of Hitler's Germany. Yet as long as Mussolini remained in power, no Jews were deported from Italy or from Italian-controlled territories. Only after his fall in 1943, and the subsequent German invasion and occupation of Italy, was there a serious attempt to round up and deport Italian Jews. Even then, most were rescued as a result of efforts by the Italian people to protect them.

Racial laws were introduced into Italy in 1938 shortly after *Kristallnacht*. Jews could not teach or study in public schools, although separate schools were permitted. Foreign Jews could not establish residence in the country, and those who had come after 1919 were deprived of their citizenship. The Italian laws, however, were a pale imitation of German racial law, and Italians were less than diligent about carrying them out.

The Italians interpreted the laws with great latitude. They found it difficult to discriminate systematically against Jews on the basis of blood: the Italian government was unwilling to provoke the Roman Catholic Church, which spoke out on behalf of those who had converted. (The pope saw fit to protest the racial laws only as they affected Jews who had converted to Catholicism.) Still, to forestall possible intervention by the papacy, offspring of mixed marriages were given time to have themselves baptized in order to avoid being defined as Jews.

The Italians were generally casual about conducting inquiries into who was Jewish. In Germany, family courts meticulously reviewed the ancestral background of those seeking to prove their Aryanism, but no proof of lineage was ever required in Italy. Bribery was routine, and official documents were easily concocted. Susan Zuccotti, a historian of Italy and the Holocaust, wrote that through corruption, the Italians seemed to be "honoring the most corrupt and penalizing, by default, the most worthy," those who refused to lie about their backgrounds.

Italy entered the war in June 1940, after

the summer of 1942 to implement the Final Solution in Finland, Prime Minister Johann Wilhelm Rangell said: "We have no Jewish question." Eight Jewish refugees were turned over to the Germans by the head of the Finnish State Police. The remainder of the small Jewish refugee population was sent to Sweden.

The Jews of Italy can trace their roots to the era before the Roman conquest of Judea and the destruction of Jerusalem in 70 C.E. Jews lived in Rome long before St. Peter, the first bishop of Rome.

In the twentieth century, Jews constituted only one-tenth of one percent of the Italian population. Thoroughly assimilated, they were the Nazi victories in Belgium, the Netherlands, and France. Foreign Jews, virtually all of whom were refugees, were arrested and sent to internment camps at Ferramonti and Campagna. Italian Jews were subject to a mild form of house arrest. Jews in Italy were treated with increasing gentleness, in marked contrast with other Axis countries, where persecution became more severe as the war went on.

While Bulgaria deported Jews in the occupied territories of Thrace and Macedonia, Jews in regions occupied by Italy in Croatia, Greece, and France were protected. In Italian-occupied southern France, Jews were far safer than they were under the French-run Vichy government. Deportations in Greece began only after Italian troops left, and in Croatia the Italian occupation forces were artful practitioners of obfuscation and delay as they avoided rounding up the Jewish population. Never warm allies of the Germans, Italians were singularly uncooperative participants in the Nazi efforts to carry out the Final Solution.

The [London] *Times* of January 21, 1943, reported:

Vichy Order Cancelled by Italians

Before the German troops in some French departments were relieved by Italians, Vichy, at the instigation of Berlin, instructed the prefects of the departments to force all domiciled Jews whenever appearing in public always to wear the prescribed yellow badge, [with] letter J as elsewhere under German domination.

Last week in the Italian occupied departments of Savoie, Haute Savoie, Basses Alpes, Hautes Alpes, Alpes Maritimes, and Var, the Italian commanding Generals notified the prefects that it is irreconcilable with the dignity of the Italian army that in the territories occupied by Italians Jews should be compelled to appear in public with this stigmatizing badge, and consequently notified the prefects that Vichy's orders were to be cancelled.

When the embarrassed prefects asked Vichy what they were to do, they were told to comply with the Italian instructions.

In 1943, Mussolini was overthrown and a non-Fascist regime came to power briefly. Even then, anti-Jewish measures were not rescinded in fear of provoking a German reaction. In the fall of 1943, Germany invaded Italy and restored Mussolini to power as a puppet. With the Germans in control, anti-Jewish policies were finally implemented.

In October, as Denmark was saving its Jews, the roundup and deportation of Jews from Rome began. Jewish leaders had been alerted to the impending deportation, but unlike Danish Jewish leaders, they did not heed the warning or pass on the information to the Jewish community. The signs of imminent action were clear. The office of the Jewish community in Rome was plundered, its funds, library, and archives confiscated. Above all, lists of the Jews of Rome were taken. Still, it was mistakenly believed that the Germans would not deport the Jews of Rome, the pope's backyard.

Other Jewish leaders outside Rome took the warning seriously. In Venice, Dr. Giuseppe Jona, the leader of the Jewish community, burned his lists of Venetian Jews and committed suicide. Many of his people escaped. In Ancona, Rabbi Elio Toaff, who was told of the deportation, advised his community to hide and not come to Yom Kippur services. In Florence, Rabbi Nathan Cassuto, a physician and the son of a renowned biblical scholar, went from house to house urging Jews to hide. Only four hundred Jews were deported from Florence.

The Vatican also had been informed of the planned deportations, but the pope failed to issue private protests or public disapproval either before or after the fact. The German ambassador to the Holy See commented to his foreign ministry that the pope had not allowed himself to be drawn into any demonstrative censure of the deportations. The pontiff appeared to be more concerned with preserving his own institution. Nevertheless, hundreds of priests and nuns, bishops, and ordinary clerics did come to the aid of Jews. Priests hid Jews in churches; monks and nuns opened monasteries and convents to them.

In 1963, a play by Rolf Hochhuth called *The Deputy* created a storm over the pope's knowledge of and inaction in response to the Holocaust. Despite attempts by papal apologists, criticism of Pope Pius XII's role was intense. The fact that Vatican archives have been fully opened only to select researchers so an independent assessment could be made has only fueled scholarly suspicions.

During the final stage of anti-Jewish persecution, the Italian police were responsible for arresting Jews. The roundup continued throughout the fall and winter of 1943 / 44. Despite these efforts, eight out of ten Jews escaped capture. Of the forty thousand Jews in Italy, eight thousand were killed.

Simple gestures of human decency were the hallmark of Italian rescue efforts even by Italian police officials who were forced to cooperate with the deportation. For example, Susan Zuccotti reports that on December 1, 1943, when the Republic of Salò decreed that all Jews were to be deported, a local *carabinieri* commander visited the winery in Catagnole where Augusto Serge and his family were staying. He spoke with the employer. "Then without greeting Serge whom he knew well, he left abruptly." The employer spoke sympathetically of the *carabinieri*: "He's a fine man; he came here to tell me, 'My heart bleeds to have to arrest an honest person, but tomorrow morning at 8:00 I have to arrest the lawyer and his family.'" Needless to say, Serge and his family fled.

Similarly, a woman on a train seeking to escape with some of her wealth was wearing too much jewelry to pass inspection. She was told by the official: "Put your baby to sleep and I will return." She was thus given the opportunity to put her valuables out of sight where the inspector could overlook them.

Carlo Rosselli, a Bologna lawyer, testified in 1945:

I was arrested by the German SS in via S. Chiara and taken to the prison of S. Giovanni in Monte, where, after three weeks, I was transferred to the concentration camp of Carpi (Modena). I was taken to the prison by public security agent Gervasi, in uniform, who although he was a public security agent, showed much understanding of my situation, so much so that he went to my home several times to convey my news. Also during my several SS interrogations, Gervasi, while bringing me from the SS office to the prison of S. Giovanni in Monte, allowed me to meet with my wife in a church,

jeopardizing his own existence, since the German SS would not compromise in these matters. Gervasi also offered me financial aid, which I did not accept. The same Gervasi, when I was transferred to the concentration camp at Carpi, volunteered to accompany me to Carpi even though it was not his turn, and on his return to Bologna he carried the news to my wife. In August of the same year I succeeded in escaping from the train carrying me to Germany. And when in October the SS of Bologna began an investigation into my escape, Gervasi — who continued to serve the SS — informed my family and saw to it that they found a safe place in the event of reprisals.

Why were Italian Jews saved in large numbers? The deportation of Jews began late, when Germany's defeat seemed inevitable. In Poland, the Nazis had five years to do their work; in the Netherlands, four. In Italy, only a year elapsed between the onset of deportation and liberation by the Allies.

Like Bulgaria, Italy did not have a significant tradition of antisemitism. Jews were few in number. They were linked to other Italians by language, appearance, culture, and history. Furthermore, the Italians, according to Zuccotti, had an "amicable inclination to ignore the law," which under the pressure of war became "a determination to evade it." The Italians' casual observance of their own religious traditions gave them a certain measure of tolerance toward the outsider and contempt for authority.

When asked about their motives, Italians who saved Jews sound a familiar refrain: "I did my duty." "I did what needed to be done." Father Rufino Niccacci, the peasant priest who saved three hundred Jews in Assisi by hiding them with false identity papers and helping them to blend into the surrounding community, was troubled by the lies he had to tell.

I became a cheat and a liar — for a good cause, mind you, but nevertheless a sinner, although I am sure that I have long since made my peace with God and that He has forgiven my trespasses.

We will not be silent. We are your bad conscience.
The White Rose will not leave you in peace.

"WHITE ROSE LETTERS"

THE WHITE ROSE

There was scattered resistance to the Nazi regime even in Germany. Some opposition to Hitler came from members of aristocratic families who viewed Hitler as a crude upstart and were appalled by his policies and the transformation of Germany into a police state. The small group of active opponents put their lives on the line. Virtually all of them were killed. Men like Dietrich Bonhoeffer, a distinguished Lutheran minister, and Hans von Dohnanyi, a jurist who served in the army, were part of a conspiracy to oust Hitler. For years, a group within the German officer corps gingerly plotted Hitler's overthrow, gaining adherents as the military tide turned against Germany. These army officers planned to assassinate Hitler, seize power, and negotiate peace with the Allies. After a series of abortive plans, a serious assassination attempt was finally made in July 1944, when it no longer took any special insight to see that Hitler's continued rule was leading to Germany's inevitable defeat. Hitler escaped the bomb blast with only minor injuries. All those who were involved in the conspiracy were killed.

The White Rose movement, which culminated in a remarkable public demonstration by students against the regime, was organized and led by young people. At its head were a medical student at the University of Munich, Hans Scholl, his sister Sophie, and Christoph Probst, who were outraged by the acquiescence of educated men and women in the Nazi treatment of Jews and Poles. Their anti-Nazi campaign was guided by a philosophy professor, Kurt Huber, a disciple of Immanuel Kant, the eighteenth-century moral philosopher who taught that human beings must never be used as a means to an end.

In 1942, the group set out to break the cycle in which "each waits for the other to begin." Their first leaflet was a call for spiritual resistance against an immoral government. "Nothing is so unworthy of a civilized people as allowing itself to be governed without opposition by an irresponsible clique that has yielded to base instinct," they wrote. "Every people deserves the government it is willing to endure."

In correspondence that became known as the "White Rose Letters," the group established a network of students in Hamburg, Freiburg, Berlin, and Vienna. "We will not be silent," they wrote to their fellow students. "We are your bad conscience. The White Rose will not leave you in peace." After mounting an anti-Nazi demonstration in Munich, in February 1943, the Scholls distributed pamphlets urging students to rebel. They were turned in by a university janitor. Hans and Sophie Scholl and Christoph Probst were executed on February 18, 1943. Just before his death, Hans Scholl repeated the words of Goethe: "Hold out in defiance of all despotism."

Professor Huber was also arrested. To the end, he remained loyal to Kant's ethical teaching that one must act as though legislating for the world. Huber's defense, his "Final Statement of the Accused," concluded with the words of Kant's immediate disciple, Johann Gottlieb Fichte:

And thou shall act as if
On thee and on thy deed
Depended the fate of all Germany
And thou alone must answer for it.

Huber and other students of the White Rose were executed a few days after the Scholls.

SS soldiers near the bodies of the men of Lidice massacred in reprisal for the assassination of Heydrich. Lidice, Czechoslovakia, June 10, 1942. *Bildarchiv, Preussischer Kulturbesitz, Berlin, Germany.*

RESISTANCE AND REPRISAL: LIDICE

The Nazis were skilled practitioners of collective responsibility, the murder of an entire community as a reprisal for individual acts of resistance. Reprisals were taken against Jews and non-Jews throughout Nazi-occupied Europe. It was an effective tactic in stifling popular enthusiasm for resistance.

The annihilation of the Czech town of Lidice is one of the most notorious instances of the Nazi practice of reprisal.

On May 27, 1942, Reinhard Heydrich, head of the RSHA, the *Reichsprotektor* of Czechoslovakia, the man who had convened the Wannsee Conference only four months previously, was severely wounded in a grenade attack on his car near Prague by two Czech parachutists sent from London by the Czech government-in-exile. The two Czechs managed to leave the scene and took refuge in the Karl Borromaeus Church in Prague.

On June 4, Heydrich died of his wounds. The Nazis swore revenge: they ordered the execution of ten thousand Czechs and threatened the expulsion of millions. The Karl Borromaeus Church, where the assassins and more than one hundred members of the Czech resistance were hiding, was besieged. Everyone in the church was killed by the SS.

In Lezaky, a village east of Prague, where the assassins' radio transmitter was discovered, every adult was killed. The children were forcibly removed to Germany for "reeducation," a process that only two of them survived.

At dawn on June 10, all the residents of Lidice, a village ten miles outside Prague, were taken from their homes. They were shot in batches of ten at a time behind a barn. By late afternoon, 192 men and boys and 71 women had been murdered. The other women were sent to concentration camps. The children were dispersed, some to concentration camps, although a few who were considered sufficiently Aryan were sent to Germany. The SS then razed the town and tried to eradicate its memory. The name of Lidice was expunged from all official records.

The Czechs were stunned by the Nazis' brutality. They also came to view resistance activities with considerably less enthusiasm. The assassination was so unpopular that the Czech government-in-exile denied all responsibility for it, even after the war.

Apparently as a "tribute" to Heydrich's memory, his SS colleagues gave the code name Operation Reinhard to the Final Solution to the Jewish Problem carried out by the General-Government in Poland in the death camps of Belzec, Sobibór, and Treblinka.

Hannah Szenes and her brother Gyuri before her departure from Palestine for her last mission. Palestine, 1944.
Beit Hannah Senesh, Kibbutz Sdot Yam, Israel.

BEHIND ENEMY LINES

In Palestine, the Jewish community was eager to join the fight against the Nazis. Though Palestine was a long way from the killing centers of Europe, most Palestinian Jews had come from Europe. It was their families who were being murdered. They spoke Eastern European languages fluently and had the skills and motivation required to carry out rescue and resistance missions.

Palestinian Jews who joined the British army served in the Jewish Brigade. In 1943, they pressed the British for the opportunity to infiltrate enemy territory and organize resistance and rescue operations. After a great deal of pressure, the British government agreed to parachute a small number of Jews into occupied territories, where they would act both as British agents and Jewish emissaries to contact the Jewish communities under siege.

Twenty-three-year-old Hannah Szenes, one of only two women among the thirty-two Palestinian parachutists dropped behind the lines, began her mission just as the Germans invaded Hungary in March 1944. A native of Budapest, Szenes had left for Palestine before the war. Her mother remained behind. Her late father had been a prominent Hungarian playwright and writer.

For three months, between March and May, Hannah Szenes was stranded in the mountains of Yugoslavia with Tito's partisans. She finally left to make her way to the Hungarian border on May 12, 1944, the day that the Germans began the deportation of Hungarian Jews to Auschwitz. "Even if our chances for success are minuscule, we must go," she said.

On June 7, she reached the Hungarian border. The first stage of deportation was completed; 289,000 Jews had been sent to death camps. Before Szenes set off on what she knew was a suicide mission, she handed a crumpled slip of paper to her companion, Reuven Dafni. On it she had written:

Blessed is the match consumed in kindling flame
Blessed is the flame that burns in the secret fastness
of the heart
Blessed is the heart with strength to stop its beating
for honor's sake
Blessed is the match consumed in kindling flame.

Szenes was captured the next day and imprisoned by the Germans and Hungarians. She was tortured, and her mother's life was threatened, but she would not reveal her radio code or the nature of her mission. She never requested a pardon or mercy. She was tried and convicted in October and executed as a traitor to Hungary on November 7, 1944. She left a final message to her comrades: "Continue on the way, don't be deterred. Continue the struggle till the end, until the day of liberty comes, the day of victory for our people." Hannah Szenes has been celebrated as a hero of Jewish resistance, a symbol of the will to fight on against all odds.

RESISTANCE

These stamps were made by Gilbert Leidervarger and his brother-in-law, David Donoff, to forge documents and identification papers for the *Eclaireurs Israélites de France,* Jewish boy scouts who had joined the Resistance. The forged identification papers belonged to David Donoff (alias "André Donnet") and his sister, Lina Donoff (alias "Denise Alice Josephine Rochard"). *Photo USHMM.*

Jews fought the Nazis in the forests of Eastern Europe and the ghettos of Poland. They fought in resistance movements in the West, with Tito in Yugoslavia, and side by side with Soviet partisans. Even in the death camps of Birkenau, Treblinka, and Sobibór, Jews resisted with force. A crematorium was blown up and escapes were organized.

At first, armed resistance was not how Jews responded to Nazi oppression. They were more practiced in the art of spiritual resistance. Jews initially attempted to thwart Nazi intentions by nonviolent means, stopping short of direct confrontation in which Jews would inevitably be overpowered. Later, it became clear that death could not be evaded by cooperation, negotiation, or forbearance.

Courage and valor in the face of death took many forms in the ghettos of Europe. Korczak went to Treblinka with his children. He may have suspected his fate. Still, he stayed with the orphans to the end. Mothers and fathers stayed with their children. Resistance fighters tended to be young and single. They did not have to care for their parents or provide for their children.

Jewish resistance fighters had the odds against them. Unlike classic guerrillas, who lose themselves by blending in with the local population, Jews were neither mobile nor unrecognizable. Confined to ghettos, they were captives who were vulnerable to retaliation. Because of widespread antisemitism in Eastern Europe, the Jewish resistance could not rely on popular support.

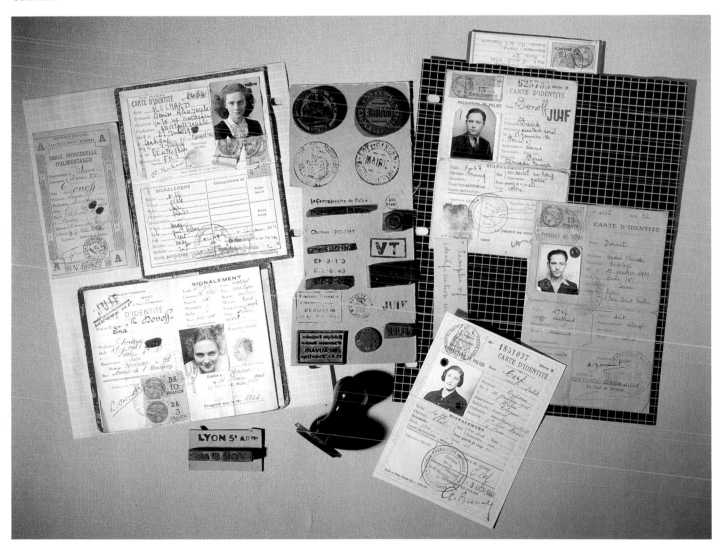

A group of Jewish partisans from Vilna. From left to right: Elchanon Magid, Jacob Prener, Bluma Markowitz (killed in a bombardment a few days after this photo was taken), Abba Kovner, Ruszka Korczak, Leib Sapirsztein, Vitka Kempner. Kneeling: Gerozan Griner, Pesach Mizerec, Motl Szames. Vilna, Lithuania, USSR, 1945. *Weiner Library, London, England.*

The call to arms in the Vilna ghetto in Lithuania was a clear statement of the determined rage that motivated Jewish resistance. Written by Abba Kovner, it was promulgated on January 1, 1942, only six months after the German invasion.

Jewish youth, do not believe those that are trying to deceive you. Out of 80,000 Jews in the "Jerusalem of Lithuania" [Vilna] only 20,000 are left. Before our eyes they took away our parents, our brothers and sisters. Where are the hundreds of men who were conscripted for labor? Where are the naked women and the children who were taken away from us on that dreadful night? Where are the Jews who were deported on Yom Kippur?

And where are our own brethren in the second ghetto?

Of those taken through the gates of the ghetto not a single one has returned. All the Gestapo roads lead to Ponar [the forest seven miles outside the city], and Ponar means death.

Ponar is not a concentration camp. They have all been shot there. Hitler plans to destroy all the Jews of Europe, and the Jews of Lithuania have been chosen as the first in line.

We will not be led like sheep to the slaughter. True, we are weak and helpless, but the only response to the murderer is revolt!

Brothers! It is better to die fighting like free men than to live at the mercy of the murderers. Arise! Arise with your last breath!

Jews did not easily blend in with the local population. Finally, it was difficult and dangerous to obtain arms. They had to be purchased and then smuggled into the ghetto pistol by pistol, rifle by rifle. Material assistance was difficult to obtain from the Allies or the underground armies in Poland.

Armed resistance was almost always an act of desperation that burst forth when all hope was lost. When Jews fully understood what the Nazis intended, any hope of survival was abandoned. At that point, the fighters were impelled by the desire to uphold Jewish honor and to avenge Jewish death.

Execution of three partisans in Minsk. One of them is a Jewish woman, Masha Bruskina, who smuggled false documents to a prison camp for Soviet POWs. Minsk, USSR, October 26, 1941.

LEFT TO RIGHT:
Bundesarchiv, Koblenz, Germany.

Central State Archives of the October Revolution. Moscow, Russian Federation.

Museum of the Great Patriotic War. Minsk, Byelorussia.

Museum of the Great Patriotic War. Minsk, Byelorussia.

GHETTO REVOLTS

Jews in the ghettos took up arms in 1942 and 1943 when liquidation was imminent. In many ghettos in Poland, Lithuania, Byelorussia, and the Ukraine, organizations were formed for the purpose of waging armed struggle. There was little hope of survival, even less of victory. Resistance was its own reward.

There were various patterns of ghetto revolts. In most ghettos, the underground was led by young people who had been trained in Zionist or Communist youth movements. Prewar political allegiances continued to divide the fighters. In Warsaw, the Zionist Irgun would not fight under the command of Mordecai Anielewicz, the leader of the Z.O.B. Some ghettos had unified commands, while others splintered along political lines. Interpretations of the past and dreams for the future could not be suspended even under the Nazi assault. Orthodox Jews rarely participated in the rebellions. The heirs of Rabban Yochanan, they tended to accept the ghetto as God's will and were far less likely to embrace the use of force. (Only in contemporary Israel, which arose from the ashes of the Holocaust, has Orthodoxy become militant and messianic.)

The underground was at odds with those *Judenrat* leaders who believed that the ghetto would survive because of its economic utility. They did not accept the doctrine, practiced by Rumkowski in Łódź and by many other *Judenrat* leaders, of salvation through work. The young leaders of underground movements worked in tandem with those *Judenrat* leaders who fully understood the implication of Nazi policy. In most ghettos the choice was stark: deportation or armed revolt. Either one led inevitably to death. In many small ghettos where revolts erupted, among them Starodubsk, Tatarsk, Kletsk, Mir, Lachva, Kremenets, and Lutsk, few survived. In Czestochowa, Bedzin, Sosnowiec, and Tarnów, Jews rebelled only on the eve of the final deportations.

A month before the liquidation of the Lithuanian ghetto of Bialystok, Mordechai Tenenbaum and Daniel Moszkowicz took command of the Anti-Fascist Fighting Bloc. They had managed to assemble a meager assortment of weapons — twenty-five rifles, one hundred pistols, a few machine guns, some hand grenades, and dynamite, bayonets, and knives. On August 16, 1943, forty thousand Jews were corralled into six narrow streets. Tenenbaum and Moszkowicz decided to storm the ghetto fence in hopes of giving at least some of the Jews a chance to flee to the surrounding countryside. The fighting lasted for four days. All but 150 Jews were killed. Tenenbaum and Moszkowicz refused to leave and died fighting.

In Lithuania and Byelorussia, ghetto residents had another choice. Where the ghettos were surrounded by dense forests, Jews could attempt to break out during the

Egon Nowak (first left) and Oskar Wertheimer (third left), Jewish partisans in the Slovak National Uprising. Slovakia, 1944. *Beth Hatefusoth Museum of the Diaspora, Tel Aviv, Israel.*

no way out of the ghetto: Ponar, where all the Gestapo roads led, was more than a metaphor for death.

But the decision to fight did not come easily to most ghetto inhabitants. Resistance meant rejecting the traditional authority of the leaders of the Jewish community: Kovner and other young fighters challenged the *Judenrat* when they urged Jews not to "believe those that are trying to deceive you."

The manifestos of the young firebrands implicitly criticized the older generations who had submitted without a struggle: "Let us not walk like sheep to the slaughter." Those who fought were clear eyed. Resistance was, at bottom, a choice between forms of dying. Whatever Jews did, they would be killed. But one could die with honor by choosing "to defend oneself to the last breath."

The dilemma of the resistance fighters is exemplified by Yitzhak Wittenberg, the commander of Vilna's United Partisan Organization. Wittenberg was betrayed by a non-Jewish Communist and arrested by the Germans on July 16, 1943. As he was being led out of the ghetto, Jewish fighters attacked the Jewish police and freed him.

An ultimatum was then given to Jacob Gens, the *Judenrat* chief. If the ghetto did not hand over Wittenberg by 6:00 the next morning, the Germans would come with tanks and airplanes and destroy the entire ghetto. A fierce debate took place within the partisan command. The choice was bleak: to fight to the end or surrender their commander. The fighters did not think that the ghetto would support them. The Jews of Vilna were not yet convinced that their last hour was really at hand. Wittenberg was given up.

The next day Wittenberg was dead, the victim of suicide or torture, perhaps both. On September 1, the ghetto was sealed. The underground mobilized its fighters and clashed with the Germans. Gens appealed for calm. To forestall the liquidation of the entire ghetto, he promised to deliver Jews for deportation. He bought only two weeks of time.

On September 14, 1943, Gens was summoned by the Gestapo and murdered immediately. The final liquidation of Vilna

confusion of battle. In Minsk, more than ten thousand Jews escaped to the forests. In Mir, only 180 would leave, even when the ghetto was about to be liquidated. In Kovno, 350 escaped with the help of Lithuanian partisans. In the ghettos of Nesvizh, Kletsk, Tuczyn, and Mizoch, which the Nazis set afire before deportation, Jews also attempted to flee to the forests.

In the Vilna ghetto, the call to arms came after three-quarters of the city's prewar Jewish population had been deported and murdered in Ponar. The call for armed resistance was made on January 1, 1942. It went unheeded for another twenty-one months, until the ghetto was on the verge of extinction. Vilna was typical in that armed resistance gained popular support only when people grasped the full meaning of Nazi intentions. There was began nine days later. Only a small group of fighters, some two hundred in all, escaped to the forests.

Those who managed to survive the ghettos in Poland and the Soviet Union were a tiny minority. Resistance was never, and could not have been, a strategy for survival. It was an existential act of honor and courage in the face of certain death.

JEWISH PARTISANS

In those areas of Eastern Europe that were covered by dense forests, Jews could flee to the forests to form their own fighting units or join partisan bands, mobile fighters who would stage fleeting attacks on the enemy. In Yugoslavia, Bulgaria, and Greece, Jews fought as equals alongside native partisans in a unified fighting movement.

In the Soviet Union, where partisan activity was widespread, Jews were welcome participants. In Byelorussia, the local population supported the partisans — even Jewish partisans — and thick forests gave excellent cover for mobile partisan bands. Jewish partisan activity often developed in parallel to Soviet movements and frequently in cooperation with them. But in Poland and the Ukraine, as in Lithuania, Estonia, and Latvia, Jews could expect little help from the non-Jewish population.

Some partisan units consisted mainly of Jews. The Jews of Vilna established four battalions — some four hundred fighters — in the forests of Lithuania. They took colorful, audacious-sounding names. The Avengers were commanded by Abba Kovner, The Struggle by Aharon Aharonovits, Death to Fascism by Yankel Prenner, and To Victory by Shmuel Kaplinski. In Lithuania where Russians comprised 21 percent of all partisans, Jews made up 7.5 percent, a large component considering the massive scale on which the Lithuanian Jews had been slaughtered.

The best conditions for partisan activities were in Byelorussia. Its forests were vast —

Partisan Boris Yochai planting dynamite on a railroad track near Vilna. He blew up twelve trains. Vilna, Lithuania, USSR, 1943–1944. *YIVO Institute for Jewish Research, New York.*

the Naliboki Forest alone covered 1,158 square miles — and guerrillas could count on a great deal of popular support as well as material supplies from the Soviet Union. In this region, organized partisan activities were conducted on a grand scale. As early as 1941, there were five thousand fighters in the region, mostly Soviet troops who had been cut off by the German army and POWs who had escaped. Before long, a partisan headquarters was set up to issue supplies and battle orders. As the tide turned against the Germans in 1943 and 1944, the number of partisans in Byelorussia rose dramatically.

Life as a partisan was difficult. Samuel Gruber recalled: "We were 22 people and 3 of our people said, 'That's enough. They don't want to go run like this. They will kill all of us and it's a hard life. We'd rather go back to the camp.'" Gruber, who had been in a concentration camp, was dumbfounded. The life of a partisan was, however, harsh and uncertain. One moved from place to place, plundered for food, fought for survival, and froze in winter.

Some eleven hundred partisan units organized into 199 brigades operated in the Naliboki Forest. Many of them were made up of Jews and had Jewish leaders. Dr. Yeheskel Atlas's unit was formed in the Derechin area; Schorr's 51 in the Slonim area; Jews escaping

Jewish partisan Mosha Pijade with his close colleague Josip Broz Tito. Yugoslavia, wartime.
Jewish Museum, Belgrade, Yugoslavia.

from Minsk formed seven different partisan units. Dr. Atlas defined the mission of his group:

> We must not settle down and take things easy. . . . Your lives came to an end in the slaughter of the 24th of July [when Derechin was destroyed]. Every additional day is not yours, but belongs to your murdered families. You must avenge them.

He asked every candidate who wished to join: "What do you want?" The answer he sought was: "To die fighting the enemy."

Early in 1944, as the Red Army went on the offensive against the Germans, the Soviet Union tightened its control of the partisans, who in effect became auxiliaries to the main fighting force. Non-Jewish commanders were assigned to Jewish commando units and the Jewish character of separate units was eroded. But with better firepower and support, the partisans were far more effective in their attacks on retreating German troops.

Most of the partisan groups consisted of single men. Because their sole purpose was to fight and inflict as much damage as they could on the enemy, membership was limited to able-bodied men prepared for battle. Those unable to fight were left to fend for themselves. But some Jewish units were unwilling to abandon those untrained or unfit for combat. Thus, another kind of partisan

unit was established: the family camp, where women, children, and old people lived with and were protected by the fighters. Perhaps as many as ten thousand Jews — men, women, and children — survived the war in family units.

Unlike the roaming bands of male partisans, family camps were large, sprawling, and necessarily immobile. They could be sustained only in areas with dense forests. The groups survived by raiding local communities for food and by serving as a civilian support system for other partisan brigades. Killing the enemy was only one of their tasks. Helping the members of the camp survive was of equal importance.

Rachel Goldfarb, an eleven-year-old child partisan in a family camp, told of her experience. "Mother did the cooking and I did whatever I was told to do. We were not with the main group. We lived sometimes in a house, sometimes under the stars. The forests were thick and had marshes. You could sink in those marshes and never come out."

In December 1941, the Nazis murdered thousands of Jews in the Barnowicz region in western Byelorussia, among them four members of the Bielsky family: mother, father, and two sons. Four other sons survived and, along with thirteen others, fled to the woods. Tuvia Bielsky sent a message to the ghetto: "Organize as many friends and acquaintances as possible. Send them to me in the woods. I'll wait for you."

At first, only eight fighters answered Bielsky's call. But over the next two years, his group grew to twelve hundred as Jews fled to the forests rather than report for deportation. Bielsky resisted calls from partisan commanders to forsake those in his group who could not fight.

In the Bielsky camp, everyone worked. A school was established for children. The forest camp was half-jokingly called Jerusalem, a sardonic comment on harsh conditions in the forests. The Bielsky brigade pillaged food and also attacked the enemy. They exacted revenge on local traitors, and for a while lived as outlaws even among the partisan groups.

A second large family camp was formed under the leadership of Shalom Zorin, a Red Army sergeant from Minsk. Zorin fled from

The Bielsky "family camp" in the Naliboki Forest. Poland, wartime.
Yad Vashem, Jerusalem, Israel.

Minsk together with Colonel Seminov, a Soviet prisoner of war who had escaped from German captivity. Zorin formed a 150-man partisan unit. Soon the group was joined by others who were not fighters. Zorin refused to abandon them. His family camp, known as Zorin's 106th Division, migrated to the Naliboki wasteland where they fought and survived until liberation in 1944.

DEATH CAMP UPRISINGS

Even in the shadow of the gas chambers of Treblinka, Sobibór, and Auschwitz / Birkenau, there were insurrections.

In May 1943, one of the last transports from Poland arrived in Treblinka. The ghettos of Warsaw and the Bialystok district had already been emptied, their Jews gassed. Only a small crew of some one thousand prisoners remained in the camp. Their assignment was to exhume and burn the bodies that had been buried in shallow pits. When it was completed, they, too, would be dispatched to join their dead brethren.

The underground group that planned the Treblinka revolt had learned of the Warsaw ghetto uprising a month earlier, and had been inspired by it. They began to acquire weapons and plan a strategy for taking over the camp, which was scheduled to be destroyed and then abandoned. Chiel Rajchman was a barber in Treblinka. One of his tasks was to cut women's hair just before they entered the gas chambers. A few days after his arrival he sorted his sister's dress. He had seen the mass graves. One of his assignments was to disperse the ashes of those who had been burned, removing the bones and pulverizing them.

The uprising was planned by Camp 1, the clothes sorting camp with 700 prisoners. . . . Originally, the uprising was planned for May 1943. They prepared gold to bribe the guards, to pay for food. We had duplicate keys to the arsenal, but the same day a trainload of soldiers arrived and the plan was postponed. The rifles and the ammunition taken from the arsenal were returned.

We informed Camp 1 that if they do not do something, we will not wait any longer and break out ourselves.

Inmates had to make do with the weapons at hand — shovels, picks, and a few home-made grenades. The arsenal was opened and a small number of weapons removed and distributed to resistance fighters. A young prisoner substituted gasoline for disinfectant in his sprayer. Late in the afternoon, a shot rang out, giving the signal to set the camp on fire. The shot was a half-hour early. It caught the inmates off guard. Grenades were thrown and prisoners dodged bullets as they fled the camp. Rajchman recalled:

We wanted to destroy the gas chambers. But we set on fire the garages, the warehouse chambers. Our plan was to get out of there and free the penal camp, but we were not able to do it. It became so chaotic. . . . After a few moments, the Germans started shooting and killing. They kept shooting and we were running wild. I was screaming, "People, save yourself." Some of them chose not to run and went back to the barracks. I was one of the last to leave. When I left many were laying on the ground, already dead.

As many as two hundred prisoners escaped and about half survived the German dragnet set to recapture them.

In the death camp of Sobibór as well, activities were also slowing down in the summer of 1943. Veteran prisoners sensed that the end was approaching. A deportation from Minsk brought to the camp a trained Soviet Jewish officer, Lieutenant Aleksandr "Sasha" Pechersky, who joined forces with Leon Feldhendler, the leader of the Sobibór underground. They worked out a daring plan. Two key SS officers would be lured into storehouses on the pretext that they were to be given a new coat and boots. Once inside, they would be set upon by the fighters and killed with axes and knives. SS weapons were to be seized, and at roll call the camp would be set on fire. All prisoners would have a chance to bolt for freedom. Once outside Sobibór's gates, they would all be on their own.

At 4:00 P.M. on October 14, 1943, the first SS man was killed with an ax. In an hour, the camp was on fire, guns were aimed at the guard towers, and the first contingent of prisoners had bolted. By dusk, more than half

Roza Robota, Jewish underground activist in Auschwitz. *Yad Vashem, Jerusalem, Israel.*

the prisoners had escaped. Only one in three was recaptured, but only dozens survived to the war's end. Rumors that the escapees carried large quantities of gold and silver made them easy prey to the local population, and few could survive the harsh Polish winter spent hiding in the forest.

At Birkenau, the revolt followed a similar pattern. By the fall of 1944, activities were also beginning to slow. The Jews of Hungary had been killed en masse during the spring and summer. Soviet forces had already liberated Majdanek, and the Allies were advancing in the west. No large Jewish community remained in Europe.

On October 7, 1944, the *Sonderkommando*, the corps of prisoners assigned to empty the gas chambers and stoke the ovens, blew up one of Birkenau's four crematoria. An elaborate underground network had been set up to smuggle dynamite to the *Sonderkommando*. The explosion was followed by the mass escape of six hundred prisoners.

Four young women accused of supplying the dynamite were hung in the presence of the remaining inmates. One of them, Roza Robota, shouted, "*Hazak v'ematz*" (Be strong, have courage) as the trapdoor was opened.

DEATH MARCHES

In the winter of 1944/45, the Nazis knew the war was lost. As the Allied armies closed in on the Nazi concentration camps — the Soviets from the east, and the British and Americans from the west — desperate SS officials tried frantically to evacuate the camps. They wanted no eye-witnesses remaining when the camps were overrun. A concerted effort was made to conceal the crimes that had been committed. The concentration camps were destroyed and buried. But Germany still needed slave labor and more time to complete the Final Solution. The inmates of the camps were moved westward in the dead of winter, forced to march toward the heartland of Germany, where their presence would be less incriminating.

In January 1945, just hours before the Red Army arrived at Auschwitz, sixty-six thousand prisoners were marched to Wodzislaw, where they were put on freight trains to the Gross-Rosen, Buchenwald, Dachau, and Mauthausen concentration camps. Almost one in four died en route. On January 20, seven thousand Jews, six thousand of them women, were marched from Stutthof's satellite camps in the Danzig region. In the course of a ten-day march, seven hundred were murdered. Those who remained alive when the marchers reached the shores of the Baltic Sea were driven into the sea and shot. There were only thirteen known survivors. One of them, Celina Manielewicz, recalled that march:

A fearful vista presented itself. Machine-gunners posted on both sides fired blindly into the advancing columns. Those who had been hit lost their balance and hurtled down the cliffside. When we realized what was happening, we and people in front of us instinctively pushed to the back. The commanding SS man, Quartermaster Sergeant Stock, picked up his rifle and came cursing towards us, shouting, "Why don't you want to go any further? You're going to be shot like dogs anyway!" He forced us forward to the precipice saying, "A waste of ammunition," and fetched each of us a terrible blow round the head with his rifle butt, so that we lost consciousness.

I don't know what happened to me; suddenly I felt something cold on my back and when I opened my eyes I beheld a mountain slope down which ever more blood-streaked bodies were rolling. I found myself in the foaming, roaring sea in a small, partly frozen bay on a pile of dead or injured, and therefore still living people.

The whole coast, as far as I could see, was covered with corpses, and I, too, was lying on such a mountain of corpses which slowly sank deeper and deeper. Close beside me lay Genia Weinberg, and Mania Gleimann and at my feet Pela Lewkowicz. Badly injured, she suddenly stood up and shouted to a sentry standing a few meters away from us on the shore, "Herr Sentry, I'm still alive!"

The sentry aimed and shot her in the head — a few centimeters away from my feet — so that she collapsed. Suddenly my friend Genia, who had also recovered consciousness in the ice-cold water, pinched me and whispered, "Don't move."

These were by no means the first death marches. In 1941, hundreds of thousands of Soviet prisoners of war had been herded along the highways of the Ukraine and Byelorussia from one camp to another.

Inmates from Dachau during a death march toward Wolfratshausen. Germany, April 1945. *Gedenskätte Dachau, Munich, Germany.*

Romanians joined the Germans as Jews from Bessarabia and Bukovina were marched to Transnistria. Thousands died en route. In 1942 Jews were marched from small ghettos to larger ghettos in Poland, only to be transported from there to the death camps.

In 1944, Eichmann was impatient to deport Hungarian Jews. He could not wait for trains to arrive in Budapest. On November 8, a death march began; tens of thousands of men, women, and children were marched to the Austrian border. Many died en route from starvation, cold, and exhaustion. The march lasted a month. Those fortunate enough to survive were sent to Dachau and Mauthausen.

There were fifty-nine different marches from Nazi concentration camps during the final winter of Nazi domination, some covering hundreds of miles. The prisoners were given little or no food and water, and hardly any time to rest or take care of bodily needs. Those who paused or fell behind were shot. Many reached the end of their strength and collapsed.

Steven Springfield recalled his experience on a death march from a satellite camp of Stutthof:

We were driven on foot through the German countryside. It was cold. It was snowing. My brother could hardly walk. I supported him as much as I could. It got so bad that he pleaded with me to let him go. "Don't," he says. "Let me die. I cannot, I really cannot handle it anymore. I want to die. Leave me here."

But it was clear that the minute I let him go, he would be shot on the spot, because anybody who couldn't keep up with the march was shot on the spot. You could see corpses all over. . . . I just couldn't give in. I just couldn't drop my brother. I carried him.

Thomas Burgenthal, at the age of nine, was one of the youngest survivors of the Auschwitz death march. He recalled:

In January the liquidation of Auschwitz happened. They lined us all up. They came in to announce that the camp was being liquidated. They gave us some food, and began to march us out of the camp. We were marched first for about three days to a town in Upper Silesia called Gleiwitz. The three of us kids were together. The children's camp group was put in front when we first marched out. But in Poland, January is very cold. After about a 10 to 12 hour walk we began to be very tired. The children began to fall back.

> But it was clear that the minute I let him go, he would be shot on the spot, because anybody who couldn't keep up with the march was shot on the spot. . . . I just couldn't give in. I just couldn't drop my brother. I carried him.

STEVEN SPRINGFIELD, STUTTHOF SURVIVOR

People from the back were pushing, that we weren't going fast enough. And whoever sat down was shot by guards at each side of the road.

The three of us developed a system of resting, which was to run up to the front, and then sort of stop almost, until we reached the back. And by that time, we had rested, and then we could run up again and we would stay warm. Suddenly in the evening they stopped the column and asked for all the children to come forward, that they were going to put us on a farm. And we wouldn't have to march anymore. Well, we had had experience. And we didn't go. All the children from that group were then taken away, and apparently shot. So we were the only three that stayed.

LIBERATION

Soviet soldiers were the first to enter a concentration camp. On July 23, 1944, Soviet troops arrived at the death camp of Majdanek, just outside the Polish city of Lublin. As the Red Army advanced to the outskirts of Lublin, the SS hastened to hide, bury, and burn the evidence of their crime. They simply ran out of time. When the Soviets entered, they found few prisoners, but ample evidence remained, including a storehouse of 800,000 shoes.

The soldiers were shocked by what they saw. Press coverage was intense. Roman Karman, a well-known Soviet correspondent, filed this report on August 21, 1944:

In the course of my travels into liberated territory I have never seen a more abominable sight than Majdanek near Lublin, Hitler's notorious Vernichtungslager, where more than half a million European men, women, and children were massacred. . . . This is not a concentration camp; it is a gigantic murder plant.

Save for the 1,000 living corpses the Red Army found alive when it entered, no inmate escaped alive. Yet full trains daily brought thousands from all parts of Europe to be coldly, brutally massacred.

In the center of the camp stands a huge stone building with a factory chimney — the world's biggest crematorium. . . . The gas chambers contained some 250 people at a time. They were closely packed . . . so that after they suffocated they remained standing. . . . It is difficult to believe it myself but human eyes cannot deceive me. . . .

The Illustrated London News apologized for twelve photographs published in October. It was not the paper's custom, it noted,

to publish photographs of atrocities, but in view of the fact that the enormity of the crimes perpetrated by the Germans is so wicked that our readers, to whom such behavior is unbelievable, may think the reports of such crimes exaggerated or due to propaganda, we consider it necessary to present them, by means of the accompanying photographs, with irrefutable proof of the organized murder of between 600,000 and 1,000,000 helpless persons at the Majdanek Camp near Lublin. And even these pictures are carefully selected from a number, some of which are too horrible to reproduce. . . .

The story as it stands is almost incredible in its bestiality, but German cruelty went further still at Majdanek. Prisoners too ill to walk into the camp . . . were dragged alive to the furnaces and thrust in alongside the dead.

Films were shot and distributed for viewing in the West. But the Soviet efforts to publicize what they found were dismissed as Communist propaganda by both Hitler and the Allies.

During the summer of 1944, Soviet forces also overran Belzec, Treblinka, and Sobibór, the killing centers that had been closed a year earlier when the annihilation of Polish Jews was virtually complete. The SS had burned Treblinka and turned it into a farm. At Belzec, pine trees had been planted to conceal the camp. Still, soldiers found bones protruding from the ground.

On January 27, 1945, Soviet forces entered

Auschwitz. The camp's last roll call had been
taken on January 17: 67,012 prisoners were
counted. Most of them were sent out on death
marches. Only those too ill to walk remained.
During the next ten days, Auschwitz was
frantically dismantled. Crematoria buildings
were blown up. SS documents and I. G. Farben
corporate records were destroyed. Dr.
Mengele left for Berlin, carrying his
"scientific" research on twins with him.
Twenty-nine storerooms were burned. In the
six that remained, the Soviets discovered
348,820 men's suits, 836,255 women's coats,
more than seven tons of human hair, and even
13,964 carpets.

The Soviets downplayed the liberation of
Auschwitz. The first press story did not appear
until May, after Soviet troops had liberated
Sachsenhausen, Ravensbrück, Stutthof, and
Theresienstadt.

The British liberated Bergen-Belsen on
April 15, 1945. The camp had been ravaged
by a typhus epidemic. Thousands of bodies lay
unburied, rotting in the sun. Sixty thousand
prisoners were still alive, many of them in
critical condition. Fourteen thousand of the
newly liberated inmates died in the first days
of freedom. Another fourteen thousand died

in the weeks that followed, despite valiant
efforts by British doctors to save them.

Even for inmates who arrived from
Birkenau, the site of massive killing, on death
marches, conditions in Bergen-Belsen were
severe. Rachel van Amerongen-Frankfoorder,
who was with Anne Frank in Belsen, recalled:

*The period in Bergen-Belsen was certainly the
most wretched. You knew so little about how the war
was going; you didn't know how long it would last,
and because of the illness you were convinced that
death was lying in wait.*

*You saw death, you noticed it so much more than
in Birkenau, where the people who were going
downhill simply disappeared. . . . You got weaker.
Especially when I got typhus, I would think, This is
it; this is the end.*

As the British entered, the camp
commandant, Josef Kramer, greeted his
conquerors in a fresh uniform. He expressed
his desire for an orderly transition and his
hopes of collaborating with the British. He
dealt with them as equals, one officer to
another, even offering advice as to how to
deal with the "unpleasant" situation. As he
toured the camp, Derrick Sington, a junior

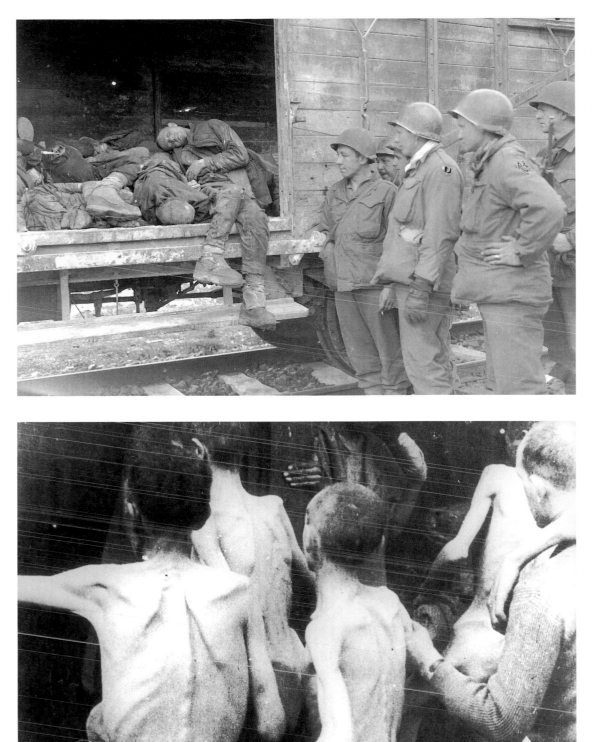

American soldiers view
corpses of Dachau
inmates who perished
in railroad cars. Dachau,
Germany, May 3, 1945.
Hulton Archive, London,
England.

**Emaciated survivors of
Dachau. Dachau, May
1945, Germany.**
KZ-Gedenkstätte Dachau Öst,
Munich, Germany.

It is your lot to begin the hard task of restoring the name of the German people. . . . But this cannot be done until you have reared a new generation amongst whom it is impossible to find people prepared to commit such crimes. . . .

BRITISH MEDICAL OFFICER, AT BERGEN-BELSEN

British officer, said to the commandant: "You've made a fine hell here." Kramer responded, "It has become one in the last few days." But the ruse could not last for long.

Peter Coombs, another British officer, wrote his wife of the appalling conditions at Belsen:

> One has to take a tour round and see their faces, their slow staggering gait and feeble movements. The state of their minds is plainly written on their faces, as starvation has reduced their bodies to skeletons. The fact is that all these were once clean-living and sane. . . . They are Jews and are dying at the rate of three hundred a day. They must die and nothing can save them — their end is inescapable, they are too far gone now to be brought back to life.
>
> I saw their corpses lying near their hovels, for they crawl or totter out into the sunlight to die. I watched them make their last feeble journeys, and even as I watched they died.

The uncontrollable epidemic was so lethal that the camp had to be burned down. Former inmates were moved to a Panzer tank corps school two miles down the road, which became the site of a displaced-persons camp. The British were horrified by what they found. Mass graves were dug, bulldozers were brought to shovel in the dead. Local civilians were marched into the camp. They, too, were taken on a tour. Before they began their visit, the colonel in charge of medical efforts spoke to them.

> You must realize that according to those wretched victims who experienced other camps, this camp was in some respects one of the better ones. Chiefly because in this camp it was possible in most cases, though not in all, to die fairly quietly from hunger or typhus. In certain other camps, the inmates were done to death and hurled into massive graves, sometimes before they were dead. . . .
>
> What you will see here is the final and utter condemnation of the Nazi Party. It justifies every measure the United Nations will take to exterminate that party. What you will see here is such a disgrace to the German people that their names must be erased from the list of civilized nations. . . .
>
> It is your lot to begin the hard task of restoring the name of the German people. . . . But this cannot be done until you have reared a new generation amongst whom it is impossible to find people prepared to commit such crimes; until you have reared a new generation possessing the instinctive good will to prevent a repetition of such horrible cruelties.
>
> We will now begin our tour.

The films the British took were broadcast throughout the world and formed indelible images of the Holocaust and the name Bergen-Belsen.

In September 1945, forty-eight members of the Bergen-Belsen staff were tried. Eleven, including Commandant Kramer, were executed in December.

American troops entered Buchenwald on April 11, 1945. Only a few days before the Americans arrived, twenty-five thousand prisoners were taken out of the camp. Many did not survive.

Americans liberated other camps in April: Nordhausen, Ohrdruf, Landsberg, Woebblein, Gunskirchen, Ebensee, and Flossenbürg. Among the soldiers entering Nazi concentration camps were Japanese-Americans whose families were incarcerated in American concentration camps in the West, and African-Americans who served in segregated units. Leon Bass recounted his experience:

> I remember going through those gates shortly after our men had gone through, and I saw the walking dead. I saw human beings who had been beaten, starved and tortured. . . . They were standing there, skin and bones, dressed in striped pajamas. They had skeletal faces with deep set eyes. They had sores on their bodies. One man held out his hands. And they were webbed together with scabs, due to malnutrition.
>
> Something happened when I walked through the gates. My blinders came off, my tunnel vision

Bulldozers clearing away corpses at Bergen-Belsen. Bergen-Belsen, Germany, April 1945. *Imperial War Museum, London, England. Courtesy of Hadassah Rosensaft.*

View of mass common graves in Bergen-Belsen. Bergen-Belsen, Germany, May 1945. *Imperial War Museum, London, England. Courtesy of Hadassah Rosensaft*

Sergeant William A. Scott II along with other American liberators view the stacked bodies at Buchenwald. Buchenwald, Germany, April 11, 1945. *United States Holocaust Memorial Museum, Washington, D.C. Courtesy of William A. Scott III.*

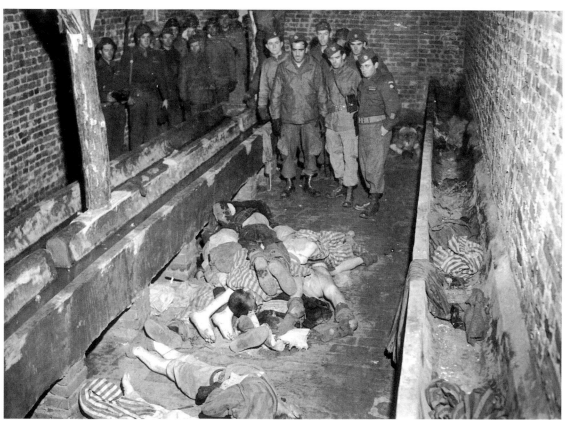

Soldiers of the American 82nd Airborne and the British 2nd Army found hundreds of dead prisoners in the concentration camp of Ludwigslust. Ludwigslust, Germany. May 6, 1945. *National Archives, Washington, D.C.*

dissipated. And I began to realize that human suffering is not delegated just to me and mine. Human suffering touches everybody. All people can suffer.

As American troops approached Dachau on April 29, 1945, Piet Maas noted the American arrival in the camp in his daybook: "17:28 [5:28 P.M.]. First American comes through the entrance. Dachau free!!! Indescribable happiness. Insane howling."

Bill Barrett, an army journalist, described the scene in the *45th Division News*:

It was late afternoon — about 4 P.M. — as the men made their way down the tracks. They knew that the camp ahead was guarded by SS troops and that they expected a hard fight. And like all men going into an attack, be they rookies or vets, these men were afraid.

They picked up the clawing stink before they reached the first boxcar. They stopped and stared and the dead stared back.

There were about a dozen bodies in the dirty boxcar, men and women alike. They had gone without food so long that their dead wrists were broomsticks tipped with claws. These were the victims of a deliberate starvation diet, and they weren't pretty.

The men looked, then shuffled on to the new car in silence. There were more dead eyes here staring out at

the German houses not 200 yards from the tracks.

Someone broke the stillness with a curse and then with a roar the men started for the camp on the double.

"I never saw anything like it," Lieutenant Moyer said later. The men were plain fighting mad. They went down that road without any regard for cover or concealment. No one was afraid, not after those boxcars. We were just mad.

Barrett concluded his front-page report, "Dachau Gives Answer To Why We Fought," with the words: "The stink of death has seeped into the ground with the blood of the murdered and Dachau must remain forever a blot on German history."

American soldiers were furious. One soldier recalls: "Control was gone after the sights we saw, and the men were deliberately wounding guards that were available and then turned them over to prisoners and allowed them to take their revenge on them." SS officers were paraded through the barracks. Prisoners were asked to judge. The questions were simple: good or bad? The judgment was carried out immediately.

The last of the camps encountered by the Americans were Mauthausen and Gusen on May 5, 1945. Three days later, the war was

Liberated inmates preparing food near the bodies of the dead. Bergen-Belsen, Germany, April 15, 1945. *Imperial War Museum, London, England. Courtesy of Hadassah Rosensaft.*

over. The army began a new, intense battle to bring the survivors back to life.

Fred Friendly, who went into Mauthausen as a correspondent, said:

Of all the sights and sounds that stunned me, the weakness of the brave men and women who survived was the most memorable. I wrote about the thousands dead and hundreds alive in barracks — six high, four men in a bed. When we walked through, they shouted in various languages, "Viva Americanski." Then, to my great embarrassment, they applauded. But their hands were so emaciated, so much without flesh, that it sounded to me . . . like seals clapping.

For the survivors, the moment of liberation was hopeful yet fearful. Hadassah Bimko, a survivor who organized medical efforts at Bergen-Belsen, wrote:

For the great part of the liberated Jews of Bergen-Belsen, there was no ecstasy, no joy at our liberation. We had lost our families, our homes. We had no place to go, nobody to hug, nobody who was waiting for us, anywhere. We had been liberated from death and from the fear of death, but we were not free from the fear of life.

Still, there was joy. Fania Fenelon wrote of the last day at Bergen-Belsen:

A new life was breathed into the camps. Jeeps, command cars, and half tracks drove among the barracks. Khaki uniforms abounded. . . . Our liberators were well fed and bursting with health, and they moved among our skeletal silhouettes like surges of life. We felt an absurd desire to finger them, to let our hands trail to their eddies as in the Fountain of Youth. . . . These men seemed not to know that one could live in slow motion, that energy was something you saved.

That evening of April 15, Fenelon slept in the abandoned SS quarters. "A table, and chairs, a clean floor and water — all you needed to do was turn on the tap. Everything we had been made to suffer," she wrote, "seemed to have sullied us. Lying in the SS sheets, we cried with happiness."

"For us," she concluded, "there will be an after." Still, that very same evening, some died of overeating. The soldiers had been generous with sweets, chocolate, and candy. Their generosity had been lethal.

Liberation was incomprehensible. Primo Levi, the Italian Jewish writer freed at Auschwitz, recalled:

The breach in the barbed wire gave us a concrete image of it. To anyone who stopped to think, it signified no more Germans, no more selections, no work, no blows, no roll calls, and, perhaps, later, the return.

But we had to make an effort to convince ourselves of it, and no one had time to enjoy the thought. All around lay destruction and death.

Viktor Frankl, a Viennese psychiatrist who pioneered existential analysis, wrote of liberation:

Timidly, we looked around and glanced at each other questioningly. Then we ventured a few steps out of the camp. This time no orders were shouted at us, nor was there any need to duck quickly to avoid a blow or a kick.

"Freedom" — we repeated to ourselves, and yet we could not grasp it.

Frankl writes of the inability to feel. "We did not yet belong to this world." He described it as depersonalization. "Everything was unreal, unlikely, as in a dream." Only later — and for some it was much later or never — was liberation actually liberating. "The crowning experience of all, for the homecoming man, is the wonderful feeling that after all he has suffered there is nothing he need fear any more — except his God."

Some survivors felt empty, even guilty that they had survived while so many others had not. Others felt nothing. Israel Lau, an eight-year-old liberated at Buchenwald, told of his meeting with an American Jewish chaplain, Rabbi Herschel Schacter, on April 11, 1945:

In my eyes he was just another person, wearing a different kind of uniform. He jumped out of the jeep, took me in his arms, weeping. I was so frightened, he started to laugh, to smile.

"How old are you, my child?" he asked.

"What difference does it make, I'm older than you," I answered.

"Why do you think you are older than me?" he asked.

"Because you cry and laugh as a child. And I stopped laughing and I can't even cry. So I must be older than you."

As the Allied armies were advancing on Berlin, Hitler retreated to the Chancellery's two-story air-raid shelter fifty feet below ground. On April 22, the Russians were in Berlin. His entourage was nervous and exhausted. Alan Bullock, Hitler's biographer, described them as near hysteria. Hitler himself was unable to sleep, afraid to be caught. His lieutenant, Albert Speer, had not carried out the order to destroy Germany. He came to the bunker to confess. Some members of Hitler's staff, including Göring, fled south. Himmler began discussions with Count Bernadotte of Sweden, who informed Himmler that the Allies insisted on unconditional surrender. Word of Himmler's attempted negotiation was leaked and reported to Hitler.

In his final hours, Hitler married his longtime companion, Eva Braun. After the ceremony and celebration, Hitler dictated his final testament. He expelled Himmler and Göring from the Nazi party, named Admiral Dönitz as president of the Reich, Goebbels as chancellor, and Bormann as party minister. His final lines were dedicated to the unfinished Final Solution.

Above all I charge the leaders of the nation and those under them to scrupulous observance of the laws of race and to merciless opposition to the universal poisoner of all peoples, international Jewry.

Within a day, Eva Braun had taken poison. Hitler shot himself in the mouth. Their bodies were burned. The Führer and his thousand-year Reich had come to an end.

CHILDREN

The ultimate crime in the Holocaust was the murder of children. A poet has said that the death of a child is the loss of infinite possibility. What then can be said of the murder of more than a million children?

Approximately one million Jewish children under fifteen were murdered by the Nazis in their attempt to achieve the "Final Solution to the Jewish Problem." Although the murder of the children was a deliberate attempt to destroy the Jewish future, children were not a direct target of Nazi anti-Jewish policies. Caught up in the web of incomprehensible events, they were the most vulnerable of all the victims of nazism.

Children in Auschwitz after their liberation by the Soviet Army. Auschwitz, Poland, after January 27, 1945. *Dokumentationsarchiv des ÖsterreichischenWiderstandes, Vienna, Austria.*

The experience of children in the Holocaust varied from country to country, city to city, and year by year, week by week. The first sting of persecution often came in the classroom or schoolyard, when children were singled out by their classmates, stigmatized and isolated. Later, they were expelled from public schools. Wherever possible, the Jewish community established separate schools. There, Jewish children felt safe, if only for a while, from the torments of antisemitic classmates and teachers.

At first, some children were shielded. Even on a train to Auschwitz, a seven-year-old French child asked his father, "What is a Jew?" He had never heard the word. "All my life I tried to protect you from the reality," the father answered. Other children had no one to protect them. In the French transit camp of Drancy, Azriel Eisenberg reported:

There were two-, three-, and four-year-olds, little ones, who did not know their names. . . . We improvised names for those who were nameless and prepared wooden disks which we suspended by strings around their necks. Later we found girls wearing boys' disks and vice-versa. Evidently, they played with these disks and often exchanged them.

In Poland and Eastern Europe, children went into the ghettos with their families. Many became smugglers and beggars. The children were always hungry. Some continued to study and live with their parents but others roamed the streets. In Vilna and Warsaw, the Jewish Council went to great efforts to provide for the children, but in Łódź, Rumkowski allowed them to be deported in order to transform the ghetto into a work camp.

Young children could sense their parents' anguish, even though they could not grasp their predicament. Doriane Kurz, who survived Bergen-Belsen at the age of nine along with her seven-year-old brother, Freddie, recalls going into hiding:

One evening we were sitting in our living room. My brother was sitting on the bay window sill and looking out. He said: "Look at the fire engine out there." My parents rushed to the window and it wasn't a fire engine. It was a truck with men sitting

Women's barracks at liberation. Mauthausen, Austria. *Photo: Ray Buch. United States Holocaust Memorial Museum, Washington, D.C.*

All the Jewish girls of this class were deported to Auschwitz, via Drancy, in July 1942. None returned. Paris, France, spring of 1942. *Fédération Nationale des Déportés et Internés Résistants et Patriots, Paris, France.*

on the outside. They all ran off and my parents grabbed us and we ran out of the house.

They ran to a storage room two floors above and escaped arrest for another eighteen months. "I remember the sound of boots coming up," she said of that night. She was only six at the time.

Children in Western Europe were sent with their families to the transit camps. In camps such as Theresienstadt and Gurs, adults made valiant efforts to create the semblance of a normal environment for the children. There were classes, games, even cultural activities. The children of Theresienstadt painted pictures and wrote poems that have survived and serve as memorials to their brief lives. The paintings of the children were a form of therapy — a means of expressing their deepest fears. Older children at Theresienstadt took an active part as actors in plays, as recruiters for poetry contests and recitations held in the evening.

Teddy — we don't know his last name or his fate — wrote of the arrival at Terezin:

At Terezin

When a new child comes
Everything seems strange to him.
What, on the ground I have to lie?
Eat black potatoes? No! Not I!
I've got to stay? It's dirty here!
The floor — why, look, it's dirt, I fear!
And I'm supposed to sleep on it?
I'll get all dirty!

Here the sound of shouting, cries,
And oh, so many flies.
Everyone knows flies carry disease.
Oooh, something bit me! Wasn't that a bedbug?
Here in Terezín, life is hell
And when I'll go home again, I can't yet tell.

Another child, Mif, wrote of the frustration:

Terezin

A fourth year of waiting, like standing above a swamp
From which any moment might gush forth a spring.
Meanwhile, the rivers flow another way,
Another way,
Not letting you die, not letting you live.

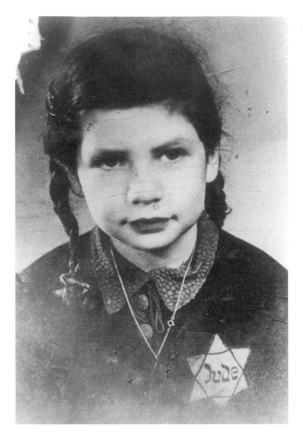

Jewish girl from Munich. She was deported to Riga. Munich, Germany, c. 1942. *Yad Vashem, Jerusalem, Israel.*

And the cannons don't scream and the guns don't bark
And you don't see blood here.
Nothing, only silent hunger.
Children steal the bread here and ask and ask and ask.
And all would wish to sleep, keep silent and just go to sleep again . . .

The heaviest wheel rolls across our foreheads.
To bury itself deep somewhere inside our memories.

But in the end, children were deported along with their parents to concentration camps. Mothers and fathers could no longer protect their young. Parents who refused to be separated from their children were sent at once to the gas chambers. Pregnant women were also selected for immediate death. Only the able-bodied and the unencumbered could hope to survive. At the ramp in Birkenau a first *Selektion* was held. Arriving Jews were divided by sex. Fathers parted from their daughters and mothers from their sons — often forever. The young children, and the parents who insisted on staying with them, went to their death.

House with Garden. A watercolor painted on the reverse side of a piece of shiny red paper. Signed in lower right corner "IV stu. Landová Marianna." Marianna Landová was born in Prague on February 27, 1932, and deported to Theresienstadt on July 2, 1942. She lived in house number 13 in the ghetto and belonged to group IV. She died on May 18, 1944, in Auschwitz. *On loan from the State Jewish Museum in Prague. Photo USHMM.*

Dwellings in Theresienstadt. Lefthand pencil drawing done on gray cardboard. Signature on back of drawing: "NOVAKJ. X 1943 13 stunde." Josef Novák was born on October 25, 1931, in Prague and deported to Theresienstadt on April 24, 1942. He lived in the boys' dormitory X and was a student of Friedl Dicker-Brandeis. He was deported to Auschwitz, where he died on May 18, 1944. *On loan from the State Jewish Museum in Prague. Photo USHMM.*

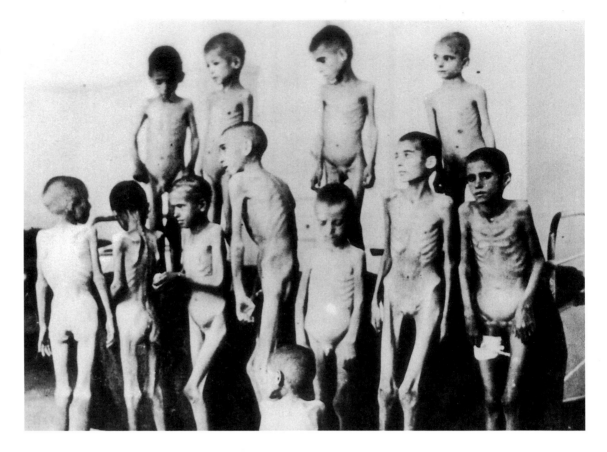

Gypsy children and twins were subject to medical experimentation by Dr. Josef Mengele, who in his zeal to breed the master race was fascinated by twins. According to one observer, Mengele was rather fond of Gypsy children. He would bring them sweets and toys. The children trusted him. They called him "Onkle Mengele." The physician would often take them to the gas chambers himself, speaking tenderly until the end.

Vera Alexander, a Jewish woman who supervised fifty sets of Gypsy twins at Auschwitz, recalled:

I remember one set of twins in particular: Guido and Ina, aged about four. One day Mengele took them away. When they returned they were in a terrible state: they had been sewn together, back to back, like Siamese twins. Their wounds were infected and oozing pus. They screamed day and night. Then their parents — I remember the mother's name was Stella — managed to get some morphine and they killed the children in order to end their suffering.

The presence of children forced their parents to make impossible choices, what the literary critic Lawrence Langer has called "choiceless choices." Throughout Europe parents had to decide if the family should stay together and face the future, or go into hiding either together or individually. Parents did not know, could not know until it was too late, that "resettlement in the East" was an almost certain death sentence. In Amsterdam, Otto Frank took his whole family, including Anne, into hiding in Amsterdam in 1942. He alone survived. In 1944, Shlomo Wiesel advised his son Elie to stay with the family rather than hide on his own with a former family maid in Hungarian-controlled Sighet. Elie Wiesel survived Auschwitz and Birkenau, as did his older sisters. His father, mother, and little sister Tzipora were killed.

Should a young child be given to non-Jewish friends, or turned over to strangers in one of the organizations in Poland, the Netherlands, and France that tried to hide Jewish children? The dilemma was difficult. Parents who knew they could not protect their children were also unwilling to part with them, and for good reason. Andrew Griffel was less than a year old when his parents gave him to a Polish couple for safekeeping. When they returned three years

later, he did not recognize and at first refused
to go with them. The Polish couple had
become his parents.

Even when a child was sent to safety,
separation was agonizing. One eyewitness to
the rescue of seventy children reports:

*The young children, who could not understand the
reasons for separation, clung to their parents and
cried. The older ones, who knew how great their
parents' anguish was, tried to control their own pain
and clenched their teeth. The women clung to the
doors of the buses as they left. The guards and even
the police themselves could hardly control their
emotions.*

Young children often endangered their
parents. A crying child could give away a
clandestine hideout and endanger the lives of
an entire group. In the concentration camp,
an infant would spell doom for both mother
and child. Judith Sternberg Newman, a nurse
deported to Auschwitz, reported the following
incident:

*Two days after Christmas, a Jewish child was born
on our block. How happy I was when I saw this tiny*
*baby. It was a boy, and the mother had been told that
he would be taken care of. Three hours later, I saw a
small package wrapped in cheese cloth lying on a
wooden bench. Suddenly it moved. A Jewish girl
employed as a clerk came over, carrying a pan of cold
water. She whispered to me, "Hush! Quiet! Go
away!" But I remained, for I could not understand
what she had in mind. She picked up the little
package — it was the baby, of course — and it started
to cry with a thin little voice. She took the infant
and submerged its little body in the cold water. My
heart beat wildly in agitation. I wanted to shout
"Murderess!" but I had to keep quiet and could not
tell anyone. The baby swallowed and gurgled, its little
voice shuttering like a small bird, until its breath
became shorter and shorter. The woman held its head
in the water. After about eight minutes the breathing
stopped. The woman picked it up, wrapped it up again,
and put it with the other corpses. Then she said to
me, "We had to save the mother; otherwise she would
have gone to the gas chamber."*

Should a child be hidden in a convent or
monastery where she or he might be
protected, but cease to be a Jew? It was easier
to hide a Jewish girl than a Jewish boy. A
circumcised boy could be identified as a Jew

Children from a Hungarian transport before being gassed. Auschwitz, Poland, spring of 1944. *Yad Vashem, Jerusalem, Israel.*

at any moment. Boys soon learned to go to the bathroom alone. Solomon Perels, whose childhood and adolescence were the subject of the film *Europa, Europa*, went to great lengths to avoid urinating or taking a shower in the presence of other boys. He could not consummate his wartime romance for fear of betrayal.

Some children spent the war years hiding in basements or attics, passed from family to family. They could not go outside or be seen in public. Others, because of the color of their hair and the absence of an accent, could pass as non-Jews. Frima Laub described her experience in the streets of Woloshisk:

Well, at that time I was infested already with lice because nobody gave me a bath and I slept in the same clothes and I lived in the same clothes and I lived in that pantry with the mice. And so I walked out of the house. And the first thing I did was go into a toy store, a religious articles store, and I bought a big cross and I spent my hundred rubles. And then I was so infested with the lice that my head, my skin was all rashes and bloody from scratching it so much.

I felt that I really needed help and I remembered this lady whom my parents were friendly with and I remembered that we used to visit them every so often.

That it's quite a bit outside the city. I didn't remember the address and I didn't remember the name. But I just remembered how we used to walk. And I . . . that's how I walked. And I made it to the house. And it was winter and cold and there was maybe five or six inches of snow. And I made it to her house and as I got to her gate, her dog started barking so she came out to see who was at the gate and she sees me and she says, "My God, come in quick. Come in quick." And she takes me to her barn because obviously she must have noticed that I have lice crawling all over me. So she wouldn't take me into her house but she took me into the barn and she . . . quickly she took off my clothes and put on other clothes and she said to me, "Where are your parents?" I said, "Everybody is killed. Everybody is dead."

Because I wanted her to have pity on me. And so she did. She took me to her bathroom. She shaved off my head. She gave me a bath. She gave me a glass of hot milk and a piece of black bread.

Children like Frima hid their true identity while leading a facsimile of a normal childhood: going to school and church, playing, taking part in family life. The very young even forgot their true identities and became who they were supposed to be. The writer Saul Friedlander, who later became a distinguished historian of the Holocaust, was about to begin training for the priesthood when a friendly priest asked him if he had heard of Auschwitz. His parents had perished there. Friedlander had been adopted by a French Catholic family.

Jana Levi reports her deepest fear:

I didn't remember anymore what my real name was. I only dreamt about it at night. When I woke up in the morning, I wouldn't remember again. I knew I had a different name, but it was so important for me to forget it that I actually did completely forget. I knew that if my parents didn't know my name they couldn't find me. . . . Nobody would know who I was. I had completely become someone else and the real person, no one would know who it was, and they didn't know who I was either.

Children living in hiding were often confused about their religion, their identity, even their gender. At a 1991 conference on the hidden child, a fifty-three-year-old man rose to tell his story. He had spent the years from age four to seven as a girl. His hair had grown out. He wore dresses. He sat on the toilet to urinate even when alone. As he told his story, the audience grew quiet. He asked if others in the room had similar experiences. Several men raised their hands. It was easier to pretend to be a girl.

THE KILLERS:
THE NUREMBERG TRIALS

In the winter of 1943, Roosevelt, Churchill, and Stalin announced that as soon as the war was over they would bring the Nazi leaders to justice. Allied outrage at Nazi treatment of civilians was fueled by the discovery of the killing centers. The Soviet army was the first to come upon the concentration camps when it liberated Majdanek and Auschwitz. Within weeks, the first trials of Nazi war criminals were held by the Soviets at Majdanek. After the war, trials were conducted by the Allies at Nuremberg and have continued sporadically to this day in countries including the United States, Israel, Poland, Germany, the Soviet Union, and France.

Two weeks after the German surrender, an agreement was reached by the Allies to conduct joint trials of those responsible for the murder of noncombatants. Justice Robert Jackson of the United States Supreme Court was named to lead the American prosecution. Nuremberg, the site chosen for the trials, was one of the few German cities that was not totally in ruins. Nuremberg had also been host to the annual Nazi party pageants.

Three kinds of crimes were specified in the indictments. First were Crimes Against the Peace, which included planning, preparing, initiating, or waging a war of aggression. Then there were War Crimes, acts that violated the laws and customs of warfare. This category covered the murder, ill-treatment, or deportation of populations for slave labor or any other purposes; the killing of hostages and prisoners of war; the plunder of private property; and the destruction of towns and cities.

The Allies outlined a subset of war crimes as Crimes Against Humanity. These were defined as the murder, extermination, enslavement, or deportation of any civilian population; persecution on political, racial, or religious grounds, whether or not these were in violation of the domestic laws of the country where the acts took place.

The first series of trials, which took place in 1946, were International Military Tribunals. Twenty-two major Nazi leaders were indicted and placed on trial by the Allies. The accused included Hitler's trusted lieutenant Hermann Göring; Nazi party officials; the foreign minister and other key cabinet officials; military leaders; the ministers of armaments and labor; ranking bureaucrats; and German occupation officials, among them Hans Frank, the governor-general of Poland and Fritz Sauckel, who had run the slave-labor program. Some Nazi leaders were missing. Goebbels and his wife committed suicide after killing their children — before the surrender, Himmler killed himself after he was captured, and one of the twenty-two indicted, Dr. Robert Ley, who headed the Reich Labor Front, hanged himself in his jail cell before trial.

Justice Jackson set the scene in his opening statement:

In the prisoners' dock sit twenty-odd broken men. Reproached by the humiliation of those they have led almost as bitterly as the desolation of those they have attacked, their personal capacity for evil is forever past. It is hard now to perceive in these miserable men as captives the power by which as Nazi leaders they once dominated much of the world and terrified most of it. Merely as individuals, their fate is of little consequence in the world.

What makes this inquest significant is that these prisoners . . . are the living symbols of racial hatreds, of terrorism and violence, and of the arrogance and cruelty of power. . . . Civilization can afford no compromise with the social forces which would gain renewed strength if we deal ambiguously or indecisively with the men in whom those forces now precariously survive.

Of the twenty-one who stood trial, fourteen were sentenced to death by hanging. The remaining seven received prison

Nazi war-criminals trial in Nuremberg. Nuremberg, Germany, 1946. *National Archives, Washington, D.C.*

sentences. Before Göring could be hanged, he committed suicide with poison smuggled into his cell. On October 16, 1946, Hans Frank was hanged in the Nuremberg prison.

After the conclusion of the Military Tribunals, a second series of trials took place in Germany. There were 185 defendants divided into twelve groups. Physicians were tried for their complicity in the selections, murder, and medical experimentation that took place in the concentration camps. Officers of the mobile killing units were prosecuted for the slaughter of civilians in Eastern Europe. Concentration camp administrators were tried for the systematic murder that occurred in the camps under their supervision. Judges were tried for their complicity in the transformation of German law into a lethal instrument of mass murder. The generals who invaded the Soviet Union were placed on trial. Top executives of I. G. Farben were tried for the sale of Zyklon B and the construction of industrial plants at Auschwitz. Alfried Krupp and the directors of his company were tried for their use of slave labor.

The defendants did not deny they had done these things. A few professed ignorance, claiming they did not know what was

happening. Some complained that they were being singled out, that many others who were still at large had done exactly the same deeds. The most common defense was to deny responsibility: those in the dock had merely followed the orders of a superior. If anyone was responsible, it was those further up the chain of command.

Judges and generals invoked the personal oath of allegiance they had sworn to Hitler. As men of morality, they were obliged to obey. They had given their word of honor to the Führer.

Proximity to the crime was taken as a measure of guilt. Those who were directly involved in the killing — doctors, concentration camp heads, *Einsatzgruppen* officers — received the most severe sentences. Industrialists were treated more leniently. Thirty-five defendants were acquitted.

While the trials were in progress, public attention shifted to the unfolding of the Cold War, the struggle between the United States and the Soviet Union that seemed to embody a worldwide battle between capitalism and Marxism. The 1948 Berlin Blockade made the future of Germany central to American geopolitical interests. The American government did not want to provoke the German people, especially when their support was vital to the future. The Korean war only intensified the desire to get on to other things. Interest in the trials faded. No sooner had they ended than clemency boards were established. In the next few years, sentences were reduced, pardons were granted, and time off was given for good behavior.

Thirty-seven death sentences were commuted in 1948. Only six of those convicted remained under sentence of death. In 1951, a general amnesty was issued by the United States high commissioner for Germany, John J. McCloy, who in 1944 as assistant secretary of war had pushed for the war-crimes trials. The archbishop of Cologne pleaded with McCloy for clemency on behalf of those awaiting their execution. These men "had acted by orders of higher headquarters." According to his biographer, Kai Bird, McCloy was initially inclined "to tell the archbishop that it was his impression that there are some offenses so shocking and so criminal . . . that it would be most difficult to find any possible bases for clemency." But after his old friend Chester McClain informed him of plans for a parole board, he kept his tongue. The pope's personal representative in Bonn appealed to McCloy for clemency. Konrad Adenauer, the leader of postwar Germany, wrote McCloy asking that the death sentences be commuted and that the widest possible clemency be granted. Former resistance fighters also intervened. A Bundestag delegation visited McCloy's office and told him that "given the political and psychological factors at a time when Western Germany was being called upon to make a military contribution to Western defense," clemency should be considered. Despite his reservations, McCloy commuted the death sentences of all but the five men who directly participated in the mass killings. Seventy-seven Nazi officials were freed, as were the most prominent industrialists. Alfried Krupp was one of those released. His personal fortune, which had been confiscated, was returned to him, and he resumed management of the Krupp industrial empire.

Why was Krupp let off so lightly? Some argued that his twelve-year sentence was disproportionate to that of other industrialists and that Krupp was singled out because of his name, charged because his ailing father could not stand in the docket. Yet the crimes of the Krupp empire were more serious than those of other industrialists, and its exploitation of slave labor was more extensive. According to Bird: "When it came to a wealthy and politically well-connected man like Krupp, he [McCloy] suspended good judgment."

The trials touched only a few of the perpetrators of Nazi crimes, generally the small number of top leaders whose roles were highly visible. Most of those who were responsible escaped judgment.

Some Nazi leaders took on new identities in Germany and Austria. Others fled to South America, and some sought refuge in the Middle East among the enemies of Israel. Still others received help from the Vatican. The escape route for Nazi war criminals (the so-called Rat Line) went from Austria and Bavaria over the mountains into Italy and from there by ship to South America. They were helped along by ODESSA, an organization of SS men formed for this purpose. In some cases they were also assisted by Western intelligence agencies that were now interested in using them in the global battle against communism.

While war criminals received assistance from individual Roman Catholic priests in places like Genoa and Trieste, Rome became the main sanctuary for the fleeing Nazis. This was due to the power of Bishop Alois Hudal, rector of the German Church in Rome. This puzzling figure had protested the deportation of Jews and even sheltered a number of them in the Monasterio dell' Anima. Yet it was he who also assisted many Nazi war criminals including Eichmann, Walther Rauff (the chief of the SS in Milan), Otto Wächter (the governor of Galicia who was responsible for the murder of 800,000 Jews), and Josef Mengele. The most popular hideout provided by the influential Hudal was the Franciscan convent on the Via Sicilia. Some war criminals, Mengele for example, were baptized as Roman Catholics. It appears that the Nazis were assisted by sympathetic (and possibly nationalistic) Roman Catholic priests, one of whom, Hudal, happened to be very influential. Some of the Roman Catholic priests serving in Rome were German nationalists sympathetic to nazism. Their personal politics shaped their attitude toward those fleeing German defeat, most especially to Roman Catholic Germans. They were fully aware of the wartime record of those seeking to escape.

It is estimated that ten thousand Nazi war criminals came to the United States in the guise of anti-Communists fleeing Soviet persecution in Eastern Europe. In the words of Alan Ryan, former director of the Office of Special Investigation, "They came through the front door with their papers in order." The U.S. government also employed Nazis and helped them enter. Operation Paperclip was a project run by the Joint Chiefs of Staff that brought sixteen hundred German and Austrian scientists and technicians, including war criminals, to the United States to work for the military and NASA. Arthur Rudolph, who directed the Saturn V moon rocket project, used slave labor at the Dora concentration camp when he headed a similar

Mittelwerk V-2 rocket factory during the war.

Operation Paperclip was duplicated by universities and private industries to recruit newly available talent. From time to time, some distinguished scholars in the humanities have been shown to have had a Nazi past. Among the most prominent were Mircea Eliade, a leading ideologue of the Romanian Iron Guard and a Romanian diplomat in Lisbon, who became a revered scholar of religion at the University of Chicago, and Vladimir Samarin, a professor of Russian language and literature at Yale, who had edited a propaganda sheet for the Nazis and urged that "all Jews be completely annihilated." Paul de Man, an English professor at Yale and one of the most influential figures in the field of literary criticism, was revealed as the writer of antisemitic, pro-Nazi articles in his native Belgium. As their pasts caught up with them, colleagues rallied round the aged scholars. They spoke of their scholarship, their achievements, their relationships with students — even Jewish students. The "follies" of their youth were best left forgotten.

It seemed as though little had been accomplished at Nuremberg. Yet, for the first time in history, leaders of a regime were held legally accountable for crimes committed in the course of carrying out their government's policy. Individuals were held responsible for their deeds. They could not shelter themselves in the defense that they were merely carrying out orders.

New standards were enunciated for the community of nations. They were often breached, but they remained recognized and much-cited standards of behavior nevertheless. In the medical profession, ethical codes were drafted for experimentation on human subjects. A Convention for the Prevention of Crimes of Genocide was adopted by the United Nations on December 9, 1948. The term *genocide* was first introduced by Raphael Lemkin in 1933, when he submitted a draft proposal to the League of Nations for an international convention on barbaric crimes and vandalism. He had a major hand in drafting the genocide convention, which was designed to overcome the claims of Nuremberg defendants that they had violated no law. The convention specifically defines the various aspects of Nazi genocide as criminal. It prohibits the killing of persons belonging to a group (the Final Solution); causing grievous bodily or mental harm to members of a group; deliberately enforcing upon the group living conditions that could lead to complete or partial extermination (ghettoization and starvation); enforcing measures to prevent births among the group (sterilization); forcibly removing children from the group and transferring them to another group (the "Aryanization" of Polish children).

The adoption of the convention was followed the next day by the adoption of a Universal Declaration of Human Rights. In 1949, the Geneva Convention on the Laws and Customs of War, enunciating the rights of prisoners of war and the conduct of armies toward the populations they control, was adopted. Although the United States had a major hand in drafting the genocide convention and signed the treaty, conservative pressures during the McCarthy era did not allow the Senate to get the two-thirds majority required by the Constitution for ratification. Conservatives argued that by ratifying the convention, the United States would be limiting its national sovereignty. Every day the Senate was in session, gadfly Senator William Proxmire of Wisconsin reminded his colleagues of the unfinished business of ratification. He gave thousands of speeches on behalf of the treaty. With the exception of Eisenhower, every American president from Truman to Carter advocated its ratification. None could muster the two-thirds vote needed for ratification. Because of conservative pressure, one-third of the Senate remained unconvinced for thirty-nine years and the treaty went unratified.

When he first assumed office, President Ronald Reagan was noncommittal about the convention. In 1987, the conservative president was persuaded to put his personal prestige behind the drive to ratify the treaty. Hearings were held in the Senate Foreign Relations Committee Room. Elie Wiesel testified as a survivor and former chairman of the United States Holocaust Memorial Council. Senator Jesse Helms, the longtime

opponent of passage, muted his criticism after that testimony, and the convention was ratified. On November 4, 1988, President Reagan signed the ratifying legislation, thus making the United States the ninety-eighth nation to ratify the convention.

EICHMANN IN JERUSALEM

In 1960, Israel captured Adolf Eichmann, the SS official in charge of the deportation of Jews, in Argentina, and brought him by clandestine means to Israel for trial in Jerusalem. Eichmann's capture was controversial because Israel had violated the sovereignty of another state. His trial before Jewish justices and the tribunal of a state that did not exist during the years of the Holocaust offended those who objected to "ex-post facto justice" and argued for an international tribunal or trial before German courts. His defense attorney argued that Eichmann could not get a fair trial in Israel before Jewish justices. The court responded: "When a judge sits on a bench, he does not cease to be flesh and blood with human emotions; but he is bidden by law to overcome these emotions. If this were not so, no judge would ever be qualified to sit in judgment in a criminal case evoking strong disgust, such as a case of treason or murder or some other heinous crime." After a long trial, Eichmann was convicted and hanged. His body was cremated — like the remains of his victims — and his ashes were scattered at sea so as not to sully Israeli soil.

Yet the aftermath of the Eichmann trial was perhaps more important than the trial itself. In Israel, a taboo had been broken. One could speak about the Holocaust. The younger generation, native-born Israelis or those from Arab lands untouched by the Holocaust, became interested in learning about these tragic events. They found the testimony of survivors riveting.

In the world of ideas, the trial had other unexpected consequences. Hannah Arendt, the distinguished German-born American Jewish philosopher, was asked to cover the trial for *The New Yorker.* Arendt made two essential points in her problematic portrayal of the trial. Her reports became a book that struck a nerve among Holocaust scholars and the Jewish community worldwide. She argued that, wittingly or unwittingly, the Jewish Councils were tools of the Nazis. Jewish leadership made the destruction of the Jewish people easier for the enemy. Her second point was no less provocative. Eichmann, she claimed, was essentially a dull bureaucrat. His deeds were not monstrous, but ordinary acts, such as arranging papers, rescheduling trains, making a bureaucracy function, fine-tuning a system of destruction. Indeed, the subtitle of Arendt's book, *Eichmann in Jerusalem,* was *A Report on the Banality of Evil.*

Arendt clearly violated the dialectic of the Holocaust in which the totality of the event is far greater than the sum of its parts. Her critics felt that if Eichmann was not the embodiment of evil, the moral significance of the Holocaust was somehow diminished. The sum total of Eichmann's many banal acts was not banality, but monstrous evil of a demonic proportion. But in the years since Arendt wrote her book, we have become more willing to examine the role of bureaucracy in perpetrating the crime and to see the bureaucrat not as someone larger than life — a mystified monster. Yet another taboo had been breached, and in Jerusalem, Berlin, Paris, and New York, scholars and writers had to face difficult questions such as what was the role of the Jewish Councils and Jewish leadership in the murder of millions of Jews. Among the issues that had to be confronted were the complicity of the victims in their own victimization and the relationship between bureaucratic evil and demonic evil. The bitter debate continues in Holocaust scholarship. At stake are not only issues of history; the pride of the living is salvaged from the conduct of the dead.

TRIALS THROUGHOUT EUROPE

Nazi war criminals were also prosecuted in other countries. Many collaborators were executed, including Prime Minister Pierre Laval of the French Vichy government, Presidents Tiso of Slovakia and Bagrianov of Bulgaria, and Marshal Antonescu of Romania and General Sztójay of Hungary. In 1943, in Krasnodar, the Soviet Union tried thirteen Soviet citizens who had served in mobile killing units. Similar trials were held in Kharkov in 1943 and in Majdanek immediately following its liberation in 1944.

Poland tried those who had presided over the destruction of Warsaw, Lublin, and Lódź. Thousands of collaborators were prosecuted. Rudolph Höss, the commandant of Auschwitz, was tried, convicted, and executed. He was hanged on a gallows erected adjacent to the gas chamber of Auschwitz I. Höss's colleague Maximillian Grabner, the head of the Political Department at Auschwitz, explained away his motivations to a court in Kraków.

I only took part in this crime because there was nothing I could do to to change anything. The blame for this crime lay with National Socialism. I myself was never a National Socialist. Nevertheless, I still had to join the party. . . .

I only took part in the murder . . . out of consideration for my family. I was never an anti-Semite and would still claim today that every person has the right to live.

The Polish Main Commission for the Investigation of Nazi War Crimes was still in operation forty-five years after the war.

In Romania and Hungary, war criminals were tried en masse. The Norwegians tried their wartime Prime Minister, Quisling. In Holland and France, trials were conducted in the years immediately following the war. In 1988, Klaus Barbie, the man responsible for the deportations from Lyon, was finally brought to trial in France.

In 1979, the United States Department of Justice established an Office of Special Investigation to track down Nazi war criminals who had found refuge in the United States. Similar investigations were conducted in Australia, Scotland, Great Britain, and Canada.

In West Germany itself, prosecutors investigated about 91,000 Germans accused of being Nazi criminals and convicted 6,479 in the criminal courts. Twelve were sentenced to death and 160 to life imprisonment. In East Germany, nearly 13,000 were convicted.

Yet in 1955, only a decade after the Holocaust, fewer than four hundred Nazi war criminals were still in German jails. Nazi business leaders had returned to their positions. Alfried Krupp's empire was flourishing and still under his control. The convicted leaders of I. G. Farben served on new corporate boards. One of them, Otto Ambros, joined the board of the American corporation W. R. Grace. Civil servants retired with their pensions intact. Former Nazi judges remained on the bench.

Few in the legal profession were untainted by the Nazi years, when the legal system had been an instrumentality of destruction. But there was no time to train a new generation of judges and lawyers, professors of law, and civil servants. Life had to continue, and a trained bureaucracy was required. The easiest way to move on was to rehabilitate all except the most ardent of Nazis. The same process of rehabilitation is currently under way in the former Soviet Union and in the Eastern European countries, where officials who had conscientiously served one regime will continue in office and conscientiously serve a democratic society whose values are the antithesis of the regime they once served.

A new democratic West Germany was born that sought to move beyond the Nazi past and begin again as a free, tolerant, and open society. For many Germans, the trials were a painful reminder of a past best left forgotten.

In 1953, after long and controversial negotiations, the West German government recognized the participation of the German people in the murder of Jews. The Federal Republic agreed to pay reparations to individual Jews, the Jewish people, and the fledgling state of Israel for the crimes of Nazi Germany. Many survivors refused on principle to accept funds that they saw as blood money.

These payments helped the absorption and material rehabilitation of many survivors in the state of Israel. Payments were offered as recompense for confiscated property, material losses, wrongful incarceration, and slave labor. Nothing was offered for the dead.

Communist East Germany never offered reparations. It regarded the Holocaust as a crime committed by Western capitalists, and therefore assumed no responsibilities toward the victims of nazism. Only after Communist rule was ended did the East German Parliament apologize to the Jews. During its first session as a democratically elected body, Parliament admitted "joint responsibility on behalf of the people for the humiliation, expulsion and murder of Jewish women, men and children." It declared:

We feel sad and ashamed and acknowledge the burden of German history. We ask the Jews of the world to forgive us. We ask the people of Israel to forgive us for hypocrisy and hostility of the official East German policies toward Israel and for the persecution and degradation of Jewish citizens also after 1945 in our country. We declare our willingness to contribute as much as possible to the healing of mental and physical suffering of survivors and to provide just compensation for material losses.

DISPLACED PERSONS

As the Allied armies swept through Europe in 1944 and 1945, they found seven to nine million displaced people living in countries not their own. More than six million returned to their native lands. But more than one million refused repatriation. Most of them were Poles, Estonians, Latvians, Lithuanians, Ukrainians, and Yugoslavs. Some had collaborated with the Nazis and were afraid of retaliation should they return home. Others feared persecution by the new Communist regimes in Eastern Europe.

Jewish survivors could not return home. Their communities were shattered, their homes destroyed or occupied by strangers. In the east, they were not welcome in the land of their birth. With nowhere to go, they were forced to live in camps set up on the sites where they had been imprisoned. For most of them, this meant a prolonged stay in Germany living in the midst of those who had sought to impose the Final Solution.

The beleaguered American army was hard pressed to juggle the multiple assignment of serving as both an occupation force and a counterforce in the new Cold War, and of dealing with the problems of the survivors. Short-term problems — housing, medical treatment, food, attempting to reunite families — were acute and demanding. The army had no long-range strategy for resettling those who could not or would not return home.

Most Jewish displaced persons wanted to begin a new life in Palestine. Although many would have preferred to emigrate to the United States, they were not willing to wait for years to qualify for admission. In 1945, most Jewish DPs were survivors of the concentration camps, partisans, or those who had spent the war in hiding. Life in the concentration camps had taken a hard toll. The survivors were destitute, and often sick. After liberation, the inhabitants of the DP camps were often dirty. If they were not depressed, they were argumentative. They were haunted by nightmares and mistrusted authority — even the American authorities who were trying to help them. Living in Germany in camps that also housed people

> *We [the United States] appear to be treating the Jews as the Nazis treated them, except that we do not exterminate them.*

EARL HARRISON, DEAN OF THE UNIVERSITY OF PENNSYLVANIA LAW SCHOOL

who openly hated Jews did little to improve their morale.

Living conditions in the camps were unpleasant. Camps were overcrowded, and although the DPs were not starved, there was never enough food. Coping again with life, with the prospect of living after everything that had been endured, was the greatest difficulty. Major Irving Heymont who directed the Landsberg displaced persons camp wrote to his wife:

The camp is filthy beyond description. Sanitation is virtually unknown. . . . The Army units we relieved obviously did nothing more than insure that rations were delivered to the camp. With few exceptions the people of the camp themselves appear demoralized beyond hope of rehabilitation. They appear to be beaten both spiritually and physically.

Britain was unwilling to permit Jewish emigration to Palestine. Trying to preserve the remnants of its empire, it was reticent to alienate the Arab world hostile to a potential Jewish state. The United States was not ready to receive an influx of refugees. Soldiers were coming home from the war. It was a time of transition from war production to a civilian economy, and there was a fear that refugees would consume scarce resources and take jobs away from Americans. Nativistic thinking did not end with World War II, even if the isolationists were silenced. Within a few weeks of taking office as president, Harry Truman dispatched Earl Harrison, the dean of the University of Pennsylvania Law School, to report on the displaced-persons camps. The report was a bombshell. Harrison concluded that:

We [the United States] appear to be treating the Jews as the Nazis treated them, except that we do not exterminate them. They are in concentration camps in

large numbers under our military guard instead of SS troops. One is led to wonder whether the German people seeing this are not supposing that we are following or at least condoning Nazi policy.

His recommendations were sweeping: the special status of Jews must be recognized; they should be evacuated from Germany swiftly; and 100,000 Jews should be admitted to Palestine. Truman, who was later to become a hero to the Jews for recognizing Israel as a state, followed his humanitarian impulses. He endorsed the report, rebuked the army, and intensified the pressure on Britain to allow 100,000 Jews to immigrate to Palestine. He also opened the United States to limited immigration. His personal sentiments were clear: "It is unthinkable that they should be left indefinitely in camps in Europe."

In response to growing international pressure, the British called for an Anglo-American Commission of Inquiry made up of six American and six British commissioners. Their strategy was to buy some time for conditions to improve and to kill the political momentum by a committee report. The commission was also shocked by conditions in the camps and was impressed by the desire of Jewish displaced persons to go to Palestine. It recommended that 100,000 be admitted to Palestine immediately, a suggestion promptly rejected by the British government. Foreign Minister Bevin wryly commented that: "The Americans wanted 100,000 Jews in Palestine because they didn't want them in New York."

Slowly, the survivors renewed their lives. At first, the DP camps consisted primarily of single men. Fewer women had survived. Life was lonely. Relief agencies such as the United Nations Relief and Rehabilitation Administration (UNRRA) took care of basic daily needs, but in the fall of 1945, Jewish relief organizations came pouring into the camps. Personnel from the Jewish Agency and the Jewish Brigade worked with the survivors. They started schools and agricultural farms. They taught Hebrew and began the preliminary organizing that would make the displaced persons a potent political force on behalf of the establishment of a Jewish state in Palestine.

I come to you with empty pockets. I have no certificates for you. I can only tell you that you are not abandoned. You are not alone. . . . I bring you no certificates— only hope.

DAVID BEN-GURION

David Ben-Gurion visiting the DP camp in Bergen-Belsen. Bergen-Belsen, Germany, February 1947. *Beth Hatefusoth Museum of the Diaspora, Tel Aviv, Israel.*

Jewish chaplains from the American army and Va'ad Haatzala, the rescue group organized by Orthodox Jews to save religious Jews and their religious institutions, conducted religious services. In 1946, the camp newspapers of Landsberg described the celebration of Purim, the Jewish festival when Haman is defeated because of the tenacity of Mordecai and the bravery of Esther:

Hitler hangs in many variants and many poses: A big Hitler, a fat Hitler, a small Hitler, with medals and without medals. Jews hung him by his head, by his feet, or by his belly. Or: a painter's ladder with a paint and brush, here a tombstone with the inscription "P.N." (po nikbar). Here lies Hitler, may his name be blotted out.

The American Jewish Joint Distribution Committee worked to improve living conditions, and the Organization for Rehabilitation through Training (ORT) began occupational training.

In October 1945, David Ben-Gurion, the leader of the effort to build a Jewish state in Palestine, visited the camps. Major Irving Heymont, the commander of Landsberg, described the visit to his wife: "To the people of the camp he is a god. . . . Never had I seen such energy displayed in the camps." To the survivors, Ben-Gurion said:

I come to you with empty pockets. I have no certificates for you. I can only tell you that you are not abandoned. You are not alone. You will not live endlessly in camps like this. All of you who want to come to Palestine will be brought there as soon as is humanly possible. I bring you no certificates— only hope.

POGROM IN KIELCE

On July 4, 1946, a mob of Poles attacked the one hundred and fifty Jews who had returned to the town of Kielce. Forty-two were killed and fifty wounded. Before the war, twenty-four thousand Jews had lived in Kielce; the one hundred and fifty who were targets of the pogrom were survivors who had come home looking for their families and their homes. The Kielce pogrom was inspired by the age-old blood libel that was part of the classic pattern of anti-Jewish violence: the mob believed that Jews were killing Christian children and drinking their blood, or using the blood to bake Passover wafers. In Kielce, the Poles were also stirred up by fear that the Jews would reclaim their lost property.

Appeals were made to church leaders and civic authorities to intervene in order to prevent a massacre. The church was silent, and the police response was to confiscate weapons held by Jews. The only priest in the town who protested the pogrom was removed from his pulpit within the week.

The news of the Kielce pogrom spread like wildfire throughout the remnant of the Jewish community in Eastern Europe. It was as though nothing had changed. Jews throughout Poland understood that it was not safe to return home; the future lay elsewhere.

Illegal emigration to the American zone of occupied Germany, which had been a trickle immediately after the war, intensified as panicked Jews sought to leave postwar Poland.

THE RETURN TO LIFE

Life inside the DP camps improved dramatically in 1946, when Polish Jews who had been released from the Soviet Union entered along with those escaping the Kielce pogrom. An UNRRA official described the site of their arrival at the Zilcheim DP camp near Frankfurt:

What appeared to be an endless queue of refugees, packs and bundles on their backs, plodding up the path toward the camp. Never had I seen such a bedraggled lot of people. Mothers held infants to their breasts, clutching the hands of tiny youngsters who stumbled alongside them. As I watched, a group halted and, throwing their bundles to the ground, literally fell in their tracks from exhaustion, unable to make the last few yards to the camp. . . . They had arrived in the last few days from Cracow and Polish Silesia, more than seven hundred miles distant. Fathers, mothers and children alike, hitch-hiked, rode trucks, jumped freight trains, slept in the forests at night and somehow managed to reach here.

Survivors married. Many who had lost a spouse remarried. Rabbis were particularly lenient in their interpretation of Jewish law to permit remarriage. By tradition, a widow may not remarry unless eyewitnesses had seen her husband dead. Such ordinary evidence of death was not possible after the Holocaust. The Chief Rabbi of Palestine, Rabbi Isaac Herzog, ruled that it was sufficient to know that a person had been deported to a death camp or selected, to assume that he or she was dead. A survivor couched his marriage proposal in words framed by tragedy: "I am alone. I have no one, I have lost everything. You are alone. You have no one. You have lost everything. Let us be alone together."

New families were formed. Mothers whose children had been murdered by the Nazis

NATURAL INCREASE of POPULATION of JEWISH CENTER BAD REICHENHALL

gave birth again. A poster in Bad Reichenhall Jewish Center proudly listed the natural increase of the population. September 1946: 8 girls, 10 boys. October: 18 girls, 17 boys. November: 8 girls, 10 boys. Life was renewed even as memories of death lingered.

Political life also began anew. By 1947, more than seventy newspapers — in many different languages and advocating every political and religious point of view — were published in the camps. Zionists organized agricultural training programs for the future settlers of Palestine. Youth movements were introduced into the camps. There were one hundred different schools, both religious and secular, serving twelve thousand students. Two high schools were established. So were vocational schools, agricultural schools, a teacher-training seminar, even a yeshiva. Collective farms — kibbutzim — were organized in preparation for life in Palestine. Yiddish was the lingua franca, but those who wanted to begin life in Palestine learned Hebrew. Political demonstrations were mounted against the British for their recalcitrance in granting independence to Palestine.

Camp life was by its nature temporary. Everyone in the camps was en route to a new home somewhere, even if it was not yet known where that home would be. A story circulated in the DP camps.

In the aftermath of the Holocaust, survivors had the courage to begin life again and to bring children into the world. This poster from Bad Reichenhall, Germany, clearly indicates the population explosion among Jews in 1946/47. On loan from YIVO Institute for Jewish Research, New York. Photo USHMM.

"Where would you like to go?" an immigration official asked a Jew.

"To Australia," he responded.

"But that's so far away," responded the official.

"From what?"

On December 22, 1945, President Truman granted preferential treatment to displaced persons who wanted to immigrate to the United States. Within the next eighteen months, 22,950 DPs were admitted, 15,478 of them Jews. But the problem of what to do with the displaced persons could not be solved merely by a minor adjustment of the quotas. Even the advocates of immigration were hesitant. An American Friends Service Committee leader, whose organization supported immigration, said:

The fact is that we are no longer the "land of opportunity" of the usual European immigrant's dream and this is especially true if we have a serious unemployment problem following the war. . . . Now that immigration to this country is not a matter of actual rescue from persecution or danger . . . we feel that plans for immigration should be given careful consideration and weighed against all possible alternatives of return to the native country, remaining in the country of current residence, or possible migration to other countries.

In the summer of 1946, with the American zone of occupied Germany flooded by the 100,000 Polish Jews newly released by the Soviet Union and by Jews fleeing Eastern Europe after the Kielce pogrom, congressional action could no longer be avoided.

The American Jewish community marshaled its allies in a successful campaign to combat the nativistic and antisemitic groups that wanted to keep the lid on immigration. The Protestant Federal Council of Churches and the Catholic publication *Commonweal* endorsed a liberalized immigration law that would bring 400,000 DPs to the United States within four years. The political struggle for a new law was ferocious.

In 1948, Congress passed a bill providing for the admission of 200,000 over four years.

Jewish refugees from Poland at an emergency reception center of the American Joint Distribution Committee. Nachod, Czechoslovakia, 1946. *American Jewish Joint Distribution Committee, New York.*

Truman called it "flagrantly discriminatory against Jews." In 1950, the act was amended to make it slightly less discriminatory. The change was too late: in 1949, most of the Jewish DPs had gone to the newly established state of Israel.

A popular joke in the DP camps spoke of those waiting to leave Europe.

Two DPs meet and one asks where the other plans to emigrate.

"Canada or Australia."

"Why not the United States?"

"Because the Americans put you on a scale, and start adding papers to the other side. When the paper equals your weight, you're ready to go."

There was a consistency to American policy before and after the war. Paper walls were erected. According to the historian of American immigration Mark Wyman: "There is truth behind this humor. A resettlement officer once laid out the documents in a single case file for entry to the United States: they stretched seventeen yards."

During the three years after the war, only 41,000 DPs were admitted to the United States. Two-thirds of them were Jews. In the four years following the passage of the immigration law of 1948, 365,223 displaced persons were brought to American shores. Half the immigrants were Roman Catholic and only 16 percent Jews. Some of the DPs openly admitted to having collaborated with the Nazis. All in all, fewer than 100,000 Jews were able to reach the United States in the years between the end of the war and the closing of the last DP camp seven years later.

In retrospect, however, the 1948 legislation was a turning point in American immigration policy. The act governing the admission of DPs was a precedent for the American response to subsequent waves of refugees, including Hungarians in 1957, Cubans in 1960, and Vietnamese in 1979.

EXODUS

Between 1944 and 1948, more than 200,000 Jews fled from Eastern and Central Europe to Palestine, crossing borders legally, semilegally, or illegally. The means did not seem to matter: the borders were crossed somehow.

The movement began spontaneously and in a small way. In the summer of 1944, three partisans, Abba Kovner of Vilna, Vitka Kempner, and Ruzhka Korczak, a former subordinate commander in Vilna, met in the Rudninkai Forest to discuss their future. They decided that every effort must be made to get to Palestine. At the same time, a survivor in Rovno, Eliezer Lidovsky, organized the first group to leave Poland, first to Romania and then to Palestine via the Black Sea.

Meanwhile, Jews who had spent the war in Central Asia tried to contact survivors in Poland. Mordechai Rosman and Shlomo Kless were sent to Poland by way of Moscow. In the railroad station they happened to meet Celia Rosenberg, Kovner's emissary. According to Yehuda Bauer:

She had no addresses, only the names of two men, Mordecai Rosman and Shlomo Kless. . . . She was in Moscow in a railway station crowded with thousands of soldiers in the last winter of the war, without documents and with no friends to turn to. She did have money, but that might turn out to be a mixed blessing if she was caught.

Jewish Brigade members sought their brethren in Romania and Hungary, and were in turn found by Jews seeking a way to Palestine. The survivors were anxious to leave Eastern Europe. The pogrom in Kielce and other manifestations of continuing antisemitism, coming after the devastation of Jewish towns and villages in Eastern Europe, sent a clear message. Those who returned were convinced there was no future in what had been home. Poland was a vast Jewish graveyard, a place of bitter memories. Jewish life still seemed to hang by a thread.

Soon the inchoate movement was organized and given a name — Bricha, the Hebrew word for escape. Bricha facilitated the

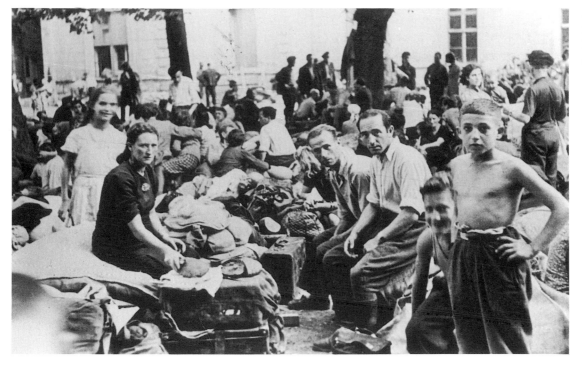

border crossings, but it did not initiate the migration. Operatives were brought in from the Jewish Brigade and the Hagana, the defense forces of Jews in Palestine. Two major routes were established. One went west from Lódź to Poznan and Szczecin, and then to the British or American sector in Germany. The other went south from Lódź to Katowice or Krakow, then through Czechoslovakia, Hungary, or Austria to Italy or Yugoslavia.

The borders were crossed by day and night, on foot and by train. Some border guards had to be bribed. Others simply turned aside and pretended not to notice. Czechoslovakia cooperated with the refugees; at times Poland did also. Most countries were quite pleased to be rid of the Jews and gladly helped them on their way. Much to the chagrin of the British, the Americans allowed Jews into their sector of Germany (including Austria).

In the summer of 1945, when Earl Harrison wrote his report, there were about 50,000 Jews in Germany and Austria. At that moment, the Jewish DP problem could easily have been solved by the issuance of 100,000 entry permits to Palestine. In the next year and a half, the number of Jews in the American sector increased fourfold, creating political pressure on both the British and the Americans that led to the establishment of a Jewish state.

Meanwhile, Jews were not content to wait while the politicians decided their fate. They set out for Palestine on their own, assisted by a Zionist underground network composed of Palestinian soldiers from the Jewish Brigade and Jews serving in Allied armies or working in Europe as civilians. Between 1945 and May 1948, 69,000 Jews made the journey by sea illegally on sixty-five boats. Only a few of the ships that ran the British blockade succeeded in reaching the coast of Palestine. Most were stopped by the British Royal Navy. The passengers were then sent to detention camps in Cyprus.

The movement of Jews to Palestine was known by several names. According to the British, it was illegal immigration. Palestinian Jews referred to it as Aliya Bet. (In Hebrew, *aliya* means a going up to the land, and *bet* is the second letter of the alphabet; hence, a second means of ascent to the land.)

Clandestine intelligence networks of Mossad (Mossad L'Aliya Bet, the agency for the Aliya Bet, which later evolved into the famed Israeli intelligence agency) operated most of the ships. The sailings, however, were anything but secret. Journalists were notified in advance. Pictures of the British forcibly removing Holocaust survivors from ships and imprisoning them yet again were sent to newspapers throughout the world as part of a

*Exodus refugee ship in
Haifa port. Haifa, Israel,
July 18, 1947. Central
Zionist Archive, Jerusalem, Israel.*

campaign to discredit the British mandate
over Palestine.

The most famous event in Aliya Bet was the
journey of the *Exodus*, a ship that set sail from
Marseilles in July 1947 carrying forty-five
hundred passengers. After a brief fight, the
ship was captured. Instead of sending the
passengers to Cyprus, the British took a "get
tough" policy and forced the ship back to
Marseilles. The passengers refused to
disembark in Europe. They went on a hunger
strike, which captured international attention.

The British cabinet would not relent in a
struggle they saw as a test of wills with the
Jews. They feared losing control of the
situation and did not understand the special
sensitivity for Holocaust survivors that would
galvanize world public opinion. The passengers
would be taken to Germany and there
returned to Bergen-Belsen against their will. It
took tear gas to force the concentration camp
survivors off the ship. For two months the
Exodus claimed the sympathy and attention of
the world. The decision to send survivors back
to a concentration camp caused international
revulsion.

Aliya Bet dramatized the indomitable will
of survivors to reach the land of Israel and
broke the back of the British mandate over
Palestine. Four months later, the United
Nations voted for the establishment of an

independent Jewish state in Palestine. Aliya
Bet provided the means of migration to
Palestine. The will to go to the Jewish
homeland was pervasive among the survivors.
I. F. Stone reported on the simple yearnings of
the survivors: "I am a Jew," he was told.
"That's enough. We have wandered enough.
We have worked and struggled too long on
the lands of other peoples. We must build a
land of our own."

Some were motivated by anger at the
non-Jewish world. Dr. Samuel Gringauz, the
head of the Landsberg DP camp's Jews, wrote
about Jewish pessimism in the camp
newspaper:

*We do not believe in progress, we do not believe in
the 2,000-year-old Christian culture of the West,
the culture that, for them, created the Statue of
Liberty in New York and Westminster Abbey on the
Thames, the wonder gardens of Versailles and the
Uffizi and Pitti palaces in Florence, the Strasbourg
Münster and the Cologne cathedral; but for us,
the slaughters of the Crusades, the Spanish
Inquisition, the blood bath of Khmielnicki, the
pogroms of Russia, the gas chambers of Auschwitz
and the massacres of an entire Europe.*

Still other survivors were desperate for hope.
Eleanor Roosevelt described her visit to a
Jewish DP camp in Zilcheim:

*Most of all, I remember an old woman whose
family had been driven from home by the war
madness and brutality. I had no idea who she was and
we could not speak each other's language, but she
knelt in the muddy road and simply threw her arms
around my knees. "Israel," she murmured over and
over. "Israel! Israel!"*

*As I looked at her weatherbeaten face and heard
her old voice, I knew for the first time what that
small land meant to so many, many people.*

On May 14, 1948, David Ben-Gurion
proclaimed the state of Israel. That evening,
the last British troops departed as the Union
Jack was lowered. In its place rose the blue
and white Star of David. That evening, Israel
was also attacked by five Arab countries. A
Jewish army was in place to defend its country.

In its Declaration of Independence, the
provisional government of the new state

Jewish demonstrators at Bergen-Belsen DP camp, during an address of Joseph Rosensaft, chairman of the Jewish Committee. Four thousand Jewish refugees demonstrated against the *Exodus* disembarkation in Hamburg. Bergen-Belsen, Germany, September 8, 1947. *Yad Vashem, Jerusalem, Israel.*

ended all restriction on Jewish immigrants. In a few days, two ships, the *State of Israel* and *To Victory*, arrived with displaced persons now coming home. In the first days of independence, the Israeli government began the evacuation of the camps in Cyprus and the DP camps in Europe. It also began an intensive recruitment effort for the Israel Defense Forces among the young and able-bodied survivors, some of whom had fought in the Allied armies or as partisans. Resistance fighters from Warsaw and Vilna soon fought in Jerusalem and the Negev.

By the autumn of 1949, Jews were leaving the DP camps of Europe at a rate of ten thousand a month. On December 17, 1950, the Central Committee of Jewish Displaced Persons was disbanded. All those who wanted to settle in Israel had arrived. In 1950, Israel passed the Law of Return, granting Jews immediate citizenship upon their arrival. Once unwanted everywhere, Jews now had a country willing to open its borders to them. Israel offered itself as a haven to Jews fleeing persecution anywhere. Under the Law of Return, Jews fleeing Khomeini's Iran, segregated South Africa, starvation in Ethiopia, and persecution in the Soviet Union have found freedom in Israel.

Jewish survivors of the Holocaust finally found a place they could call home, a country

that wanted them and that they wanted. The task of state-building was challenging and looked to the future. There were wars to be fought, cities and villages to be built, crops to be planted. These activities did not allow much time to dwell on the past. It would take a long time for the survivors to rebuild their lives from the ashes, and even more time to face the haunting memories of a painful past.

Arrival in an independent Jewish state was a defining moment. Survivors remembered from where they had come and how difficult their journey had been. Peter Somogi was a twin who had survived Mengele experiments. He was a favorite of Mengele because he was "cultural, played piano." He and his twin fled Hungary "with the Zionist movement on April 4, 1949," Somogi recalled:

Our flight was very well organized. There were about ten young people in our group, as well as a few parents. We had guides at every stage of our journey. These guides had been well-paid. In those days, there were a lot of people who made their living sneaking people out of Europe.

The border guards had been bribed, so we were able to cross without any problems. But instead of going directly south, we went up north through Czechoslovakia, and then on to Vienna.

In Vienna, we had to bribe Russian soldiers to pass through. The city was then under Russian control. We stayed in an old schoolhouse, where we were joined by scores of other Jews trying to flee.

We spent three weeks in Vienna, and then made our way to Salzburg. In Salzburg, we stayed in an old concentration camp, I don't know which one. I didn't care—and surprisingly, I didn't feel particularly bothered by that. We didn't spend too much time there.

After about a week, we went to Bari, in southern Italy. There, it was very easy to move around: Everyone accepted bribes. They let us go through even though not one of us had passports.

We waited for the boat that was to take us to Israel. There were hundreds of us by then, gathered from every corner of Europe, awaiting passage to the Promised Land.

We were all very excited. We felt for the first time that we didn't have to look behind our back and hear someone saying "dirty Jew."

First anniversary of Israel's Independence Day. Tel Aviv, Israel, May 4, 1949. *Government Press Office, Jerusalem, Israel.*

Eva Mozes was also a twin, one of Mengele's victims. For her, arrival in Israel was also a homecoming.

> It was early in the morning when our ship approached Haifa. We watched the sun rise over Mount Carmel. It was one of the most beautiful sights I had ever seen.
>
> Most everyone on the boat was a Holocaust survivor. We all stood up and started singing "Hatikvah," the Jewish national anthem.
>
> We hugged and kissed each other. We felt at last we had come home.

The birth of the state of Israel was the most significant positive consequence of the Holocaust. The independent Jewish state might have come into being because of the impetus of Jewish nationalism and the Zionist movement of return to the land of Israel. But the presence of survivors in displaced-persons camps after the war increased worldwide support and sympathy for the Jewish state and

hastened its formation. Yet Israel is not an answer to the Holocaust. Its formation could not undo the horror of the death camps. Elie Wiesel wrote: "To pretend that without Auschwitz there would be no Israel is to endow the latter with a share of responsibility for the former." It places an unbearable burden on the Israelis whose very conduct and continued survival must redeem the irredeemable evil of the Holocaust.

A NEW WORLD

Survivors of the Holocaust began arriving in the United States in 1946; they continued to arrive for another half dozen years. William Helmreich has interviewed many survivors who came to America. He described their journey to

America as the beginning of an adventure. They had left as displaced persons and found themselves treated as passengers on a ship.

I remember someone playing guitar singing "I come from Alabama with my banjo on my knee . . ." I didn't realize it then but they were beginning to acculturate us on the boat. It was the English language; it was a certain kind of music that speaks of hopefulness and abandon, the opposite of suspicion and worry and looking around the corner. To me, as a thirteen-year-old, that's what it represented. It represented sunshine, even though I was throwing up everything.

Tom Lantos, the only survivor elected to Congress, recalled his voyage as a nineteen-year-old to America:

There was a big basket of oranges and one of bananas. I wanted to do the right thing so I asked this sailor, "Should I take an orange or a banana?" And he said: "Man, you eat all the goddamn oranges and all the goddamn bananas you want." Then I knew I was in paradise.

Many recalled their arrival in the United States with joy and gratitude. Madeline Deutsch was deported to Auschwitz at fourteen. Four years later, she came to America. "And we . . . practically everybody I think . . . bent down and kissed the good old American soil because this finally meant freedom. We were finally, after all these years, free."

Arrival in the United States was a moment of intense excitement and reunion with relatives and friends. Wallace Witkowski of Kielce recalled:

I escaped from Poland to Sweden on a coal freighter on December 31, 1948, and from there I managed to come to the United States within three days of my 21st birthday when my non-quota immigrant visa was expiring. So I was lucky again. I flew from New York to Detroit and looked up my father's name in the telephone directory. . . . And called his number. There was no answer, and I stood at the counter not knowing what to do and I heard my name. He recognized me from the back.

Another survivor described the reunion of father and son on a New York pier.

When the first passengers were allowed onto the gangplank something akin to an electric shock went through the crowd. A young man ran wildly toward the expectant crowd waiting by the fence. A bone-chilling cry rang out — "My child, My child!" shouted an older man, tears streaming down his cheeks. His daughter who stood beside him looked at her brother as he took her in his arms and kissed her. Everyone around them, even the customs officials, was greatly moved. Overcome by emotions, they turned away.

Once in the United States, they were essentially on their own even though there was a vast organizational apparatus to support them. The Hebrew Immigrant Aid Society (HIAS) resettled these immigrants as they had assisted in the resettlement of earlier generations of American Jewish immigrants. Abraham Malnick recalled: "I came to this country. They [HIAS] gave me seven dollars on the ship. Dropped me off in New York without a language, without nothing, without any relatives, without anybody. And I felt pretty lonely. I still didn't know where my

Moses Frisch greets his brother and his sister-in-law who survived a Nazi concentration camp. New York, May 1946.
FPG International, New York.

aunts lived." HIAS did assist survivors to locate housing in the apartment shortage of the first postwar years. They could also help with job placement, but could not begin to deal with the wounds of the Holocaust. Organizations were supportive, friends and relatives were essential. Not all families welcomed their new arrivals: Eva Edwards, who survived the war years in France, landed in New York Harbor in May of 1948. She recalled her first months:

Well, it was bad. We were taken to a shelter. Although my uncle could have put us up, he put us in a shelter, and then his wife, fearful that we might cost too much money, put my mother and me to work in a factory. That was our introduction to the United States. I didn't speak English so I had to start all over again learning. I was eighteen at that time. So I did learn. I had to go to work to support the family but I had no skills.

In contrast, Thomas Burgenthal, who was aged nine when he went on the death march from Auschwitz, recalls: "My uncle and aunt were wonderful to me. They took me in. Obviously, it was my family. They were people who themselves work in factories and in stores." He had planned to come to the United States for a year. He remained. For other survivors, the reunion with relatives was temporary. Madeline Deutsch recalled:

My aunt and uncle took us with them to their home. They lived near Pittsburgh, Pennsylvania, and we stayed with them for a while. And they wanted us to stay there. But I had just turned eighteen at the time, and where they lived there were either the all grown-up, older people with grown children who were married and with little babies, or young married people. There was nobody that was Jewish that was my age. And at that point I could not communicate with anybody other than a Jew. I just couldn't! Everybody [else] was the enemy.

Many survivors were taken to the Hotel Marseilles, a dilapidated house on New York's Upper West Side. They were handed a key to their room and for the first time in years they were given privacy. For people who had lived for years in the overcrowded conditions of ghettos, concentration camps, and even

displaced persons camps, a private room was the first symbol of freedom.

Still, scars of their past experience remained. William Rosenwald, the well-known philanthropist who owned Sears, Roebuck, recounted how a group of children had arrived at a shelter. The youngest were dispatched to an infants' home. It took a few days for the others to gather enough courage to ask if the infants had been sent to the gas chambers. They did not believe the social worker until they were taken to see the children.

Young people were also hampered in their struggle for an education. For many, their formal training had stopped in 1941 or 1942. They were poorly trained in English and much older than their classmates. They had a lot of catching up to do. David Bergman, who was fourteen years old when he entered Auschwitz, was a graduate of concentration camps before he entered high school.

I started high school. I was looked at like I came from another world because I was their age. They were all nice but they didn't know how to approach me. In their minds they had just seen the movies, the horrors. So I was looked upon as somebody who had come from another world.

I was too old for junior high school and I missed the background of junior high school, so I was not ready to be in high school. So what do they do? They sent me to both. Talk about having a rough road, but I managed to keep up.

Rene Fritz was born in Vienna. She survived in hiding with false identities.

I had to go to public school because here I am almost thirteen and I belonged in eighth grade. I don't understand one word. Nobody speaks Yiddish there. I don't know anything. I never had a day of math in my life. Zero. But I am a novelty because I could sing the French national anthem.

They devised a plan. Every day I would spend half an hour in the first grade, a half hour in the second, a half hour in the third. Well it was a little humiliating because here I am with these seven- and eight-year-olds and I am almost thirteen but there was no other way to get caught up.

I wanted to be like the rest of them. I remember buying sheet music and standing in front of the mirror and practicing how to lose this accent.

Young survivors had lost their childhood. They had to acculturate to American society and to learn new mores. Even when successful, it was not simple. Thomas Burgenthal said:

I came in December. In January I was in high school in Paterson, New Jersey. I enjoyed it very much. I was treated very well. I had a wonderful college advisor who gave me a list of ten colleges, all small, that I should write to. And she told me what to write, asking for admission and a scholarship. Most of the colleges on seeing my record didn't know what to do with this kid who had no school except basically two and a half years in Germany and about a year of high school in New Jersey.

One college I'd written to was Bethany College in West Virginia. I received their catalogue . . . and it said this is a Christian college. Coming from Europe with my experience I thought it meant they didn't want me.

One day I got called to my counsellor's office and she said: "There is somebody from Bethany College who would like to meet you."

The first thing the person says to me: "You wrote to Bethany; why didn't you send in the application?" I hemmed and I hawed. I didn't quite know how to explain it. Finally I told him the truth and he said: "Oh this isn't the case at all. I can tell you that if you apply to Bethany College we'll give you a scholarship and a job. You won't need a penny in order to graduate."

Thus, the career of one of the nation's eminent lawyers was launched. Burgenthal completed Bethany and went on to become a professor of law, dean of American University's School of Law, and one of the nation's authorities on human rights.

Survivors had an ambivalent sense of being in America. Some felt that they should have gone to Israel, but after the hardships they had endured, the United States was the only place where they had relatives, and they looked forward to a less difficult life. Unlike earlier generations of immigrants who came in search of the American dream, the survivors' experience of America was bittersweet. They remembered a dark side of American history, the failure of the United States to serve as a haven before or during the war, the refusal to bomb Auschwitz. The

United States had not been their rescuer or protector during their hour of greatest need. David Bergman recalled being drafted into the army. "I was just getting on my feet, starting college, when I get a letter from Uncle Sam. That was when the Korean war was happening. They told me I would be drafted and then I tried to explain to them that I just went through hell."

Yet survivors soon developed a fierce love for America. They embraced American values. They relished the ordinary freedoms of American life. Lilly Malnick, a sixteen-year-old survivor of Auschwitz who married another survivor, recalled:

We worked very hard in this country. We were young. It's true we could not speak the language when we came but we learned as fast as we could and we built a new family and a new life. America gave me the opportunity to live as a human being again.

They could go to synagogue without fear; they could approach men in uniform without hesitation. David Chase, a Hartford industrialist, spoke of his love for America:

America gave us a home when we had none. America embraced us when we felt rejected. It gave us a feeling when we were stateless. . . . The initials "D.P." which identified us as Displaced Persons years ago have taken on a new meaning. Today the letters "D.P." identify us as Delayed Pilgrims. We are proud to be Americans.

The reception of survivors was not always easy or uneventful. Some survivors did not blend smoothly into the melting pot that had been the metaphor of American acculturation for generations past. Madeline Deutsch felt out of place.

Everybody was different. They . . . they didn't go through what we went through. We were different people. It was like . . . I don't know whether it was that they were green people with little horns or we were the ones. Couldn't decide which except that we were completely different. So I had nothing in common with any of the young people.

My aunt and uncle tried to put me back into school so I learned something and I couldn't do that because I saw all the teachers the way I saw them

Families waiting for their Jewish relatives from Europe to disembark. New York, 1948. *Beth Hatefusoth Museum of the Diaspora, Tel Aviv, Israel.*

afraid that the Nazis are still out there. I was having nightmares for years and years. For many years, I was still reliving everything. The trip to Auschwitz, the beatings, the killings, the dead people that were taken off the train, the . . . the beatings and the . . . the dogs that were released and just jump on the people and tear them apart. I lived with this. Years and years! I still live with it, but I don't have these horrible nightmares anymore except occasionally. . . . But this was for years. And it was a horrible, horrible thing.

Unlike earlier immigrants, their presence was a constant reminder not only of the American dream but of the American failure to rescue them in time. Helen Lebowitz Goldkind, a teenager in Auschwitz, came to the United States afterward and was unprepared for what she saw.

We came here and we saw children on the street and they were free. They were running around and they played in the playgrounds. And we saw the people and they . . . you know, I keep on asking are they Jewish. Are they Jewish? Because I thought all the Jews, that [the Holocaust] happened to all the Jews. And they says, "Ya, all." So, you know, we had to deal with that. You know that there are Jewish kids that survived.

They soon learned that if they wanted to have friends in America, the past had to be forgotten. Helen Lebowitz Goldkind remembered:

I couldn't talk about it for a long time. I did not talk about it for a long time. And I made a decision when I had my first child that I will not talk about it. The reason why I didn't want to talk about it is because I was afraid I will talk about it so much. And to me it was if my kids will hear what I have gone through that Hitler will get to them too and I wanted sort of like to save them from that. They guessed. They knew that something isn't right because during the day I could control my emotion and I was busy. I was very busy. I worked. I was trying to raise a family and so I could control what's there behind my head, the past. But sometimes I would just go in and cry for weeks.

They often were met with reproach, with unexpected resentment. Beneath the surface

back home: antisemites and making things miserable and unhappy, so I didn't want to go back to school.

So we stayed there from March until the 4th of July. And then we went . . . to New York to visit my mother's aunt and cousins who came in the 1920s to the United States. And so we visited them just supposedly for a few days, but then we saw that there were a lot more Jews in New York, more people my age that I could possibly communicate with and learn from and start a life. Because I was 18, but I was, in fact, only thirteen because those years were nothing. Those were erased from my life. So I was thirteen years old in an eighteen-year old girl's body. And I didn't know anything.

I was a frightened little girl. I could not communicate with anybody except the immediate family, my mother's sister and brother-in-law and their son, their only son. And then we went to New York again. My mother's aunt and her cousin. I couldn't go out to the street. I was petrified. I was

was always the unasked question, "Why did you survive when so many others perished?" They swam with the American tide and bowed to the American pressure to get on with the future. Still, they had an enduring sense of being different, and of loss. Cecilie Klein-Pollack was born in Czechoslovakia and deported to Auschwitz in 1944. As she reflected upon her years since the war, she said:

We survived but our lives were destroyed. Though we look like you, we can never be like you. We wear nice clothes like you. We take vacations like you. We make beautiful affairs [and invite many friends], but the ones I wanted most, they never arrived. And we go to funerals and we cry for the ones that we never buried. The first grave that I have is now of my husband. I always wake up at night and think of them.

I wanted to have lots of children because each child I thought I am bringing back from Auschwitz.

But in the end, survivors could not keep silent. It didn't work for them or for the generation that followed. They felt themselves responsible to the past and for the future Helen Goldkind's experience was not atypical for survivors.

I had to have help because of the nightmares. The nightmares were terrible. The nightmares were very exhausting. And you can't control them. You cannot control a nightmare. . . .

The reason why I decided to talk about it is because I really think it's important. I know I cannot bring back my family, my little brother, the million and a half children that were destroyed, that were gassed, but perhaps maybe I could reach some people and make them understand that this did happen and it can happen again if we are not going to be aware of our surroundings.

I think that every person on earth should examine this, what has happened in the Holocaust because a thing like that can happen again and we need to watch that it should never happen again to any minority. And therefore I feel I need to get this across to the world, maybe even to our future generation and tell them that this cruelty has been done to people from other people and to watch out.

There is an urgency to survivors' testimony. Almost a half century after the Holocaust, time is running out. Within a decade or two, the last of the survivors will be gone.

They were bidden to speak by those they left behind. And so they did, despite the temptation of silence, despite their fear that words were inadequate to convey what they had experienced. They understood that silence consigned the victims to oblivion and their murders to even greater meaninglessness. Only remembrance could salvage some meaning from the ashes of Auschwitz. The dead had died merely for the accident of their Jewish ancestry. Their deaths could serve as a warning, but only if the story was told from generation to generation.

Sergeant William Best greets nineteen-year-old Joseph Guttman, survivor of Buchenwald, whom he adopted. New York, December 24, 1948. *National Archives, Washington, D.C.*

AFTERWORD

The central theme of the story of the Holoaust is not regeneration and rebirth, goodness or resistance, liberation or justice, but death and destruction, dehumanization and devastation, and, above all, loss.

Millions were murdered, worlds were shattered, cities were without Jews and soon even without the memory of Jews. The center of Jewish life had shifted from Europe to the United States and Israel. For those who speak a Jewish language, the language had changed from Yiddish to Hebrew. The main body of Jewish scholarship was written in English and no longer in German. And throughout Europe, the ashes of the dead were all that remained of the past. The losses were overwhelming in number — two out of three European Jews were dead; nine out of ten in Poland, Lithuania, Latvia, Czechoslovakia.

Behind each loss was a person whose life was ended tragically and prematurely. And for those who survived, there were the burdens of memory, haunting memories, nonheroic memories of worlds shattered and destroyed, of defeat, and of life in its aftermath.

The killers were civilized men and women of an advanced culture. They were both ordinary and extraordinary, a cross section of the men and women of Germany, its allies, and their collaborators as well as the best and the brightest. Their deeds were a paradigmatic manifestation of human evil intensified by the power of the state, fueled by technological and scientific achievement, and unchecked by moral, social, religious, or political constraints.

Whether restricted to the past or a harbinger of the future, the killers demonstrated that systematic mass destruction is possible. Under contemporary conditions, the execution of such a policy would only be easier.

But what of those of us who were not there? The Holocaust cannot be reduced to order, or even to a sense of overriding meaning. The event defies meaning and negates hope. How, then, are we to approach it?

Our first task is comprehension, understanding what at first seems incomprehensible. The philosopher Hannah Arendt, herself a refugee from Nazi Germany, called the Holocaust the burden of our century. Arendt wrote of the challenge of coming to an understanding of the Holocaust, the need to face the reality without closing ourselves off to the sorrow that comes with knowledge:

Comprehension does not mean denying the outrageous, deducing the unprecedented from precedence, or explaining phenomena by such analogies and generalities that the impact of reality and the shock of experience are no longer felt.

Comprehension is an act of involvement:

It means, rather, examining and bearing consciously the burden which our century has placed on us — neither denying its existence nor submitting meekly to its weight.

Our second task is to deal with the meaning of the Holocaust and the absence of meaning: to confront the fact that mass murder was a self-justifying goal of state policy. There is a natural tendency to seek simple answers and assign a singular meaning to these events in order to cushion the horror and shield us from its assault on the mind and the emotions. Some have sought solace in the creation of Israel and the return of the Jewish people to their ancient homeland. Others have sought to find a sense of meaning in the tenacity of the human spirit. The eminent literary critic Terrence Des Pres closed his moving study of life in the death camps with the words of a survivor: "It wasn't the ruthlessness that enabled an individual to survive. It was an intangible quality . . . an overriding thirst — perhaps, too, a talent for life, and a faith in life."

Some commentators, among them Rabbi Harold Schulweis and sociologist Samuel Oliner, find even in the evil of the Holocaust some redeeming goodness. They point to the altruistic person and the power of men and women to do good, to resist evil, to save and to rescue. Yet however great the nobility, no matter how significant the gestures of solidarity, the Holocaust is a bleak story, an unrelenting tale of evil and woe. It leads to anger, to rage, and to a feeling of impotence. So many died, so little was done, so few were saved.

We tend to back away from the real story, to shield ourselves from the darkness as a way to preserve our self-esteem as human beings, to fortify our confidence in humanity itself. Thus the Israelis speak of Holocaust and Resistance Day, as if the one somehow balanced the other. Germans and Austrians seek to recover instances of resistance, moments of decency amid the evil. Americans speak of survivors and not of victims; we want to know about the righteous, but not the collaborators, the cowards, or those who were indifferent. Yet truth is orphaned when we try to mitigate the awesome evil of the Holocaust.

According to Lawrence Langer, the apparent meaninglessness of the Holocaust defies our need to make sense of the past:

History assures us that man is superior to time when he can explain the unexpected, account in this instance for the extermination of a people, uncover a system for surviving and thus reduce the event to a partial intellectual order that somehow theoretically balances the price in human lives paid for that order.

But because "the disorder of meaningless death contradicts the ordering impulses of time," we cannot close the account. "Those who died for nothing during the Holocaust," Langer writes, "left the living with a perpetually present grief." He suggests that we are increasingly haunted by the Holocaust "as the event recedes into the past," because "there is no inner space or time to bury it in." In my own work, I have repeatedly used the image of a void — emptiness and absence — where presence had been. We must face that void.

Our third task is to live in the aftermath of the Holocaust: to live authentically, creatively, meaningfully. But how?

Historian Yehuda Bauer enunciated three commandments as the human imperative of the Holocaust. "Thou shalt not be a victim. Thou shalt not be a perpetrator. Above all, thou shalt not be a bystander."

Emil Fackenheim, a survivor of Sachsenhausen, was permitted in 1939 to emigrate to Canada, where he became one of the preeminent Jewish philosophers of our time. His understanding of the Holocaust underwent change over time, a change that reflected the growing interest in the event by scholars and the general public alike. Fackenheim first attempted to prove that history must not change the content of faith. He confessed to failure in 1967. Fackenheim then set out to find a moral imperative in the ashes of Auschwitz. The "commanding voice of Auschwitz" said that Hitler must not be granted "posthumous victories," Fackenheim wrote. But over time, even this magisterial response was not sufficient. For Fackenheim and his fellow post-Holocaust thinkers, the event has become a defining moment of twentieth-century humanity, a moment which all too starkly reveals what we can become.

In his recent writings, Fackenheim has concluded that the Holocaust was a rupture of philosophy, faith, history, and culture — a rent in the very fabric of society and civilization itself. The task of those who live in its aftermath is to mend, to patch together by creative deeds the fabric of our own humanity. Fackenheim knows the dictum of Rabbi Nachman of Bratzlav: "Nothing is as whole as a heart that has been broken." He also understands that stitching by the seamstress makes the mended place the strongest part of the garment. Where there has been this kind of repair — such as the Vatican II proclamation on the Jews — we may find hope.

Elie Wiesel, the bard of the Holocaust, has also offered an image of how to live in its aftermath: "In a world of absurdity, we must invent reason, we must create beauty out of nothingness. And because there is murder in the world . . . and we know how helpless our battle may appear, we have to fight murder and absurdity and give meaning to the battle, if not to our hope." Irving Greenberg, a leader of modern Jewish orthodox thought, has embraced Wiesel's existential logic and given it a theological cast. In a world where the images of God and humanity have been shattered, he believes, we must recreate the divine image in the world and restore our sense that humanity is created in the divine image. God is shattered; so, too, creation.

Richard Rubenstein, whose pioneering work, *After Auschwitz*, first raised theological questions about the Holocaust and thus set the agenda for post-Holocaust thought, believes the ultimate question left by the Holocaust is how nations will treat those people who are superfluous, who have no rightful economic place in society. The mass murder of "superfluous" people is the perennial temptation of the modern state. In the United States, we have such people — the old, who no longer work; the young, who do not work; the unemployed, who cannot find work; the despairing poor, many of them minorities, who live from generation to generation without work. We have established a covenant of social justice where the working population educates the young, gives social security to the elderly, and provides minimum services for the needy. Will the strains of economic dislocation, now even more stressful than when Rubenstein first wrote *The Cunning of History*, break the covenant?

The Holocaust transforms our understanding. It shatters faith — religious faith in God and secular faith in human goodness and progress. The memory of the Holocaust has been seared into our consciousness. Its truth has been told not to provide answers, but to raise questions. To live authentically in its aftermath, one must be aware of the reality of radical evil and its startling triumphs, and fight against that evil and that triumph.

How then do we build on the ashes? Slowly, tenderly, humanely. With humility, perhaps with hope. We must teach ourselves and our children by example and by deed about suffering. Suffering itself is not the key to greatness or accomplishment. It confers no honors, yields no virtue. Suffering demands confrontation and, above all, alleviation. To ennoble suffering is to condone it in some measure. It must never be rationalized. In a world where life is precarious, lives must become ever more precious. The Holocaust cannot be allowed to numb us to evil, but it must sensitize us and alarm us. It must sharpen our insights into the importance of human rights and human dignity everywhere.

For Israelis, confrontation with the Holocaust has led to a renewed understanding of their own national goals: a homeland for Jews seeking a haven; a place to recreate life and live in freedom; an end to Jewish vulnerability; and the quest for national security through self-reliance and self-defense. It has also led to deep insecurity about the world. The Israelis take threats seriously and promises ever so lightly.

For some Germans and Austrians, the past is best forgotten, buried, or "normalized." Thus, Kurt Waldheim and many of his countrymen developed amnesia about "those" years; Helmut Kohl as Chancellor of Germany sought to get on with the business of state-building, to look toward the future and not to the past. They were not alone. On November 9, 1989, when the Berlin Wall fell, the jubilant mayor of Berlin proclaimed that that date will live in German history, as if the ninth of November had not already entered German history fifty-one years earlier when the synagogues of Germany were set ablaze during *Kristallnacht*. For other Germans, such as Günter Grass and Richard von Weizäcker, an authentic wrestling with the past is essential to any German future, to the rebuilding of German culture, values, literature, and philosophy. Von Weizäcker wrote of the German people that "their forefathers have bequeathed them a heavy legacy."

It is not a matter of overcoming the past. One can do no such thing. The past does not allow itself to be retrospectively altered or undone. But whoever closes his eyes to the past becomes blind to the present. Whoever does not wish to remember inhumanity becomes susceptible to the dangers of new infection.

The most profound change in Christian teaching toward the Jews was initiated by Vatican II, the convocation of bishops convened by Pope John XXIII on October 11, 1962. At the final session of the council three years later, a new teaching, the Declaration on the Relationship of the Church to Non-Christian Religions, *Nostra Atatae*, was promulgated on October 28, the seventh anniversary of Pope John XXIII's election. In this document, proclaimed by Pope Paul VI, the Roman Catholic Church revamped its teaching on the Jews. With the Holocaust as backdrop, it ended many centuries of teaching that the Jews were responsible for the crucifixion of Jesus:

What happened in His passion cannot be blamed upon all the Jews then living without distinction nor upon the Jews of today.

Vatican II denounced the teaching of contempt and called for a change in preaching and teaching regarding the Jews.

The Jews should not be presented as repudiated or cursed by God. . . . All should take pains, then, lest in catechetical instruction and in the preaching of God's word they teach anything out of harmony with the truth of the gospel and the spirit of Christ.

Antisemitism was condemned:

The Church repudiates all persecutions against any man. Moreover, mindful of her common patrimony with the Jews and motivated by no political considerations, she deplores the hatred, persecutions and displays of anti-Semitism at any time and from any source.

Though the teaching stopped short of affirming the ongoing life of the Jewish people and their integrity as a continuing religion, it did recognize the roots of Christianity in Judaism and "the spiritual bond linking the people of the New Covenant with Abraham's stock." The synod sought to foster and recommend that mutual understanding and respect which are the fruits of all biblical and theological studies, and of brotherly dialogues. Thus, centuries of Christian teaching were transformed and one of the major sources of antisemitism was removed at least from formal Church teaching.

For Americans, confronting this European event brings us a new recognition of the tenets of American constitutional democracy: a belief in equality and equal justice under law; a commitment to pluralism and toleration, particularly at a time when our society is becoming more diverse than ever before in our history; a determination to restrain government by checks and balances and by the constitutional protections of unalienable rights; and a struggle for human rights as a core national value and a foundation for foreign policy. The Holocaust must shatter the myth of innocence. It has implications for the exercise of power. Those who wrestle with the darkness know it can happen again — even in the most advanced, most cultured, most civilized of societies — but if we are faithful to the best of American values, the most sterling of our national traditions, then we can have confidence that it won't happen here.

The call from the victims — from the world of the dead — was to remember. From the survivors, initial silence has given way to testimony. The burden of memory has been transmitted, and thus shared. From scholars, philosophers, poets, and artists — those who were there and those who were not — we hear the urgency of memory, its agony and anguish, its meaning and the absence of meaning. To live in our age, one must face the void.

Israel Ba'al Shem Tov, the founder of Hasidism, once said: "In forgetfulness is the root of exile. In remembrance the seed of redemption." Whether we can share his hope is uncertain. His fears, we understand all too well.

Let us return to Sachsenhausen once again and listen to the words of one who was there:

I have told you this story not to weaken you
But to strengthen you.
Now it is up to you.

BIBLIOGRAPHICAL NOTE

This account of the Holocaust is based on a wide variety of source material and secondary interpretations. The following note includes the major works drawn upon in the narrative. It also suggests other books for readers who want to learn more about various aspects of the Holocaust.

For those who wish to study further, the material is vast and can be overwhelming. A word of advice may help. Interweaving history with biography and reading primary material in conjunction with secondary sources are good ways to strike a balance between the bleak depersonalization of Holocaust history and the vivid power of individual stories. Diaries and memoirs, oral histories and novels should be read alongside the standard works in the field. These personal accounts make the textbook history come alive and inspire the discipline often required to tackle more extensive reading. The many films that convey the reality of life during the Holocaust are also an important contribution to our understanding.

There are several major histories of the Holocaust. Each has strengths and weaknesses, but they offer the reader an in-depth view of the events described in this work. The most influential of these histories is Raul Hilberg's *The Destruction of the European Jews: Revised and Definitive Edition* (New York: Holmes and Meier, 1985), a three-volume study that has also been condensed into a one-volume college edition. It provides an unequaled insight into how the Holocaust was perpetrated. The work

is considered magisterial by many scholars of the Holocaust. Hilberg used German documentation as his major source. He has been criticized by scholars for what they consider an overreliance on German material as well as his depiction of Jewish leadership as inept in responding to the events of the Holocaust. No one, including those who criticize, has written a better or more enduring work. First published more than thirty years ago, it has stood the test of time.

Lucy Dawidowicz, in *The War Against the Jews* (New York: Holt, Rinehart and Winston, 1975), fills in the story of ghetto life from Jewish documentation. Dawidowicz ends her work at the edge of the death camps, where any attempt at autonomous Jewish history came to an end. Despite its weaknesses, her work is a major exposition of the intentionalist school of Holocaust historiography. According to Dawidowicz, the annihilation of the Jews was central to Hitler's thoughts and plans from 1919 onward.

Martin Gilbert's *The Holocaust: A History of the Jews During the Second World War* (New York: Holt Rinehart and Winston, 1985) is a narrative history of the Holocaust woven from the words of those who were there — victims, perpetrators, and bystanders. What it lacks in analysis, it more than makes up in texture and its conveyance of the emotional power of the event. Gerald Reitlinger's *The Final Solution* (Norvale, NJ: Jason Aronson, 1988), first published in 1953 and updated a decade later, is remarkable for the early understanding it provided of the Holocaust. Much of what Reitlinger wrote less than a decade after the Holocaust has been confirmed by subsequent research.

A multidisciplinary study of the Holocaust combining history and political science, sociology, psychology, literature, and theology is found in *Approaches to Auschwitz*, by Richard L. Rubenstein and John Roth (Atlanta: John Knox, 1987). The work is both comprehensive and insightful, a fine introduction for a beginning student of the Holocaust. Yehuda Bauer's *A History of the Holocaust* (New York: Franklin Watts, 1982) is an excellent textbook that covers the Holocaust with precision and learning. It, too, is a fine place to begin. Nora Levin's *The Holocaust: The Destruction of European Jewry 1933–1945* (New York: Schocken Books, 1973) is strongest in its treatment of resistance. Finally, Leni Yahil's work *The Holocaust: The Fate of European Jews* (Oxford: Oxford University Press, 1991) is comprehensive and insightful. Written by a fine scholar late in her career, it is built on the strong foundation of both earlier works and a generation of research. It is a work of passion and power.

Michael Marrus's *The Holocaust in History* (Hanover and London: Brandeis University Press, 1987) is an excellent assessment of what is known about the Holocaust and what remains unknown. Unlike some other texts, it is a model of clarity and brevity. The collection of essays by John Roth and myself, *Holocaust: Religious and Philosophical Implications* (New York: Paragon Books, 1990), brings together more than a score of the major essays on the Holocaust and is designed to introduce readers to a diverse field of learning.

On American responses to the Holocaust, David Wyman's two books, *Paper Walls* (New York: Pantheon Books, 1985) and *The Abandonment of the Jews* (New York: Pantheon Books, 1984), treat both the prewar years and American wartime policy. Each work stands on its own as an instructive treatment of American policy and the forces that shaped it. Taken together, they provide overwhelming evidence of inaction, indifference, and inattention. Henry Feingold, in *The Politics of Rescue* (New Brunswick: Rutgers University Press, 1970), offers a good understanding of the political context in which American policy developed. Alan M. Kraut and Richard Breitman's *American Refugee Policy and European Jews* (Bloomington and London: Indiana University Press, 1987) is a balanced treatment of American policy. An early work by Arthur Morse, *While Six Million Died* (New York: Hart Publishing, 1967), first called attention to American inaction and to the role of the American Jewish community during the Holocaust. Martin Gilbert's *Auschwitz and the Allies: A Devastating Account of How the Allies Responded to the News of Hitler's Mass Murder* (New York: Holt, Rinehart and Winston, 1981) treats the evolution of knowledge of the final solution and inaction on three continents.

Three works on the American press are also of significance. Deborah Lipstat's *Beyond Belief: The American Press and the Coming of the Holocaust* (New York: The Free Press, 1986) details American press coverage of the Holocaust. Robert W. Ross, in *So It Was True: The American Protestant Press and the Persecution of the Jews* (Minneapolis: University of Minnesota Press, 1980), chronicles the response of the Christian press to the Holocaust as it was taking place, and Haskel Lookstein has detailed the response of the American Jewish press in his work *Were We Our Brother's Keepers?* (New York: Hartmore House, 1985). In the early 1980s, former Justice Arthur J. Goldberg was asked to chair a commission inquiring into the role of American Jews and their organizations during the Holocaust. In the end, the commission could not agree on a joint report, but it did publish a series of papers that shed light on the issues confronting the American Jewish community. Yehuda Bauer's ongoing studies of the American Jewish Joint Distribution Committee in *My Brother's Keeper: A History of the American Joint Distribution Committee* (Philadelphia: Jewish Publication Society, 1974) and *American Jews and the Holocaust* (Detroit: Wayne State University Press, 1981) are models of judicious and balanced understanding. Ironically, this chief defender of American Jews is an Israeli. Rafael Medoff, *The Deafening Silence: American Jewish Leadership and the Holocaust* (New York: Shapolsky Publishers, 1987) and Monty Penkower, *Jews Were Expendable* (Urbana and Chicago: University of Illinois Press,

1983), are less charitable in their treatment of American Jews.

The World Must Know begins with the American entry into Nazi concentration camps. Robert Abzug's *Inside the Vicious Heart* (Oxford: Oxford University Press, 1985) is an invaluable account of the American liberation of the camps. Dwight David Eisenhower's *Crusade in Europe* (Garden City, NY: Doubleday, 1948) describes his visit to Ohrdruf. *The Liberation of the Nazi Concentration Camps 1945* (Washington: United States Holocaust Memorial Council, 1987), by colleagues Brewster Chamberlin and Marcia Feldman, contains valuable original testimony. So do the oral history collections of the United States Holocaust Memorial Museum and the Crawford Center at Emory University in Atlanta.

The sources for our understanding of the background of Jews before the Holocaust are extensive. Only a few can be cited. For an understanding of antisemitism, see Rosemary Reuther, *Faith and Fratricide: The Theological Roots of Antisemitism* (New York: Seabury Press, 1974); Norman Cohn, *Warrant for Genocide: The Myth of a Jewish World Conspiracy and the Protocols of the Elders of Zion* (Providence: Brown Judaic Series, 1981); Alan T. Davies, *Antisemitism and the Foundations of Christianity* (New York: Paulist Press, 1979). Leon Poliakov's *A History of Antisemitism* (New York: Vanguard Press, 1975) is rightfully regarded as a major work. The first part of Hannah Arendt's *The Origin of Totalitarianism* (Cleveland: World Publishing, 1951) and Richard Rubenstein's *After Auschwitz: Radical Theology and Contemporary Judaism* (Indianapolis, Bobbs-Merrill, 1966) offer important insights into antisemitism and the death camps. Robert Wistrich's work, *Antisemitism: the Longest Hatred* (New York: Pantheon, 1992), is both scholarly and easily accessible to the nonscholarly reader. Franklin Littel's *The Crucifixion of the Jews* (New York: Harper & Row, 1975) and A. Roy Eckardt's *Elder and Younger Brothers: the Encounter of Jews and Christians* (New York: Charles Scribner's Sons, 1967) are attempts to confront the implications of this long history of antisemitism for contemporary Christians. Paul van Buren's extended theological work in books such as *Discerning the Way: A Theology of the Jewish-Christian Reality* (New York: Seabury Press, 1980), and *Christ in Context: A Theology of Jewish-Christian Reality* (San Francisco: Harper, 1988) is the most compelling reexamination of Protestant thought in the aftermath of the Holocaust.

For the Nazi ascent to power, Karl Dietrich Bracher's *The German Dictatorship: The Origins, Structure and Effects of National Socialism* (New York: Praeger, 1970) and Martin Brozat's *Hitler and the Collapse of Weimar Germany* (New York: Berg, 1987) are important works. William Sheridan Allen's *The Nazi Seizure of Power: The Experience of a Single German Town* (New York: Franklin Watts, 1973) traces the rise of nazism in Thalburg. Other studies of Hitler's rise include Henry Turner's *German Big Business and the Rise of Hitler* (New Haven: Yale University Press, 1985) and Richard F. Hamilton, *Who Voted for Hitler* (Princeton: Princeton University Press, 1982).

Karl A. Schleunes's *The Twisted Road to Auschwitz* (Urbana and Chicago: University of Illinois Press, 1970) contains an important discussion of the anti-Jewish boycott and the formative years of the Nazi regime. The work of Raul Hilberg is also significant in detailing the evolution of Nazi policy.

Maurice Friedman's middle volume of his three-volume biography, *Martin Buber's Life and Work: The Middle Years 1923–45* (New York: E. P. Dutton, 1983), is an invaluable source on Buber's life during the Holocaust years. Leonard Baker's *Days of Sorrow and Pain: Leo Baeck and the Berlin Jews* (Oxford: Oxford University Press, 1978) and Albert Friedlander's *Leo Baeck Teacher of Theresienstadt* (New York: Holt, Rinehart and Winston, 1968) are fine, if overly laudatory, accounts of the life of German Jewry's leader.

The Evian Conference is treated in David Wyman, *Paper Walls*; Henry Feingold, *The Politics of Rescue*; and Saul S. Friedman, *No Haven for the Oppressed* (Detroit: Wayne State University Press, 1973). Irving Abella and Harold Troopers, *None Is Too Many* (New York: Random House, 1983), which discusses Canadian policy toward the Jews, is an excellent source.

The segment on enemies of the state is based on the author's work, *A Mosaic of Victims: Non-Jews Persecuted and Murdered by the Nazis* (New York: New York University Press, 1990) and on other works about each victim group.

Bohdan Wytwycky's *The Other Holocaust: The Many Circles of Hell* (Washington, DC: The Novak Report on the New Ethnicity, 1980) provides an excellent framework in which to understand the multiplicity of Holocaust victims. Richard Plant's *The Pink Triangle* (New York: Holt, 1986) and Ruediger Lautmann's article "The Pink Triangle: The Homosexual Male in Concentration Camps," in *The Journal of Homosexuality* vol. 6 (1981), are significant sources on the Nazi persecution of homosexuals. Donald Kendrick and Grattan Puxon's *The Destiny of Europe's Gypsies* (New York: Basic Books, 1973) is an important source on the Gypsies. In addition, I have relied upon the work of Sybil Milton, a resident historian at the museum, a report prepared for the museum by Gabrielle Tyrnauer, and extensive correspondence with Ian Hancock of the University of Texas, who has been vigilant in pressing for the inclusion of the Gypsies in any discussion of the Holocaust. Christine King's work *The Nazi State and the New Religions* (New York: E. Mellen Press, 1982) describes the Jehovah's Witnesses. Also recommended is Ian Krenshaw's *Popular Opinion and Political Dissent in the Third Reich: Bavaria 1933–45* (Oxford: Oxford University Press, 1985). John Conway's *The Nazi Persecution of the Churches 1933–45* (New York: Basic Books, 1968) is an important source for religious persecution by the Nazis.

Important works on Nazi racism are George Mosse's *The Crisis of German Ideology: Intellectual Origins of the Third Reich* (New York: Grosset and Dunlap, 1964), Leon Poliakov's *The Aryan Myth: A History of Racist and Nationalism Ideas in Europe* (New York: New American Library, 1974), and Fritz Stern's *The Politics of Cultural Despair: A Study in the Rise of Germanic Ideology* (Berkeley: University of California Press, 1961). Robert Jay Lifton's *The Nazi Doctors: Medical Killing and the Psychology of Genocide* (New York: Basic Books, 1986) is a major study of the development and practice of Nazi medicine by an eminent American psychoanalyst and ethicist. Robert Proctor's *Racial Hygiene: Medicine Under the Nazis* (Cambridge: Harvard University Press, 1988) and Benno Müller-Hill's *Murderous Science: Elimination by Scientific Selection of Jews, Gypsies, and Others, Germany 1933–1945* (Oxford: Oxford

University Press, 1988) are also helpful in understanding scientific racism, eugenics, and euthanasia.

The best material on the Expansion without War is Radomir Luza's *Austro-German Relations in the Anschluss Era* (Princeton: Princeton University Press, 1975) and Gehard Botz's article "The Jews in Vienna from the Anschluss to the Holocaust," in Ivan Oxaal, ed., *Jews, Antisemitism and Culture in Vienna* (London: 1987).

Richard Lukas, *The Forgotten Holocaust: The Poles Under German Occupation, 1939–1944* (Lexington: University of Kentucky Press, 1986), and Yisrael Gutman and Shmuel Krakowski, *Unequal Victims: Poles and Jews During World War Two* (New York: Holocaust Library, 1986), provide two conflicting but important assessments of the victimization of the Poles. Gutman and Krakowski argue for a differentiation between the victims and Lukas sees many parallels between Nazi policy toward the Jews and the Poles.

The Holocaust in France is covered in Michael R. Marrus and Robert O. Paxton's *Vichy France and the Jews* (New York: Basic Books, 1981) and Robert Aron's *The Vichy Regime*. Jacob H. Boas's *Boulevard des Misères: The Story of Transit Camp Westerbork* (Hamden, CT: Anchor Books, 1985) and Jacob Presser's *The Destruction of Dutch Jews* (Detroit: Wayne State University Press, 1988) are critical to understanding the subject.

The final days of Anne Frank are chronicled by Willy Lindwer, who has compiled extensive interviews with her friends and colleagues in *Anne Frank: The Last Seven Months* (New York: Pantheon Books, 1991).

There are many studies of the Warsaw ghetto. The most authoritative is Yisrael Gutman's *The Warsaw Ghetto* (Bloomington and London: Indiana University Press, 1982). There are wonderful original sources on the Warsaw ghetto including several major diaries. The most important are *Notes from the Warsaw Ghetto: The Journal of Emmanuel Ringelblum* (New York, Schocken Books, 1958); Janusz Korczak, *Ghetto Diary* (New York: Holocaust Library, 1978); *The Warsaw Diary of Chaim A. Kaplan* (New York: Collier Books, 1965); and *The Warsaw Diary of Adam Czerniaków* (New York: Stein and Day, 1979), with an introduction by Raul

Hilberg. The subtitle of this edition, *Prelude to Doom*, is an apt phrase for Czerniaków's agony. Hilberg's respected article "The Ghetto As a Form of Government," which appeared in John Roth and Michael Berenbaum's *Holocaust: Religious and Philosophical Implications*, provides a clear depiction of the problems faced by the leader of the largest ghetto in Europe. Betty Jean Lifton's *The King of the Children: A Biography of Janusz Korczak* (New York: Farrar Straus Giroux, 1988) is a passionate, moving exposition of his life and an excellent source for both the experience of children in the Holocaust and life inside the doomed ghetto. Reuben Ainsztein's *The Warsaw Ghetto Revolt* (New York: Holocaust Library, 1979) is an important description of the uprising. Vladka Meed's *On Both Sides of the Wall* (New York: Holocaust Library, 1979) is a vivid description by a woman who was an arms courier for the resistance.

All studies of the Jewish Councils have benefited greatly from Isaiah Trunk's masterful treatment, *Judenrat: The Jewish Councils in Eastern Europe Under Nazi Occupation* (New York: Macmillan, 1972), an exhaustive treatment of Jewish Councils throughout Eastern Europe. Undertaken in part to refute Hannah Arendt's depiction of Jewish leadership, Trunk nevertheless substantiates her accusations as often as he dismisses them. After Trunk's work, simple generalizations about the *Judenrat* are much more difficult to make, while their plight is much more understandable. For Lódź, Lucjan Dobroszycki's English edition of *The Chronicle of the Lódź Ghetto 1941–44* (New Haven and London: Yale University Press, 1984) stands as the definitive source. *The Lódź Ghetto: Inside a Community Under Siege*, edited by Alan Adelson and Robert Lapides, provides excellent additional source material. Gila Flam's book *Singing for Survival: Songs of the Lódź Ghetto 1940–45* (Urbana and Chicago: University of Illinois Press, 1992) approaches the Lódź ghetto from the perspective of its music. *Surviving the Holocaust: The Kovno Ghetto Diary* by Abraham Tory (Cambridge: Harvard University Press, 1990) is an important work. Tory was an official of the *Judenrat* and a firsthand observer and chronicler. The commentary by Dina Porat is a model of how to make complicated technical information accessible to a nonscholarly audience.

On Theresienstadt, Ruth Bondy's work, *Elder of the Jews: Jacob Edelstein of Theresienstadt* (New York: Grove Press, 1989), is significant. The most authoritative source is H. G. Adler's German-language work on Theresienstadt. For the children of Theresienstadt, see *I Never Saw Another Butterfly* and Elena Makarova's *From Bauhaus to Terezin: Friedl Dicker-Brandeis and Her Pupils* (Jerusalem: Yad Vashem, 1990).

Christopher Browning's *Ordinary Men: Reserve Police Battalion 101 and the Final Solution in Poland* (New York and San Francisco: Harper Collins, 1991) is a very valuable study of the Einsatzgruppen. His work *Fateful Months: Essays in the Emergence of the Final Solution* (New York: Holmes and Meier, 1985) has also proved helpful in narrowing the debate as to when the decision on the Final Solution was made. Charles Sydnor, Jr., *Soldiers of Destruction: The SS Death Head Division 1933–45* (Princeton: Princeton University Press, 1977), is an important study of the killers. *The Black Book*, edited by Ilya Ehrenburg and Vasily Grossman, which details the Nazi destruction of Soviet Jews, was suppressed by Stalin. Parts of their report were published by the Holocaust Library in New York, and an unexpurgated version will soon be published in Russia and Jerusalem. It provides important information on the Einsatzgruppen, as does Ernst Klee, Willi Dressen, and Volker Riess's account of the perpetrators in *The Good Old Days: The Holocaust as Seen by Its Perpetrators and Bystanders* (New York: Free Press, 1988).

Radu Ioanid's *The Sword of the Archangel: Fascist Ideology in Romania* (Boulder: Eastern European Monographs, 1990) is the initial work of a promising scholar who continues to research the Holocaust in Romania.

Raul Hilberg's study of the German railway system, "The Role of the German Railroads in the Destruction of the Jews," is still the major work in the field. It was published in *Society* (November / December 1976).

Benjamin Ferencz, *Less Than Slaves: Jewish Forced Labor and the Quest for Compensation* (Cambridge: Harvard University Press, 1979), and Edward Homze, *Foreign Labor in Nazi Germany* (Princeton: Princeton University Press, 1967), are valuable in describing the Nazi use and abuse of slave labor.

Yitzhak Arad's work *Belzec, Sobibór, Treblinka: The Operation Reinhard Death Camps* is an invaluable resource on the death camps. The literature on Auschwitz is extensive. The museum's collection of essays, *Auschwitz* (New York: Hill and Wang, 1993), includes the fruit of major contemporary research. Danuta Czech's *Auschwitz Chronicle* (New York: Holt, 1990) is an important work now available in English. There are many important memoirs written about Auschwitz. The classic memoirs are Elie Wiesel's *Night* (New York: Hill and Wang, 1960) and Primo Levi's *Survival in Auschwitz* (New York: Collier, 1986). Charlotte Delbo's *None of Us Will Return* (New York: Grove Press, 1968) is a fascinating account by a non-Jewish woman. Dr. Miklos Nyiszli's *Auschwitz* (Greenwich, CT: Fawcett Crest, 1960) is written by a physician, as is Elie Cohen's *The Abyss* (New York: W. W. Norton, 1973). Two other works among the many memoirs should also be explored. Viktor Frankl's *Man's Search for Meaning: An Introduction to Logotherapy* (New York: Pocket Books, 1963) is a sensitive, brilliantly simple account of life inside the inferno. Isabella Leitner's *Fragments of Isabella* (New York: Dell, 1983) describes the life of a young Hungarian Jewess who arrived in the camp and survived.

Samuel P. Oliner and Perl M. Oliner's *The Altruistic Personality: Rescuers of Jews in Nazi Europe: What Led Ordinary Men and Women to Risk Their Lives on Behalf of Others* (New York: Free Press, 1988), is an interesting study of the sociology and psychology of rescuers and their values. Carol Rittner, RSM, edited *The Courage to Care* (New York: New York University Press, 1986), which covers the conference on rescuers sponsored by the United States Holocaust Memorial Council. Leni Yahil's *The Rescue of Danish Jewry* (Philadelphia: Jewish Publication Society, 1969) is still the definitive work on the subject. Leo Goldberger, who was among those rescued, has edited a fine work, *The Rescue of the Danish Jews: Moral Courage Under Stress* (New York: New York University Press, 1987). Helen Fein's *Accounting for Genocide* (New York: Free Press, 1979) is an excellent sociological account on how genocide happens. Her concept of the universe of moral obligation is most helpful in describing why some chose to rescue while others remained indifferent.

OJGABE FUN JIDISZN CENTRAL-KOMITET FAR DER AMERIKANISZER ZONE IN ESTRAJCH

Post-Holocaust poster. A political plea for justice, this poster reads: "If there is justice in the world, let it appear immediately." Jewish Central Committee for the American Zone in Austria. 1947. *On loan from YIVO Institute for Jewish Research, New York. Photo USHMM.*

Philip Hallie's *Lest Innocent Blood Be Shed: The Story of the Village of Le Chambon and How Goodness Happened There* (New York: Harper & Row, 1979), is still the best study of the small French village. The museum now has an oral history collection on Le Chambon supplemented by the recollections of our librarian, a child saved in the village. A study of the White Rose should begin with a book by that name, Inge Scholl's *White Rose* (Middletown: Wesleyan University Press, 1983). Emil Fackenheim's *To Mend the World* (New York: Schocken Books, 1989) contains an important description of Professor Huber's work.

David Wyman's work on the War Refugee Board in *The Abandonment of the Jews* is significant. So, too, are the personal papers of Josiah Dubois, to which I had access when they were deposited at the Museum of American Jewish History in Philadelphia. Jan Karski, my colleague at Georgetown University, has been kind enough to grant me access to his papers as well as his oral history presentations to the museum and in Claude Lanzmann's masterpiece, the film *Shoah*. An understanding of Gerhard Riegner's role is clear in his oral history now on deposit in the museum and in Walter Laqueur and Richard Breitman's intriguing portrait of Eduard Schulte in *Breaking the Silence* (New York: Simon and Schuster, 1986). Laqueur's other work on the Holocaust, *The Terrible Secret: Suppression of the Truth about Hitler's Final Solution* (Boston: Little, Brown, 1980), is an authoritative treatment of what was known by the perpetrators, the victims, and the bystanders (including the Allies and the Vatican) and what was done with that knowledge. Laqueur's distinction between information and knowledge is pivotal to our understanding of inaction.

Any study of Hungarian Jews and the Holocaust must begin with Randolph Braham, *The Politics of Genocide: The Holocaust in Hungary* (New York: Columbia University Press, 1981). Per Anger's *With Raoul Wallenberg in Budapest* (New York: Holocaust Library, 1981) is a fine firsthand account. John Bierman's *Righteous Gentile: The Story of Raoul Wallenberg, Missing Hero of the Holocaust* (New York: Viking Press, 1981) is a respected biography of the Swedish hero.

Susan Zuccotti's *The Italians and the Holocaust: Persecution, Rescue, Survival* (New York: Basic Books, 1987) is a balanced treatment of the Italian record. Ivo Herzer's *The Italian Refuge: Rescue of Jews During the Holocaust* (Washington: Catholic University Press, 1989) is a fine collection of essays on the Italian rescue.

Hannah Szenes is the subject of an excellent biography by Peter Hay, *Ordinary Heroes: Chana Szenes and the Dream of Zion* (New York: G. P. Putnam's Sons, 1986). *Hannah Senesh: Her Life and Diary* (New York: Schocken Books, 1973) provides insights into her life and struggle. Callum MacDonald has written a fascinating, detective-like thriller in *The Killing of SS Obengruppenfuhrer Reinhard Heydrich* (New York: Free Press, 1989), the event that triggered the destruction of Lidice.

On resistance, Yuri Suhl's *They Fought Back* (New York: Crown, 1987) is a valuable collection of firsthand accounts of resistance and a fierce polemic against Raul Hilberg. Yitzhak Arad's work *Belzec, Sobibór, Treblinka: The Operation Reinhard Death Camps* contains valuable material on resistance in Sobibór and Treblinka. Richard Strauss and Chiel Rajchman's oral histories at the United States Holocaust Memorial Museum are also invaluable. Richard Rashke's *Escape from Sobibór: The Heroic Story of the Jews who Escaped from a Nazi*

Death Camp (Boston: Houghton Mifflin, 1982) is informative.

As to the displaced persons and Bricha, Yehuda Bauer's *Flight and Rescue: Bricha* (New York: Random House, 1970), Leonard Dinnerstein's *America and the Survivors of the Holocaust* (New York: Columbia University Press, 1982), and Mark Wyman's *DP: Europe's Displaced Persons* (Philadelphia: Balch Institute Press, 1988) provide important background information on the DP camps. William Helmrich's unpublished work on survivors who resettled in the United States and Herbert Friedman's unfinished memoirs have also been valuable.

On liberation, two works have been most helpful: Robert Abzug, *Inside the Vicious Heart* (Oxford: Oxford University Press, 1985), and John Bridgman, *The End of the Holocaust: The Liberation of the Camps* (Portland: Areopagitica Press, 1990). The resources of the museum's oral history collection are invaluable.

For the Nuremberg Trials of Nazi war criminals, Robert E. Conot's *Justice at Nuremberg* (New York: Harper & Row, 1983) is a fine treatment. Kai Bird's biography of John J. McCloy, *The Chairman: John J. McCloy, The Making of the American Establishment* (New York: Simon and Schuster, 1992), enables us to understand the role of politics and pressure that led to commuting the sentences of the Nazi war criminals. Michael Musmanno's *The Eichmann Kommandos* (Philadelphia: Macrae Smith, 1961) and Victor Bernstein's *Final Judgment* (London: Latimer House, 1947) are most helpful. The multivolume publication of the proceedings of the International Military Tribunal are indispensable.

John Loftus's *The Belarus Secret* (New York: Alfred Knopf, 1982), Charles Ashman and Robert J. Wagman's *The Nazi Hunters* (New York: Pharos Books, 1988), and Alan Ryan's *Quiet Neighbors* (New York: Harcourt Brace Jovanovich, 1984) tell the story of the escape of Nazi war criminals and their resettlement as free men.

There are excellent biographies of Hitler. Among the best are Alan Bullock's *Hitler: A Study in Tyranny* (New York: Harper & Row, 1964); Gerald Fleming's *Hitler and the Final Solution* (Berkeley: University of California Press, 1984); and Robert G. L. Waite's *The Psychopathic God: Adolf Hitler* (New York: Basic

Books, 1977). Richard Breitman's *The Architect of Genocide: Himmler and the Final Solution* (New York: Alfred Knopf, 1991) is a valuable new addition to the field.

The controversy surrounding the Eichmann trial and Hannah Arendt's interpretation of Eichmann's role was a watershed in the historiography of the Holocaust. Jacob Robinson's polemical response, *And the Crooked Shall Be Made Straight* (New York: Macmillan, 1965), was the first of many works to deal with the Arendt controversy. Gideon Hausner, Eichmann's prosecutor, wrote his memoir of the trial in *Eichmann in Jerusalem* (New York: Schocken Books, 1966). Elizabeth Young-Bruehl's *Hannah Arendt: For Love and the World* (New Haven and London: Yale University Press, 1982) presents a sympathetic treatment from Arendt's perspective. Gershom Scholem's exchange with Arendt reprinted in *On Jews and Judaism in Crisis* (New York: Schocken Books, 1976) offers quite a different account.

Nicholas Balabkin's *West German Reparations to Israel* (New Brunswick: Rutgers University Press, 1971) is an excellent treatment of the subject. So, too, is Joseph Borkin's *The Crime and Punishment of I. G. Farben: The Startling Account of the Unholy Alliance of Adolf Hitler and Germany's Great Chemical Combine* (New York: Free Press, 1978). Martin Bergman and Milton E. Jucovy's *Generations of the Holocaust* (New York: Basic Books, 1982) is a collection of important articles on the enduring burden of children of the Holocaust. Helen Epstein's *Children of the Holocaust* (New York: G. P. Putnam's Sons, 1979) is a well-written and moving account of the struggles of children of the Holocaust. Aaron Hass's *In the Shadow of the Holocaust* (New York: Cornell University Press, 1990) is a psychological profile of the second generation of survivors.

Regarding children, the best sources are the hundreds of children's diaries and adult recollections of their childhood experience now extant. Deborah Dwork's *Children with a Star* (New Haven and London: Yale University Press, 1991) collects the diverse children's experiences and gives them some order and coherence. It provides a valuable framework with which to approach the original material. My work in issuing the second edition of

I Never Saw Another Butterfly (New York: Schocken Books, 1993) has brought me new insights about the children of Theresienstadt through their poems and poetry. Yehuda Nir's *Lost Childhood* (New York: Harcourt Brace Jovanovich, 1989) is one of the least romanticized and brutally frank accounts of childhood during the Holocaust. Lucette Matalon Lagnado and Sheila Cohn Dekel's *Children of the Flames: Dr. Joseph Mengele and the Untold Story of the Twins of Auschwitz* (New York: William Morrow, 1991) docs what it sets out to do. It tells the story of the twins.

Two important works on oral history and survivors' testimony are Lawrence Langer's *Holocaust Testimonies: The Ruins of Memory* (New Haven and London: Yale University Press, 1991) and Shoshana Felman and Dore Laub's *Testimony: Crisis of Witnessing in Literature,*

Post-Holocaust poster. "Come to ORT. Don't stand idle on the side! Work! Learn a trade for life." This was posted in displaced persons camps in the American sector. *On loan from YIVO Institute for Jewish Research, New York. Photo USHMM.*

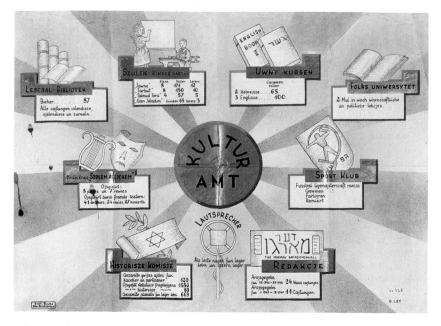

Cultural life exploded in the camps. This poster illustrates the character of life in the DP camps. The books read, schools and classes, the courses in Hebrew and English (for immigration to Palestine and the United States); the folk university; drama performances; sports clubs; historical committee; and newspapers. Bad Reichenhall Germany, 1947. *On loan from YIVO Institute for Jewish Research, New York. Photo USHMM.*

Psychoanalysis and History (New York: Routledge, 1991). Both are drawn from material in the Fortunoff Archive for Holocaust Testimony at Yale University. Langer's other important books are *Versions of Survival: The Holocaust and the Human Spirit* (Albany: State University of New York Press, 1982) and *The Holocaust and the Literary Imagination* (New Haven: Yale University Press, 1975). Several other major works of literary analysis are worth noting. Sidra Ezrachi's *By Words Alone: The Holocaust in Literature* (Chicago: University of Chicago Press, 1980) and Alvin Rosenfeld's *A Double Dying* (Bloomington and London: Indiana University Press, 1980). Terrence Des Pres's *The Survivor: Anatomy of Life in the Death Camps* (Oxford: Oxford University Press, 1980) is an important treatment of survival and its implications. David Roskies's scholarship on Jewish literary responses to catastrophe is informative and sensitive. His works include *Against the Apocalypse: Response to Catastrophe in Modern Jewish Culture* (Cambridge: Harvard University Press, 1984) and his anthology *The Literature of Destruction: Jewish Responses to Catastrophe* (Philadelphia: Jewish Publication Society of America, 1989). Steve Lipman's *Laughter in Hell: The Uses of Humor During the Holocaust* (Norvale, NJ: Jason Aronson, 1991) and Eliezer Berkovits's *With God in Hell: Judaism in the Ghettos and Death Camps* (New York and London: Sanhedrin Press, 1979) explore a variety of forms of Jewish response to catastrophe.

Yehuda Bauer's *Flight and Rescue: Bricha* (New York: Random House, 1970) is central to our understanding of the border crossings en route to Palestine. In Bauer's other works, *From Diplomacy To Resistance* (Philadelphia: Jewish Publication Society, 1970) explores the history of Jewish Palestine between 1939 and 1945, and *Jewish Emergence from Powerlessness* (Toronto: University of Toronto Press, 1979), traces the emergence of Jews from passivity to militancy during and after the Holocaust. Ze'ev Hadari and Z. Tzahor's *Voyage to Freedom: An Episode in the Illegal Immigration to Palestine* (London: Valentine Mitchell, 1985) and Jon and David Kimche's *The Secret Roads* (London: Secker and Warburg, 1954) provide valuable information on illegal immigration to Palestine. Bernard Wasserstein's *Britain and the Jews of Europe, 1939–1945* (Oxford: Oxford University Press, 1979), and Ronald Zweig's *Britain and Palestine during the Second World War* (Woodbridge, UK: Boydell Press, 1987), provide a much wider context for our understanding of the issue.

As to the meaning of the Holocaust, an interested student might first turn to my study, co-authored with John Roth, *Holocaust: Religious and Philosophical Implications.* The twenty-fifth anniversary (second edition) of Richard Rubenstein's *After Auschwitz* (Baltimore: Johns Hopkins University Press, 1992) is another good starting point. Emil Fackenheim's major works include *God's Presence in History* (New York: New York University Press, 1969); *Encounters Between Judaism and Modern Philosophy: A Preface to Modern Jewish Thought* (New York: Basic Books, 1973); *The Jewish Return into History: Reflections in the Age of Auschwitz and a New Jerusalem* (New York: Schocken Books, 1978), as well as *To Mend the World.* Other works of mine, *After Tragedy and Triumph: Modern Jewish Thought and the American Experience* (Cambridge: Cambridge University Press, 1991) and *The Vision the Void: Theological Reflections on the Works of Elie Wiesel* (Middletown, CT: Wesleyan University Press, 1979), explore the religious and philosophical implications of the Holocaust. Anne Roiphe's *A Season for Healing: Reflections on the Holocaust* (New York: Summit Books, 1988) teaches us how to grapple with and perhaps heal the wounds of the Holocaust.

ABOUT THE MUSEUM

The initiative for the creation of the United States Holocaust Memorial Museum came from President Jimmy Carter who, in 1978, appointed a President's Commission on the Holocaust. Under the guidance of its chairman, distinguished writer Elie Wiesel, the commission considered the feasibility of an American Holocaust memorial. After intense deliberation, it recommended that a "living memorial" be established (in the form of a museum and educational center) in Washington, D.C., to preserve the memory of one of the twentieth century's darkest moments so that future generations might learn from the lessons of the past.

In 1980, following upon the commission's findings and by unanimous act of Congress, the United States Holocaust Memorial Council was established and charged with two principal tasks: to conduct an annual national observance for the victims of the Holocaust known as "Days of Remembrance," and to plan and build a national institution dedicated to Holocaust education and remembrance.

In 1987, President Ronald Reagan appointed Harvey M. Meyerhoff to succeed Elie Wiesel as chairman of the Holocaust Memorial Council. A Baltimore-based philanthropist and developer, Meyerhoff oversaw the development phase of the museum. William J. Lowenberg served as his vice-chairman. Albert Abramson chaired the Museum Development Committee, which oversaw the physical construction of the museum building and the exhibition. Miles Lerman chaired the International Relations Committee and the Campaign to Remember, and Benjamin Meed chaired the Content and Days of Remembrance Committee.

In 1989, Jeshajahu Weinberg, who had created Israel's Museum of the Diaspora, was appointed Museum Director to head the professional staff. Weinberg, who pioneered the idea of a story-telling museum in Israel, gave a unique focus to the creation of a historical museum.

Most of the museums and monuments on the national mall celebrate the fruits of democratic freedoms. Yet, by virtue of its contents, the United States Holocaust Memorial Museum reflects the opposite: the disintegration of civilized values and the perversion of technological achievements. Housed in a building designed by architect James Ingo Freed of Pei, Cobb, Freed & Partners, the museum has been built on public lands with funds donated by the American people. Though the central tragedy of the Holocaust did not take place on American soil, this museum's core messages are very much intended for American audiences.

The museum is far more than a memorial to the Jewish genocide. It stands as a testament, and perhaps as a challenge, to the central issue of any democratic society: the responsibility of individuals in a free society, and of a nation dedicated to democratic values, when human freedoms are placed at grievous risk.

View of the Hall of
Witness, United States
Holocaust Memorial
Museum, during
construction, July 1992.
Photo: Alan Gilbert.

The building itself serves as an
introduction to the Holocaust "universe,"
providing subtle architectural metaphors and
reminiscences of historical experience. Four
towers on the north side of the building
evoke the watch towers of the death camps;
triangular shapes repeat throughout the
building, a reminder that prisoners in the
camps were marked with a variety of triangles
to denote their status. The central atriumlike
gathering place of the museum — the Hall of
Witness — is defined by its distortions: a
skewed and twisted skylight; a glass fissure
running the length of the floor. In the idiom
of architectural poetry, the building reflects
the rupture of civilization that took place
during the Holocaust.

In addition to the permanent exhibition,
two special exhibition galleries present
changing installations on complementary
subjects. "Remember the Children," an
exhibition inspired by Mrs. Adeline Yates and
the Committee to Remember the Children of
the United States Holocaust Memorial
Council, tells the story of one child of the
Holocaust, Daniel, a composite but historic
figure who represents the millions of children
who endured similar experiences. "Remember
the Children" provides a continuing,
participatory educational experience for
young visitors ages nine to twelve. A separate
Children's Wall, with thousands of tiles
hand-painted by American schoolchildren,
also commemorates the more than a million
children who perished in the Holocaust.

A multifaceted institution, the United
States Holocaust Memorial Museum addresses
various audiences. An Education Center serves
students, teachers, and interested adults, many
of whom will first encounter the Holocaust
when they visit this museum. A film theater
and auditorium extend the museum's services

through educational programs, cultural events, and film screenings. In the Learning Center, an interactive, computer-based educational facility, visitors pursue self-directed inquiry and learn more about the Holocaust by accessing text, graphics, maps, film footage, movies, and music.

A collection of over thirty thousand Holocaust-related items is catalogued and preserved by the museum's Collections Department. Providing an ever-growing resource for exhibition use as well as loans to other museums, this collection has grown through donations from survivors, liberators, former soldiers, and their families, and through gifts from foreign governments and other sources abroad.

Also housed in the museum facility is the Holocaust Research Institute, a center for scholarship and academic research, which contains a comprehensive library, a large archival collection specializing in the Holocaust, a photo and film archive, and a vast collection of video testimony by Holocaust survivors, perpetrators, and liberators. An active publications program is sponsored by the Research Institute, which publishes The Journal of Holocaust and Genocide Studies.

Serving scholars, researchers, university libraries, regional Holocaust centers, schools, and the general public, the museum's library has developed a specialty collection in the expanding field of Holocaust studies. The Holocaust Archives collects, preserves, organizes, catalogues, and makes available to bona fide researchers original material as well as copies of archival material from Eastern European countries previously inaccessible to Western scholars. The archives also houses the Benjamin and Vladka Meed National Registry of Jewish Holocaust Survivors, which contains the names, cities of birth, camps of incarceration, places of liberation, and communities of resettlement for more than seventy thousand survivors who came to the United States in the aftermath of the Holocaust.

Because remembrance is at the heart of the museum's mission, a solemn and inspiring Hall of Remembrance — designed as a place for both individual contemplation and formal ceremonies — serves as the national memorial to the victims of the Holocaust. During the annual "Days of Remembrance" commemoration, while ceremonies take place in town halls and legislative chambers throughout the nation, a central national observance takes place in our nation's capital within the walls of the Hall of Remembrance.

Too often, the events of the Holocaust seem too enormous to be comprehended. For many, the sheer number of victims — six million Jews, millions of others — cannot be fully understood. By personalizing the history, it comes within our grasp. At the United States Holocaust Memorial Museum, visitors do not learn at a distance; rather, they are brought inside the story. On entering the museum, visitors can punch into a computer and receive an identity card — for an actual person of the same age and gender, who lived at the time of the Holocaust. As visitors move through the exhibition, they can find out what was happening at a given historical moment to their exhibition "twin" — and visitors learn, before they leave the exhibition, whether that person survived or perished. The personalization of experience brings the visitor face to face with history.

The museum confronts difficult questions, questions whose answers are still being formed: what could we have done differently to combat nazism; how could Americans have responded more humanely to European refugees; what course of action, beyond decisive and unconditional military victory, could have been taken in pursuit of rescue?

Standing 1,500 feet away from the Washington Monument in the heart of our national capital — at what columnist George Will has called "the epicenter of our collective life" — the United States Holocaust Memorial Museum reminds each of us how fragile democracy is, and how vigilant we must all remain in defending the core American values — indeed, the core human values — of individual dignity, social justice, and civil rights.

ACKNOWLEDGMENTS

Words of gratitude are in order.

First of all, I must thank Jeshajahu Weinberg — colleague, friend, and the director of the United States Holocaust Memorial Museum — who has shaped the museum in profound ways. Under his diligent and demanding leadership, the singular approach to the Permanent Exhibition was determined and brought to completion. And it is from this exhibition that this book has taken its form.

The design team for the exhibition was headed first by Martin Smith and later by Raye Farr, both brilliant documentary filmmakers who gave completely of themselves. They worked directly with Ralph Appelbaum and his design associates. Their innate individual talents were enhanced by the synergy of the team that was formed. We worked in harmony, in tension, and in constant dialogue with one another. From these efforts, the exhibition was born. I have learned much from our common endeavors.

The museum is blessed with a fine staff, and they have helped shape this work in addition to their ordinary museum assignments. Arnold Kramer is a talented photographer and an excellent photo editor. His temperament makes working with him a pleasure. His assistant, Tina Rosenbaum, has always been helpful and skilled.

Dr. Joan Ringelheim and the research staff of the museum — past and present — have been invariably helpful. Two fine scholars have earned special mention. Dr. Severin Hochberg's research briefs were most informative and often challenging. Dr. David Luebke is a young and promising scholar whose research briefs were informed and often original. His captioning of photographs was meticulous, detailed, and blessedly concise.

Dr. Radu Ioanid, Sara Ogilvie of the museum's photo research teams, Genya Markon, director of the museum's photo archives, and Marcy Zelmar have been most helpful in selecting and authenticating the photographs used in this book. Their research is impeccable.

Holly Snyder, Rebecca Leader, Colette Thayer, and Linda Harris have offered every conceivable cooperation of the Oral History Department to include the significant resources of the museum's collection of oral histories in this work. Their efforts were reliable and timely. They have been most gracious.

Our librarians, Elizabeth Koenig and Olga Shargorodska and William Connelly, have been particularly cooperative. Jacek Nowakowski and the Collections Department he directs have been unusually helpful. Martin Goldman has solved many problems, seemingly effortlessly. Aleisa Fishman and Karen Wyatt have assisted with quotes and copyrights.

Ronald Goldfarb, a distinguished attorney, skilled writer, and wise counsellor, has helped this work in so many ways. He has represented the museum publications program with skill, drive, and humor. We have become fast friends, even family.

Barbara Wolfson has been skilled and patient, intelligent and diligent in working with me on drafts of this work. She has been a wonderful sounding board and a fine intellectual colleague.

Yisrael Gutman, editor of the *Macmillan Encyclopedia of the Holocaust*, was kind enough to read this work. His comments were most helpful.

Lydia Perry, my assistant and friend, has kept this work on track. She has run interference to protect my time. She has taken so much off my shoulders so this work could be done. Moreover, she has read this work many times. As always, even during the most difficult of times, she handles all that is thrown at her with grace and competence. Betsy Chock has stepped in to help out without being asked.

My children, Ilana and Lev, have paid a heavy price for all that I have done. Increasingly, they understand its importance. Increasingly, I understand its cost to them. We are finding a more appropriate balance between all-consuming work and a deeply deserving family. Their love sustains me. It is deeply cherished.

Finally, Fredrica Friedman, the executive editor of Little, Brown, has been all a writer can hope for in an editor: demanding, intelligent, sharp, timely. She has reshaped this work, heated it up, and insisted that the voices of the victims be heard.

I am grateful to all who have contributed to this work. Their generosity of time and spirit is deeply appreciated.

Responsibility for any errors or shortcomings in this work are mine and mine alone. For in the end a scholar, even when assisted by researchers, employed by an institution or directing its creative work, writes the truth he or she knows — and in my case, the truth I live and the responsibility I bear are one.

Michael Berenbaum
Director, United States Holocaust
    Research Institute
Hymen Goldman Adjunct
    Professor of Theology,
    Georgetown University

INDEX